SECRETS OF
SAND HILL ROAD

Virgin BOOKS

SECRETS OF
SAND HILL
ROAD

Venture Capital
and How to Get It

SCOTT KUPOR

Virgin BOOKS

1 3 5 7 9 10 8 6 4 2

Virgin Books, an imprint of Ebury Publishing,
20 Vauxhall Bridge Road,
London SW1V 2SA

Virgin Books is part of the Penguin Random House group of companies whose
addresses can be found at global.penguinrandomhouse.com

Penguin
Random House
UK

First published in the United Kingdom by Virgin Books in 2019
First published in the United States by Portfolio in 2019

www.penguin.co.uk

A CIP catalogue record for this book is available from the British Library

ISBN 9780753553961

Printed and bound in India by Thomson Press India Ltd.

Penguin Random House is committed to a sustainable future for
our business, our readers and our planet. This book is made from
Forest Stewardship Council® certified paper.

MIX
Paper from
responsible sources
FSC® C018179

To all the women in my life—Laura, Ashlee, Alexa, and Amanda—who put up with my silly antics, yet remind me every day of how lucky I am to enjoy their love

CONTENTS

FOREWORD

Scott Kupor's *Secrets of Sand Hill Road: Venture Capital and How to Get It* is motivated by the desire to democratize opportunity. It demystifies venture capital, laying out how this crucial part of the startup ecosystem works for anyone who picks it up. It examines the VC startup life cycle from every angle, including how VCs decide where to invest, how to pitch, and all the many, many legal and financial details and players involved in forming and growing a startup. (Its exposition of the term sheet alone makes it worth far more than its cover price, and I wish I'd had it available to me when I was first looking for startup funding.) It understands that hard decisions sometimes have to be made and that deals can be confusing, and ends with a look at the IPO process. All of this information is presented as a means of reframing the relationship between startups and their investors as a true partnership, rather than an uneasy alliance. Scott has seen the process from both sides of the table, as a startup executive and as an investor, and he's distilled his experiences and his perspective into an accessible, straightforward guide. Its purpose is to help build on the progress that's already been made in taking entrepreneurship from a career path open to the few and the privileged, to one that's open to anyone with an idea and the will to see it to fruition. This is the most urgent obligation of the startup movement as a whole, as we work to help build a more equitable society, but it also has huge implications for the continuing economic success and survival of our country, where new businesses account for almost all net new job creation and nearly 20 percent of gross job creation overall. Leaders like Scott are moving us all closer to fulfilling that obligation.

For most of the twentieth century, entrepreneurship wasn't seen as a career. It was more like a path followed by people who didn't fit into one of the traditional professions open to them and could afford to do something different. Although some succeeded, being an entrepreneur was as much a curse—or maybe more of one—as an exciting opportunity. Even many initially successful entrepreneurs ended their careers in poverty or were forcibly removed from their creations. Now, though, conditions favor entrepreneurs. Barriers to entry are being reduced everywhere, thanks to the semiconductor revolution, the rise of globalization, and the influx of new talent into every industry and sector. Think about this: venture-backed companies now spend 44 percent of the entire R&D budget for American public companies. The 665 public companies that are VC-backed make up a fifth of the total market capitalization of public companies. They employ four million people. Those are significant numbers, but I believe this is just the beginning. The startup movement can—and must—grow to have a much larger impact. When we pour so much money into such a limited range of companies, we can't effectively tackle the challenges we face. That's why one of my favorite things about this book is the way it so clearly parses out the incentives and systems behind venture capital. This will help all entrepreneurs navigate the maze of venture investors and decipher their behavior. The system works the way it does for a reason, and now that reason is comprehensible.

But there are other, larger lessons to glean as well. As you'll learn in this book, most venture firms invest money on behalf of larger institutional asset managers, like university endowments and retirement funds. Most of these asset managers use a formula to determine how much money to allocate to different types of investments, including the high-risk, highly-illiquid sector of venture. (This approach to portfolio construction was pioneered by David Swensen at Yale, whose methods have been widely adopted, as you'll read about in chapter 2). What that means is that the amount of resources our society currently invests in innovation is based on the percentage of assets that need to be invested according to this formula, *rather than on the number of investable opportunities that exist*. When too much money is chasing too few deals, there's only one possible result: Because we have too few entrepreneurs, we can't put enough money to work. Instead, it's wasted on bidding up the prices of the few available assets rather than funding the kinds of organizations that are actually needed. The problem is even more pressing when you consider it from a diversity point of view. Not only are there not enough startups, but the ones that do exist aren't nearly wide-ranging enough to build the kinds of companies our present and future call for. Possibly for the first time in history, we're talent-constrained instead of capital-constrained. Scott's book is an important step in making the opportunity to build a venture-scale business available to everyone so we can change that. The information about how to seek out and secure funding shouldn't be limited to an elite club. Every startup is about a single idea, but taken together, all startups have a common purpose as well: to shape a better world for all of us. And a better world is one in which everyone is represented and served well by the companies and systems we create.

That's why *Secrets of Sand Hill Road* is so valuable, and so timely. It's for people interested in venture capital, of course, but it's also for anyone who cares about the ability of the US to remain competitive, create new jobs, and continue on the path of economic growth. Those people include policy makers, academics, government officials in the US and elsewhere, civic leaders in startup hubs around the country and globe—who are already helping to democratize startups geographically—and people who work in corporate innovation (who can look to the VC world for inspiration on how to fund and grow projects within their organizations). Finally, *Secrets of Sand Hill Road* is for all the entrepreneurs who might not see themselves as a part of Silicon Valley—everyone who might not be considering trying to start a company based on their crazy concept, but really should be thinking about it. Given the chance, any one of those ideas could well become a reality that changes the way we live, and those are ideas we need to support. I believe Scott's book is destined to change the equation when it comes to who gets funded. It's leading us into a fairer, more robust future, and I can't think of a wiser person to take us there.

Eric Ries, *author of* The Lean Startup *and* The Startup Way

SECRETS OF
SAND HILL ROAD

Introduction

I am writing this book from my office on Sand Hill Road, the hallowed Silicon Valley street that holds as much promise for entrepreneurs as Hollywood Boulevard does for actors, Wall Street does for investment bankers, and Music Row does for country music artists. And, as with most of the storied streets, it's not much to write home about—Sand Hill Road is a drab collection of modest, low-rise office buildings, upstaged by its much more famous neighbor, Stanford University.

But I'm not writing it from on high. This is no sermon, no stone tablet passed down. This book isn't intended to be the venture capital (VC) bible. There are far too many important nuances in the field, with lots of different firms that invest at different stages, under different investment theses, with different portfolio constructions, and different return expectations. Not to mention different personalities.

And that's just on the venture capitalist side of things. More importantly, no two entrepreneurs are the same. The innovative, often world-changing companies they create always come with a unique set of opportunities, challenges, and conditions to be navigated.

ledge the personal biases I bring to the
experience, hard-won, on the startup side
years at LoudCloud and then Opsware. The other
personally developed, on the VC side, in my role as
partner at Andreessen Horowitz, or a16z, where I have
since the firm started in 2009. This means I've had the opportunity to see VC from multiple vantage points.

And, in fact, my hope is to help us stop thinking divisively in
terms of one side or the other, one side *versus* the other. Entrepreneurs and VCs are not on opposing sides, the way one soccer team
tries to crush another in the World Cup. Rather, we are partners,
and once we agree to work together (and even if we don't), we
are on the same side. What we share is a desire to create benign
businesses, see them have an impact on and improve the world,
and together realize some financial benefit along the way.

The story of venture capital is really a *subset* of the story of entrepreneurship. As venture capitalists, we raise investment funds
from a broad range of limited partners (LPs), such as endowments, foundations, pension plans, family offices, and fund of
funds. The capital raised from LPs is then invested in great entrepreneurs with breakthrough ideas.

Venture capitalists invest anywhere from the very early stage,
where the startup is little more than an idea and a couple of
people, to growth-stage startups, where there is some decent revenue coming in and the focus is on effectively scaling the business. Generally, a company leaves the venture ecosystem one of
three ways: via an initial public offering (IPO), a merger or acquisition, or bankruptcy and a wind down.

There is often a misconception that venture capitalists are like
other investment fund managers in that they find promising investments and write checks. But writing the check is simply the
beginning of our engagement; the hard work begins when we
engage with startups to help entrepreneurs turn their ideas into
successful companies.

For example, at Andreessen Horowitz, we often work with our companies to help them identify talented employees and executives to bring into the company or to identify existing companies that can serve as live customer test sites for their products. The reality is that those who are successful in our field do not just pick winners. We work actively with our investments to help them throughout the company-building life cycle over a long period of time. We often support our portfolio companies with multiple investment rounds generally spanning five to ten years, or longer. We serve on the boards of many of our portfolio companies, provide strategic advice, open our contact lists, and generally do whatever we can to help our companies succeed.

All that being said, VCs are only as good as the entrepreneurs in whom they have the privilege to invest. And nobody should confuse the tireless heavy lifting that the entrepreneurs and their teams do to build a successful business with the investing activity of a VC. Simply put, entrepreneurs build businesses; VCs don't. Great VCs help in any way they can along the company-building path, but it is the entrepreneurs and their teams who tread that path every day and make the difference between success and failure. And while all VCs hope that each of our companies succeeds against huge risks and grows into a successful business, the reality is that the majority fail.

Entrepreneurship is inherently a risky endeavor, but it is absolutely essential to the American economy. Successful venture-backed companies have had an outsize positive impact on the US economy. According to a 2015 study by Ilya Strebulaev of Stanford University and Will Gornall of the University of British Columbia, 42 percent of all US company IPOs since 1974 were venture backed. Collectively, those venture-backed companies have invested $115 billion in research and development (R&D), accounting for 85 percent of all R&D spending, and created $4.3 trillion in market capitalization, which is 63 percent of the total market capitalization of public companies formed since 1974. Furthermore, specific to the impact on the American workforce, a 2010 study from the Kauffman Foundation found that young startups, most venture backed, were responsible for *almost all* of the twenty-five million net jobs created since 1977.

What does all this mean? Simple. We need you. We need your ideas and your guts. We need your companies and your commitment to growth.

What I want to do most with this book is help entrepreneurs. Access to capital is critically important to the success of a startup, and at one time or another you have to (or will) consider whether or not your business can and should raise VC. I hope this book helps to democratize access to the information about what makes the venture business tick—to the benefit of you, the entrepreneur.

The decision to raise capital from a venture firm is a huge one, and should not be undertaken without a full consideration of the benefits and risks of this source of capital. For example, is your business even appropriate in the first instance to raise venture financing? Is the market size big enough that the business at scale has the prospect of being a home run, and thus moving the needle for a venture capitalist in terms of her overall fund returns? How can you better understand the economic incentives of the VC industry in order to determine whether you are in fact looking for capital in all the right (or wrong) places?

If you choose to raise venture money, how do you think about the appropriate balance of economic and governance terms with your VC financier? What trade-offs are you willing to make, and what are the downstream implications of those decisions, particularly if you need to raise subsequent capital when the business develops at a different pace than you expect? And how will you and the board work effectively to achieve the long-term goals of the business?

It's an unfair truth that VCs get a lot of at bats, lots of chances to invest in a home-run company, while most entrepreneurs get to step up to the plate only a few times. Or to mix my sports metaphors, you get only a few real shots on goal in your lifetime while we VCs get several. Because of this imbalance, specifically re-garding investment decisions, information asymmetry can come into play (often at the expense of the founder). The VCs are repeat players and thus have the benefit of lots of years of developing their understanding of the various mechanics (especially when negotiating term sheets), whereas founders have been through the process only a handful of times, at most. What I hope to lay out for founders is a better understanding of and appreciation for the interplay between VCs and founders in order to level the playing field. Information asymmetry should not pollute the foundation of a marriage that could last ten years or more.

Does that timeline surprise you? That you are likely entering into a (minimum) ten-year marriage of sorts with your venture partners? It's longer now than ever before, yet for too long there has been a lack of transparency into the inner workings of that partnership.

That is why I want to give you, a founder, some insider infor-mation, secrets, and advice so that you can best navigate your way through your interactions with venture capital firms, from the initial pitch session all the way through to an IPO or acquisition.

I've now had the opportunity to see VC from both perspec-tives—as a member of a startup and now as the managing partner for Andreessen Horowitz. While my seat has changed—and cer-tain elements of the venture business have evolved—the funda-mentals remain the same: VCs seek investment opportunities with asymmetric upside payoff potential (and capped downside—after all, you can only lose the money you invest), and entrepreneurs who are funded by VCs seek to build industry-changing and valu-able stand-alone companies. And every so often when these in-centives align, magic happens.

Entrepreneurs need to understand their own goals and objec-tives and see whether they align with those of the funding sources they want to tap. To determine that calculus, entrepreneurs would be wise to understand how the VC business works, what makes VCs tick, and what ultimately motivates (and constrains) them. After all, we are each motivated by the incentive structures that our industries engender; understanding those is in many ways a key part of the entrepreneurial journey.

Start by Asking the Right Questions

Have you ever seen those Charles Schwab commercials about how to talk to your financial advisor? Unless you watch a lot of golf on TV or actually pay attention to YouTube ads, you probably haven't. Here's the premise.

Your average middle-aged couple goes through a series of life events. They ask their home contractor to explain why she recommends cedar versus synthetic wood for a remodel. They meticulously debate the merits of a particular school for one of their kids. They grill the car salesman on whether the 467- or 423-horsepower car is more appropriate. But then, in the final vignette of the commercial, the couple sits across a large mahogany desk from a well-dressed financial advisor who tells them, "I think we should move you into our new fund." The couple glance blankly at each other for about a second—pregnant pause—and then immediately accede to the request. No questions asked.

The commercial's narrator benignly reminds the viewers: "You ask a lot of good questions . . . but are you asking enough about how your wealth is managed?" The implication, of course, is that we all feel empowered to dig deep into many important life decisions, but for some reason we give a free pass to others if it's a topic we don't understand or feel intimidated by, no matter how important the decision.

This book is not about how to solve that underlying problem—we'll all need to search in the psychology book section on Amazon for answers to that issue.

But this book is about helping you to ask the right questions about one of the most important life events for entrepreneurs—your startup and your career—so that you can make an informed decision about how best to proceed.

Why?

Because if you are going to raise money from VCs or join a company that has venture money, the only way to know if that is a good idea is to **understand why VCs do the things that they do. In other words, know your partner before you get married.**

Having a deep understanding of a prospective partner's motivations will help you anticipate their moves and (hopefully) interpret them correctly when they happen. More importantly, it will help you determine whether entering into the partnership is the right path to pursue in the first place.

The VC Life Cycle

This book follows the VC life cycle as it relates to and informs entrepreneurs. The first section of the book deals with the formation of a VC firm—who are the players who fund them, what incentives (and constraints) do they provide for the firms, and how do the partners within a firm interact with each other. To understand how VCs choose to invest in certain companies and how they might act once involved with a company, we also need to look upstream to understand the motivations of the funders of such firms. For if VC firms fail to satisfy the needs of their masters, there will be no more money with which to invest in new startups.

Next, we'll explore startup company formation. We'll look at all the things that founders need to think about when deciding to start a company—from dividing up founder equity, to deciding who sits on the board of directors, to how to incent employees, and much more. A lot of the ultimate decision about whether to seek VC financing will be influenced by decisions that founders make at the time of company formation.

We'll spend a big chunk of time on the VC financing process itself—in particular, the term sheet. This is the Magna Carta of the industry, as it ultimately defines the economic and governance rules under which the startup and the VCs will operate.

Then, with funding in hand, founders will need to be able to operate within the economic and governance constraints that they agreed to. Thus, we'll talk about the role of the board of directors and how it influences the path of the startup and potentially the ability of the founder to keep steering the ship. Boards, including the founder, also have to operate under various well-defined legal constraints that can materially affect the degrees of freedom of a company.

In the last section, we'll complete the circle of life. In the beginning, money comes into the VC firm through the investors in the fund. That money in turn goes into startup companies. Finally, the money comes back (or not) to the investors in the fund in the form of initial public offerings or acquisitions. If enough money doesn't make it through the full cycle, then life, at least as we know it in VC land, ceases to exist. The financing spigot dries up, which can have downstream effects on the rate of funding for new startup ideas. Hopefully, everyone in the ecosystem does her part to avoid that.

Of course, not all VCs are the same, and, as I mentioned earlier, what I write about here is heavily influenced by my experiences at Andreessen Horowitz. So your mileage may indeed vary. That said, I've tried to broaden the conversation to make this book more general for the overall venture industry.

This book may not answer all the questions you have and is not intended to be a comprehensive source on the topic. There are plenty of academics who teach semester-long classes on VC, and of course there are lots of VCs and others in the venture capital ecosystem—entrepreneurs, lawyers, accountants, and other service providers—who spend their professional lives learning and perfecting their craft.

Nonetheless, I hope this book shines a light on how VC works and why, in order to create more and better company-building opportunities.

CHAPTER 1

Born in the Bubble

In the interest of unlocking the somewhat opaque doors of venture capital, behind which are the inner workings, incentives, and decision-making processes of VCs, let me start by more properly introducing myself.

The first thing to know about me is that if I weren't a venture capitalist, I would sing country music in Nashville. But lucky for everyone who is a real country music fan—and for my ability to support my family financially—I somehow found my way into the VC business! I live in Silicon Valley, not Tennessee, so the best I can do is wear cowboy boots to work and play the guitar in my spare time. Both of which I do, as often as possible.

Let me give you a little bit of context about what the tech and investment world was like when I was getting started in in the 1990s.

Some of the big tech names back then were E.piphany, NetIQ, VA Linux, Commerce One, Razorfish, and Ask.com. It's possible you haven't heard of any of these companies, but they—like me—were products of the 1999–2000 tech bubble that produced roughly nine hundred initial public offerings of venture-backed tech companies. It was a great time to be starting out in the tech industry, as there seemed to be no end to the promise of technology and to the amount of wealth creation that was available to everyone involved.

Netscape had gone public in 1995, a mere *eighteen months* after its founding, receiving a huge amount of media attention and heralding the beginning of the dot-com boom. Google wouldn't be founded until 1998, but Silicon Valley was already fired up with dot-com fever. New internet startups were appearing daily. The tech world was abuzz.

Venture capitalists (VCs) were investing in new companies at an unprecedented pace relative to historical norms. About $36 billion went into new startups in 1999, which was approximately double what had been invested the prior year (although that's now less than half of what was invested in 2017). Additionally, limited partners committed more than $100 billion of new capital to the venture capital industry in 2000, a record that hasn't come close to being broken since! By comparison, limited partners committed about $33 billion in funding in 2017.

Startups were also getting to an IPO faster than ever during the dot-com bubble. On average, it was taking companies about four years from founding to go public, which was a huge acceleration of the historical trend of taking six and a half to seven years to IPO. Today, that time period often exceeds ten years, for reasons we'll get into later in this book.

In addition to a record number of IPOs, the public markets were also exuberant. On March 10, 2000, the Nasdaq index, the barometer for technology stocks, peaked just above 5,000. More interesting, the price-to-earnings ratio (P/E ratio) of the companies listed in the Nasdaq index stood at 175. This means that stock market investors were valuing one dollar's worth of a company's earnings at $175.

While it's generally the case that investors value a dollar of earnings today at some multiple greater than one because a company's stock price is intended to reflect the present value of the cumulative cash flows of a business into the future, a 175 multiple is a historical anomaly. For comparison, the Nasdaq P/E ratio today is under 20, which is generally in line with the long-term historical trends for the index.

At the time, Cisco was anticipated by many to become the first $1 trillion market capitalization company. Alas, Cisco's market cap peaked at about $555 billion in March 2000; today it stands around $200 billion. Early in 2018, Amazon became the first $1 trillion market cap company, albeit for a brief time, and as of this writing, sits at around $800 billion. (Fun fact: In March 2000, Amazon's market cap was a mere $30 billion).

What Could Possibly Go Wrong?

So, back in 2000, everyone was on a collective sugar high to end all sugar highs. What could possibly go wrong? As it turns out, a lot.

The Nasdaq index began a precipitous decline from its March 2000 peak, falling all the way to its nadir of just above 1,300 in August 2002. While there is much Monday-morning quarter-backing about the impetus for the decline, many market analysts point to the Federal Reserve's aggressive interest rate tightening in early 2000, which created a big debate as to the sustainability of heavy borrowing that many technology infrastructure companies had undertaken. Regardless of the ultimate cause, in about two and a half years, the index lost nearly 80 percent of its value, tech companies laid off record numbers of employees, VCs stopped investing in new companies, and the few companies that had sufficient cash to sustain themselves were focused purely on self-preservation at the expense of everything else.

That's why you probably don't remember most of the companies I mentioned before. Yet this was the environment in which I began my professional career.

Despite graduating from Stanford University in 1993 and Stanford Law School in 1996, sitting right at the epicenter of the tech boom the whole time, I was largely oblivious to what was happening around me. So, after graduating from law school, I left Silicon Valley to spend a year in my hometown of Houston, Texas, clerking for the Court of Appeals for the Fifth Circuit. This was an incredible learning experience and a fun way to spend a year, but, as it would turn out, it had zero relevance to my longer-term career.

I moved back to Silicon Valley to work for Lehman Brothers. Lehman, of course, was later a victim of the global financial crisis, suffering an ignominious bankruptcy in September 2008. My job at the time, in addition to being an all-around grunt, was to help life sciences companies raise capital, go public, and make acquisitions. Those were noble things to do, but for the fact that despite the raging bull market in technology in Silicon Valley, the investor appetite for life sciences was largely dormant.

Lucky for me, a friend had just taken a job at Credit Suisse First Boston, a scrappy investment bank that had brought on Frank Quattrone to build out their technology banking practice. Frank is a legend in the technology banking world, having started his career at Morgan Stanley, where he led IPOs for companies such as Apple and Cisco and advised on a huge range of important mergers and acquisitions. He is still a dominant figure in the technology space, having founded in March 2008 a leading mergers and acquisitions advisory firm named Qatalyst.

So I joined Credit Suisse First Boston and drank from the fire hose of the developing tech bubble. A few years into my job, on the eve of finishing an IPO for E.piphany, one of the marketing executives I had worked with to help them prepare for the IPO told me he was leaving to join a new startup called LoudCloud. Cofounded by Marc Andreessen, the already revered cofounder of Netscape, LoudCloud was trying to create a compute utility (much like Amazon Web Services has now created). Among the other cofounders was Ben Horowitz.

This was the fall of 1999, and the dot-com excitement was in full swing. I had finally opened my eyes to what was happening around me, and I wanted to be a part of it. When my friend at E.piphany offered me the chance to meet Marc Andreessen and

Ben Horowitz and see what they were doing, it was too much to pass up. My wife, who was about five months pregnant at the time with our first child and who was busy closing on the first house we were buying together, didn't see it quite the same way. She had a pretty good argument, to be honest. Why quit a great job with Credit Suisse First Boston where the business was going gangbusters, meaning the chance for both financial and professional success was palpable, in order to join a startup where I'd get paid next to nothing in salary for the promise of some equity appreciation in the future from stock options? She did, however, ultimately acquiesce, likely against her better judgment at the time.

I'll never forget my interview with Marc. Although I had never met him before, like everyone in the tech industry I knew of his accomplishments and media fame. So when he asked me to meet him at a little Denny's restaurant in Sunnyvale for my interview, I was a bit surprised.

But it didn't take long to get excited about the LoudCloud market opportunity. Marc took a napkin from the table and began drawing some barely decipherable sketch of how LoudCloud was going to take over the computing world. Only now, with the benefit of more than eighteen years of working with Marc, have I come to learn that doodling in all its glory is among his many skills.

The idea of LoudCloud was elegant in its simplicity; it turned out that the execution of the business was anything but. In basic terms, Loudcloud sought to turn computing power into a utility. Just as when you plug your phone charger into the wall socket you don't need to know (or care) about how the electricity got there, you just use it, LoudCloud's mission was to do the same for computing capacity. As an engineer, you should be able to develop your custom application and then just "plug it in" to the compute utility that could run the application seamlessly for you. You shouldn't have to worry about what kind of database, networking equipment, application servers, etc., underlie the utility; it should simply work. It was a great idea—one that Amazon Web Services has built into a multibillion-dollar business today.

LoudCloud was probably about ten years ahead of its time, an oft-repeated lesson, by the way, in the startup world. Though timing isn't everything, timing is definitely something—it's a big reason why we now see many ideas that failed in the dot-com bubble being reincarnated as successful businesses two decades later. As market conditions change—in the case of the dot-com businesses, the market size of available customers was simply too small relative to the cost of acquiring those customers—business models that previously failed can become viable. Marc likes to remind us that when he was building Netscape, the total size of the internet population was about 50 million people, nearly all of whom were accessing the internet on clunky dial-up connections. Thus, no matter how much utility the browser provided, the end-user market simply wasn't that big. Contrast that to today, where we have about 2.5 billion smartphone users with ubiquitous connectivity to the internet and the potential for that number to double over the next ten years. All of a sudden, businesses that couldn't work profitably at 50 million users take on a very different look when they can appeal to a mass-market audience.

After meeting with Marc, I also interviewed with a number of other members of the team, including cofounder Ben Horowitz. The setting for that interview was more normal, as we met on a Saturday at the company's offices. But I remember being surprised by Ben's attire—he was fully decked out in Oakland Raiders garb, including T-shirt, watch, and baseball hat. I now know, after many years of working side by side with Ben, that his attire was completely in character. In fact, to this day, Ben keeps a life-size dummy of a fully outfitted Oakland Raiders football player in his office. For the uninitiated, that can be quite a surprise!

LoudCloud's Atypical Success

I got the job as a business development manager at LoudCloud. This title was the euphemistic way of saying, "You were an investment banker in your previous job and might have some skills to add to the company, but we're not quite sure yet exactly what those will be." (Over my seven-year tenure at LoudCloud, I had the opportunity to take on a number of different roles, including running financial planning and investor relations, corporate development, some engineering teams, customer support, and field operations, which included support, professional services, and pre-sales engineering.)

I was in, I was thrilled (my wife was less so), and we at Loud-Cloud set out to build the first compute utility, flush with what we thought was plenty of cash. In its first few months, the company had raised nearly $60 million of debt and equity. But then again it was early 2000 and we were all living the dot-com dream. VC money was raining from the rafters.

We naturally decided to raise more money—$120 million, to be exact. In some respects the money was free (as the valuation at which we were able to raise was over $800 million—this for a less-than-one-year-old company!). But it was not in fact free, for with it came the expectations of growth for which the VCs had provided the money.

And grow we did. We topped six hundred employees before the company was even two years old. We decided to go public in March 2001, which was definitely not the greatest timing, right in the wake of the dot-com meltdown. In fact, LoudCloud was one of only a very small number of tech companies to go public that year (fewer than twenty tech IPOs happened in 2001, versus nearly five hundred in the prior year). The portfolio managers with whom we met during the IPO road show of back-to-back meetings could not have been more shell-shocked about the decimation they were seeing in their portfolios. They looked at us as if we had three heads when we dutifully gave the LoudCloud IPO pitch. Recall that Nasdaq was at about 2,000 at this time, down significantly from its roughly 5,000 peak a year prior, but still not at the bottom it would reach in August 2001.

But we went public because it was the only viable source of capital available to LoudCloud. We desperately needed the additional funding to continue to run the business. Despite having raised a lot of money to date, we were dangerously low on cash due to the post-2000 dot-com collapse. This was because we had originally targeted our service offerings to other startup companies; they seemed like a natural customer base given that they could benefit from being able to pay LoudCloud to worry about their computing infrastructure while they focused their activities on the internal development of their custom applications.

For us to provide this service, however, we had to procure significant amounts of data center space and a ton of computer equipment. We paid for this infrastructure up front with the idea that we would amortize the payback of these costs as we grew our customer base. That worked for the first year or so until the cascading effects of the air being let out of the dot-com balloon caught up to us. As a result, our dot-com customers started going out of business and naturally had no VCs willing to fund their on-going operations. We were stuck with a very high fixed cost base of capital infrastructure against a diminishing base of customers—a recipe for significant cash consumption.

And, as noted above, by this time, the VCs had essentially stopped writing checks, so the only other option for us was to raise money from more buyout-oriented investors. Buyout investors are different from VC firms in a few ways. Namely, they tend to invest in companies that are beyond pure startup stage, and they generally make what are called "control" investments. Control means that they often own a majority of the company and control a majority of the seats on the board of directors; this gives them the ability to be the major determiners of the company's strategy. Buyout capital can often be more expensive than VC because the upside opportunity for these investors is more constrained given the later stage at which they invest. This was the case for us, meaning that the valuation at which they would fund the company was much lower, and thus the amount of ownership we would have to give up was much higher. In addition, the control aspects of the buyout alternatives we had were less palatable than our desire to preserve more degrees of freedom in running the business.

In an odd way, therefore, going public seemed to provide the lowest available cost of capital and the apparent path of least resistance. We originally intended to sell shares to the public at a range of ten to twelve dollars per share. (When companies file to go public, they put what's known as an "initial filing range" out to the market to signal the price range at which they hope to sell shares to the public. IPOs that are in demand are often oversubscribed, meaning there is more institutional demand to purchase shares than there are shares to sell, and naturally in that case the company will increase the filing range accordingly.) But the stock market continued to deteriorate over the course of our IPO marketing period, and we ultimately sold stock to the public at six dollars per share. This is definitely not your typical IPO story. But, the IPO allowed us to raise sufficient capital to give ourselves a shot at success without having to give up day-to-day control of the business.

"Live to fight another day" is another great startup mantra to always keep front and center in your mind. Of course, as John Maynard Keynes reminded us, this applies to almost every financial endeavor: "The markets can remain irrational longer than you can remain solvent." Cash is undoubtedly king in the startup world—and in the business world more generally.

But perhaps the most poignant phrasing of this lesson that I ever heard came from the late Bill Campbell. Bill is a Silicon Valley legend (Apple, Intuit, GO Corporation, Google, etc.) and in his later years was referred to as "Coach," for he spent tireless hours coaching entrepreneurs as they were building their businesses. He was also once a "real" coach of the Columbia University football team, but suffice it to say that his coaching record there paled in comparison to his many business successes over a long career. We were privileged to have Bill on our board at LoudCloud, where he constantly reminded us in very simple terms of the critical role that cash plays in a startup's life cycle: "It's not about the money. It's about the F-ing money." Enough said.

In 2002, we ultimately sold most of the LoudCloud business to Electronic Data Systems (EDS) and essentially restarted as an enterprise software business named Opsware. In addition to being the new name of the company, Opsware was also the name of the software we had developed to use internally when we were running the LoudCloud business—the name was a contraction of "Operations Software." Because as LoudCloud we had to manage a whole series of servers, network devices, storage devices, and applications, we developed the Opsware software to reduce the amount of manual labor needed by automating a variety of the technology management tasks. When EDS acquired the LoudCloud business, it licensed the Opsware software but allowed us to retain the core intellectual property. So we did what any enterprising startup would do and created a new business selling the Opsware software to other large-enterprise customers who could benefit from automating their own technology management processes.

And we did all this while still being a publicly listed company, albeit with a nascent business and a market cap that appropriately reflected that (im)maturity. The stock hit a low of thirty-four cents, but we stuck with it for another five years and ultimately built a nice software business at Opsware that Hewlett-Packard purchased in 2007 for $1.65 billion. My partner Ben has written extensively about the transformation of the business in his own book, The Hard Thing about Hard Things, which I highly recommend. (And that's not just because he's still my boss!)

Immediately following the sale of Opsware to Hewlett-Packard, many of us had the opportunity to stay on as part of the HP Software business. At the time, HP Software was a roughly $4 billion division within the broader HP mother ship (HP sold everything from printers and ink cartridges to desktops, servers, networking equipment, and storage devices) that had been built on the foundations of HP OpenView, a set of software products that, like Opsware, helped companies manage their IT assets.

Over the years, HP Software had acquired a number of other software businesses in the broader IT management space, and thus the product line, employees, and customer base were very diverse and geographically dispersed. I had the opportunity to manage the integration of the Opsware team into HP Software and then to run the roughly $1 billion global software support business. With 1,500 employees scattered across every major global market, I logged more airline miles in that job than I have ever done in my professional lifetime to date. But it was a fun and exciting opportunity to manage a team at scale, as jobs and learning experiences of that kind can be hard to come by in the earlier-stage startup world.

Change Is Afoot in Silicon Valley

Following the 2007 sale of Opsware to HP, Marc and Ben began investing in earnest as angel investors. Angels are traditionally individuals who invest in very-early-stage startups (generally known as "seed-stage companies"). In Silicon Valley in 2007, the angel community was pretty small, and there were not many institutional seed funds, meaning professional investors who raised money from traditional institutional investors to invest in seed-stage companies. Rather, angel investing was dominated largely by a loose collection of individuals who were writing checks out of their personal accounts. Interestingly, Marc and Ben made their angel investments through an entity known as HA Angel Fund (Horowitz Andreessen Angel Fund), a reversal of the now-well-known brand name for their venture fund.

Marc and Ben started investing at an exciting time when change was afoot in Silicon Valley. To understand this change, you have to understand a bit of the history of the VC industry.

As we'll dive into deeper in subsequent chapters, the Silicon Valley VC business started in earnest in the 1970s and was characterized for most of the next thirty-odd years by a relatively small number of very successful firms that controlled access to startup capital. In simple terms, capital was the scarce resource, and that resource was "owned" by the then-existing VC firms, many of which are still very successful and active players in the current VC marketplace. Thus those who wanted access to that capital— the entrepreneurs—needed to effectively compete for that capital. The balance of power, therefore, as between the VC firms and entrepreneurs, was squarely in favor of the former.

Beginning in the early 2000s, though, there were a few significant transformations in the startup ecosystem that would change things in the entrepreneurs' favor.

First, the amount of capital required to start a company began to decline; this continues in earnest even today. Not only did the absolute cost of servers, networking, storage, data center space, and applications begin to fall, but the procurement method evolved from up-front purchasing to much cheaper "renting" with the advent of what is known as cloud computing. As a startup, these changes are very significant, as they mean that the amount of money you need to raise from VCs to get started is much less than in the past.

Y Combinator Cracks Open the "Black Box"

The second material transformation in the startup ecosystem was the advent of an incubator known as Y Combinator (or YC for short). Started in 2005 by Paul Graham and Jessica Livingston, YC basically created startup school. Cohorts of entrepreneurs joined a "YC batch," working in an open office space together and going through a series of tutorials and mentorship sessions over a three-month period to see what might come out the other end. Over the past thirteen years, YC has turned out nearly 1,600 promising startups, including some very well-known success stories such as Airbnb, Coinbase, Instacart, Dropbox, and Stripe.

But that's not the most significant impact that YC has had on the VC ecosystem. Rather, the import of YC, I believe, is that it has educated a whole range of entrepreneurs on the process of starting a company, of which raising capital from VCs is an integral part. That is, YC cracked open the "black box" that was the VC industry, illuminating to entrepreneurs the process of startup company formation and capital raising.

In addition, YC created true communities of entrepreneurs among which they could share their knowledge and views both on company building and on their experiences working with VC firms. Prior to this time, the entrepreneurial community was more dispersed, and therefore knowledge sharing between members of the community was decidedly limited. But with knowledge comes power, thus the second material driver of the changing balance of power between entrepreneurs and VCs.

Something More

And that takes us to the founding of Andreessen Horowitz, started in 2009 by Marc Andreessen and Ben Horowitz. What Marc and Ben saw was this fundamental shift in the landscape that would no longer make access to capital alone a sufficient differentiator for VC firms. Rather, in their view, VCs would need to provide something more than simply capital, for that was becoming a commodity, and instead, in this post-2005 era of VC, firms would need to compete for the right to fund entrepreneurs by providing something more.

What that "something more" would be was informed by their thinking around the nature of technology startup ventures. That is, tech startups are basically innovative product or service companies. In most cases, tech startups represent an amalgamation of engineers who identify some innovative way to solve an existing problem or create a new market by introducing a product or service that consumers didn't even know could exist. This affinity between the identification of the problem to be solved and the development of the product or service that in fact solves the problem is a key component of successful tech startups. No doubt that effective sales and marketing, capital deployment, and team building, among others, are also crucial ingredients to success, but fundamentally tech startups need to "fit" a market problem to a compelling market solution to have a shot at success.

Thus, to increase the odds of ultimately building a widely successful and valuable company, Marc and Ben had a thesis that founders should ultimately be product/engineering types and that there should be a tight coupling between the product visionary and the individual responsible for driving the company's strategy and resource allocation decisions. Those latter responsibilities are typically the province of the CEO. Therefore, Marc and Ben had a predilection for backing CEOs who were also the source of the company's product vision.

But, while technical founding CEOs might be great at product development, they might often lack the rest of the skills and relationships required to be all-around great CEOs—technical recruiting, executive recruiting, PR and marketing, sales and business development, corporate development, and regulatory affairs, among others.

As a result, the "something more" that Marc and Ben decided to build Andreessen Horowitz around was a network of people and institutions that could improve the prospects for founding product CEOs to become world-class CEOs. And I was lucky enough to become employee number one as we launched the firm in June 2009.

Over the past ten years, we've gone from $300 million in funds under management and a three-person team to managing more than $7 billion in funds and roughly 150 employees. Most of our employees focus on that "something more," spending their days building relationships with people and institutions that can help improve the likelihood of our founder CEOs building enduring and valuable companies.

An Ode to Entrepreneurs

We've been fortunate enough to invest in many great companies, some of which are household names today—Airbnb, Pinterest, Instacart, Oculus, Slack, GitHub—and many that we hope will become household names in the future. And we've learned a lot, sometimes by making the right decisions but also by making mistakes as we've built the business. We believe in being innovative and experimenting in our own business. In fact, we consistently tell our team to "make new mistakes," which we hope translates into taking informed risks, iterating on product and service offerings, and learning from previous mistakes to avoid treading down the same dead-end path. Throughout the course of this book, we'll spend more time on many of the lessons learned.

Most importantly, we believe deeply in the sanctity of the entrepreneurial process and work hard every day to respect the very difficult journey that aspiring entrepreneurs walk on their hopeful path to success. We know that the odds of success for most entrepreneurial endeavors are small and that the ones that make it do so due to a unique combination of vision, inspiration, grit, and a healthy dose of luck.

It is their stories, and those of LoudCloud, Opsware, and Andreessen Horowitz, that are in many ways the story of this book.

Startups thrive (or die) based on the availability of capital from VCs, particularly at the formative stages of their lives when the business itself is in growth mode and can't support itself through operating cash flow. And VC, like all types of capital, is a great form of financing where the needs and desires of the entrepreneur and the VC are aligned; there is a mutual pact the two organizations enter into with an agreed-upon set of objectives they hope to accomplish together. Money from public, institutional investors can also be an important part of the financing equation as a startup gets to a later point of maturity and can then satisfy the demands for predictable earnings growth that such investors require.

In a similar vein, when interests diverge between entrepreneurs and VCs, the world is not a very fun place to be.

As I've already mentioned, the best way to set up a successful marriage between entrepreneurs and VCs is to level the playing field and make sure everyone understands how VC works. So now it's time to roll up our sleeves and dig in.

CHAPTER 2

So Really,
What Is Venture Capital?

Let's start at the beginning—what is venture capital and when is it an appropriate form of financing for a new company?

Most people think of venture capital as a source of financing for technology startups. That's certainly true. VC money has funded many very interesting technology startups, including Facebook, Cisco, Apple, Amazon, Google, Netflix, Twitter, Intel, and LinkedIn, to name just a few. In fact, if you look at the five largest market capitalization companies today (though this could well be out of date by the time you read this book!)—Apple, Microsoft, Facebook, Google, Amazon—all of them were funded by venture capital. Not too bad for an industry that, as we will see, is a pretty tiny part of the overall world of finance.

But not all venture-funded companies are technology companies. Among the very successful nontechnology businesses that were also funded by VCs are Staples, Home Depot, Starbucks, and Blue Bottle Coffee.

So what, then, is really the purpose behind venture capital, and how best should we think about the scope of companies for which VC might be the most relevant source of financing?

Is VC Funding Right for Your Startup?

We'll get into this a lot more in later chapters of this book, but one way to think about VC is that it is a source of funding for companies (whether technology based or not) that are not otherwise good candidates to get funding from other, more traditional financial institutions.

There are other institutions that are in fact the source of "startup" capital for most new businesses; they're called banks. Small-business loans, particularly among community-based banks, have for a long time been the lifeblood of new company formation. This is why, among the many problems caused by the global financial crisis of 2008, job growth and new company formation stalled out—banks were simply unwilling (or in some cases, didn't have the deposit base) to extend loans to new businesses. It's also part of the reason why we saw the growth of alternative lending plat-forms (such as LendingClub) in the post–financial crisis years; they were in part filling a hole in small-business financing created by the exit of traditional bank lenders from this space.

But even if banks are in a lending mood—which they luckily have been for the last few years—loans are not always the best form of financing for all companies. That is because loans are not part of the permanent capital structure of a company. In lay-person's terms, this means they actually have to be paid back at some point (and often with interest along the way). Thus, loans are best suited for businesses that are likely going to be generating near-term positive cash flow sufficient to pay interest and, ultimately, the principal amount of the loan.

However, equity—in the form of a financial investment in exchange for an ownership interest in the company—doesn't suffer from this limitation. It is in fact permanent capital—meaning that there is no defined time period or mechanism by which the company has to return that capital to its investors. A company that is generating excess cash flow may wish to return capital to its equity holders in the form of a dividend or a buyback of shares, but there's no requirement to do this (at least not in the vast majority of VC equity financings). Rather, the equity holder is making an implicit bet at the time of the investment that the value of the equity will grow commensurate with the financial progress of the business, and the most likely method by which the equity holder will realize that value is by selling that equity at some future date.

Debt or Equity, Which Would You Choose?

So if you are a founder of a company, assuming you had a choice between debt and equity, which would you choose? Well, the answer is that it really depends on the type of business you are seeking to build, and how you want to think about the constraints that different forms of capital entail.

If you think you can generate near-term cash flow, or at least are willing to reduce investment in some areas of the business to make available cash to pay interest (and ultimately principal) on debt, then bank lending may be your best source of capital. After all, using debt means you don't have to sell any of the equity in your company to others, and thus you retain complete control of the business. Of course, bank loans do exert some control in the form of covenants—often financial metrics that you need to maintain to avoid being in default on the loan—but the bank itself is not a board member or voting shareholder of the company.

But if you think you are going to need to invest all your cash into the expenses of the business and don't see a near-term ability to generate cash flow (or don't want to be constrained by the fact that you have nonpermanent capital in your business), equity financing may be the better bet.

Now, of course, equity financing doesn't come for free—you are at a minimum going to have to give up an ownership position in the company to your equity holders. And if you decide to take equity from VCs—as we'll see in this book—you are going to have to live with their involvement in certain decisions of the company and, in many cases, as part of the board of directors of the company.

Nonetheless, equity-based financing is often the better choice for businesses that (1) are not generating (or expecting to generate) near-term cash flow; (2) are very risky (banks don't like to lend to businesses where there is real risk of the business failing, because they don't like losing the principal balance of their loans); and (3) have long illiquidity periods (again, banks structure their loans to be time limited—often three to five years in length—to increase the likelihood of getting their principal back).

We should go back to our definition of "VC" and clarify that it is not just any form of financing for businesses that may not be good candidates for traditional bank financing; it is equity financing specifically. And it is equity financing that the investors are willing to hold on to for a long time (that's what we mean when we say "long illiquidity periods"), but only on the assumption that they will ultimately get paid for the risk they are taking in the form of significant appreciation of the equity value.

You may have heard that some VCs invest in companies through notes. Isn't that really debt?

Yes and no. It is true that many early-stage investors—we call them angels or seed investors—often invest in companies via notes, but they have a distinguishing characteristic that makes them look more like equity: they are convertible notes. What does that mean? The initial investment looks like debt—it has an interest rate (most of the time) and a date by which the principal amount of the debt is expected to be repaid. That looks and smells like the bank debt we were talking about earlier.

But the debt also has a conversion feature—that is, a mechanism by which, in lieu of getting the principal back, the investor converts its debt into equity. Thus, the conversion feature turns nonpermanent capital into permanent capital. The conversion is often tied to equity-based financing for the company. In most of the cases we are concerned about in this book, the debt will in fact get converted into equity, so for the time being we are going to lump it into our discussion of equity. We will return to a broader discussion of convertible notes in chapter 9.

Before we dive deeper, let's spend a few minutes discussing some high-level themes about venture capital.

This is oversimplified, but there are basically three types of people involved in VC. There's an investor (institutional, "limited partners"—I promise we'll unpack these definitions soon) who invests in a venture firm's fund. Then the venture capitalist, usually a general partner at the firm, takes that money to invest in (hopefully) upward-bound startups. And the entrepreneur uses that money to grow her company. Those are the three: the investor, the VC, and the entrepreneur.

Now that we've got that out of the way, let's look at how investors consider VC funds to put their money into.

Venture Capital as a (Not-Very-Good) Asset Class for Investors

In simple terms, an "asset class" is a category of investments to which investors make an allocation. For example, bonds are an asset class, as are public market equities; that is, investors often choose—as part of a balanced portfolio—to invest some portion of their monies into bonds or stocks of publicly traded companies. Hedge funds, VC funds, and buyout funds, among others, are also examples of asset classes.

Institutional investors (i.e., professionals who manage large pools of capital) often have a defined asset allocation policy by which they invest. They might for example choose to invest 20 percent of their assets in bonds, 40 percent in publicly traded equities, 25 percent in hedge funds, 10 percent in buyout funds, and 5 percent in VC funds. There are numerous other asset classes for consideration and x-number of percentage allocations between the assets classes that institutional investors might pursue. As we'll see when we talk about the Yale University endowment, the objectives of the particular investor will determine the asset allocation strategy.

So, if we agree that VC is an asset class, why is it not a "good" one? Simply because the median returns are not worth the risk or the illiquidity that the average VC investor has to put up with.

In fact, as recently as 2017, the median ten-year returns in VC were 160 basis points below those of Nasdaq. A "basis point" is just a fancy way of saying 1/100th of a percentage point—so 200 basis points means 2 percentage points.

What does that mean? Unfortunately, it means that if you invested in the median returning VC firm, you would have tied up your money for a long time and have generated worse investment results than if you had just stuck your money in a Nasdaq or S&P 500 index fund. And you could have bought or sold your index holdings on any given day if you decided you needed to use that money—whereas had you needed to get your money out of the VC fund, good luck!

What explains this? Well, there are a few things at work here. Most significantly, VC returns do not follow a normal distribution.

You're probably familiar with the concept of the bell curve, which says that the distribution of *anything*—in this case we are talking about investment returns—is symmetric (meaning that half of the points are to the left of the median and half are to the right) and with defined standard deviations from the median (for example, in a normal distribution, 68 percent of the points fall within one standard deviation of the median).

If VC returns followed a bell curve, then you would have lots of firms—specifically, 68 percent of them—that were clustered within one standard deviation of the median. That is, most institutional investors could choose a manager to invest in and have a high expectation that that manager's returns would fall within that distribution.

Instead, VC firm results tend to follow more of a power-law curve. That is, the distribution of returns is not normal, but rather heavily skewed, such that a small percentage of firms capture a large percentage of the returns to the industry.

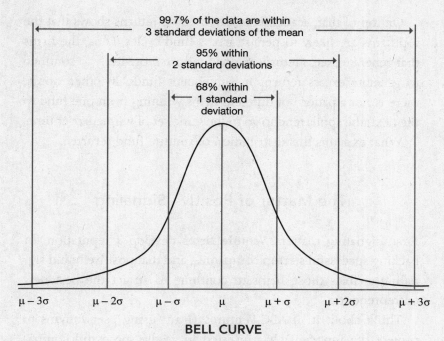

99.7% of the data are within
3 standard deviations of the mean

95% within
2 standard deviations

68% within
1 standard
deviation

$\mu - 3\sigma$ $\mu - 2\sigma$ $\mu - \sigma$ μ $\mu + \sigma$ $\mu + 2\sigma$ $\mu + 3\sigma$

BELL CURVE

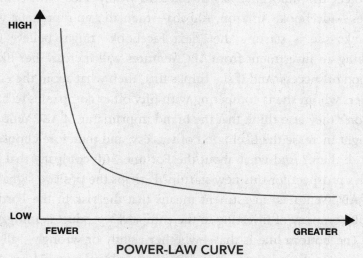

HIGH

LOW

FEWER

GREATER

POWER-LAW CURVE

So if you are an institutional investor in this paradigm, the likelihood of your investing in one of the few firms that generates excess returns is small. And if you invest in the median firm, the results generated by that firm are likely to be in the long tail of returns that are subpar.

On top of that, academic research on VC returns shows that the top firms are likely to persist across fund cycles. Thus, the firms that generate excess returns in one fund are more likely to continue to generate excess returns in subsequent funds. In other words, there is not a pattern of different firms winning from one fund to the next; the spoils tend to go to the same set of winners over time.

What explains this distribution of venture fund returns?

The Matter of Positive Signaling

First, signaling matters. Venture firms develop a reputation for backing successful startup companies, and that positive brand signaling enables those firms to continue to attract the best new entrepreneurs.

Think about it: if ABC Ventures (I am using pseudonyms to protect the innocent) has invested in wildly successful companies—Facebook, Amazon, Alibaba—then the entrepreneur who thinks she is starting the "next Facebook" might believe that taking an investment from ABC Ventures will increase her likelihood of success. And if she thinks that, then what about the engineers whom she is competing with fifty other companies to hire? Won't they also think that the brand imprimatur of ABC Ventures might increase the likelihood of success, and therefore choose to work there? And what about the Fortune 500 company that is a sales prospect for this new startup? Perhaps the positive signaling of ABC Ventures' investment means that the risk to the Fortune 500 company of investing in the company's product is mitigated.

The bottom line is that—whether rightly or wrongly—all the players in the ecosystem are doing a simple calculus: Those ABC Ventures folks must be smart. After all, they've invested in Facebook, Amazon, and Alibaba, to name a few—so by the transitive property, the entrepreneur building the next Facebook must be smart, and thus the risk of failure is lower for this company. Hence, past success begets future success.

Before you dismiss this as crazy, it's no different than any other signaling mechanisms people use throughout society. Why do lots of companies recruit heavily from Ivy League universities, even though we know there are lots of smart students who graduate from non–Ivy League schools? Well, because they've had success before with hiring Ivy League graduates and believe that the university itself has done a good job in the admissions process of screening the student for high intellect and good character.

Essentially, we often use signaling as a shorthand way of informing judgments. And as with all forms of generalization, sometimes we have false positives. This happens when we overfit on the curve and ascribe success to individuals or companies that might in fact not be as good as we have presumed them to be. We can also have false negatives, when we underfit on the curve and thus eliminate great candidates without having fully evaluated their skill sets.

In the venture context, as we'll see when we discuss incentives, underfitting is the far more serious mistake. If you invest in a company that turns out to be worse than you anticipated (false positives), the worst that you can do is lose all your invested capital. For people investing their life's savings, this is a very disheartening outcome. But as we'll see, for VCs this is simply part of their day job. But failing to invest in a *winner* means that you forfeit all the asymmetric upside that comes along with that investment. Missing the next Facebook or Google is no doubt painful, and depending on the rest of your portfolio, can be career ending for a VC.

VC Investing Is a Zero-Sum Game

Another reason that success in venture capital seems to cluster is that VC investing is largely a zero-sum game. Let me explain this by analogy to public market investing.

If you and I both think that Apple is a great stock to buy, we can both decide to buy it. Of course, if one of us is a really big buyer, the act of buying it might move the price such that my price might be different from yours (depending on which of us gets there first). But regardless, the general investment opportunity of buying Apple stock is available to each of us, independent of what the other does. The stock market is a democratic institution open to anyone who has money and a brokerage account.

Contrast that with VC investing. In most cases, when a company raises VC money, there is one "winner" (or maybe two) and a lot of losers. I put "winner" in quotes because we all think that we've won when we are able to invest in what looks like a very promising startup. But we often learn later that in some cases it can be more appropriately described as the "winner's curse"—a phenomenon whereby buyers in auctions get emotionally attached to the buying process or have imperfect information, such that they value the asset more than it's actually worth. In a VC deal, competition can certainly drive what we call "deal heat," a sometimes irrational response that causes investors to overpay for an asset. And no doubt information is nearly always imperfect in the evaluation process of an early-stage company.

Regardless of whether the asset is properly priced, there is often one VC firm that is the "lead" investor in the financing round and, as a result, invests the lion's share of the money in the company for that particular round. Sometimes, there are other nonlead investors who might participate in smaller amounts in the same financing round, but in no case is the round made available on a public stock exchange for any random investor to participate.

Once that investment round is completed, in most cases that investment opportunity is gone forever. There will never be another first round of financing for Facebook. So whatever return is ultimately generated from that first round of investment accrues to a very small set of fortunate investors.

There are of course often subsequent financing rounds—e.g., the "B" round of financing for Facebook—but the valuation of the company presumably has increased by that time and thus the eventual return to that set of investors will trail that of the first round's investors.

So if you couple the positive signaling we discussed earlier with this discontinuous nature of financing rounds and the winner-take-all notion, hopefully you can see how the overall returns in the industry often accrue to a limited (and often persistent) set of VC firms.

Investing in VC Is Restricted

The other special characteristic of venture investing is that it is restricted to what are known as "accredited" investors only. Accredited investors are basically people who have achieved some level of financial success (the current rules require that you have a $1 million net worth or have earned for the last two years, and have an ongoing prospect of earning, at least $200,000 annually). The theory of accreditation is that wealth equates to investment sophistication; it's an admittedly overbroad and underinclusive definition, but one in which the US securities laws seem to have much faith.

When a private company wishes to raise money to fund its operations, it must comply with US securities laws and thus needs to respect the accredited investor definition. Under the law, a company can sell securities only if it follows the registration requirements of securities offerings (which generally means that the company needs to be publicly registered) or it must have some exemption from the securities laws that allows it to sell securities without being a public company. That exemption generally comes in the form of agreeing not to sell securities broadly to unaccredited investors but rather to restrict the sale to accredited or qualified—an even higher form of wealth, generally in excess of $5 million of net worth—investors.

Investors in VC funds themselves also need to comply with these restrictions. Thus, you will not be invited to make an investment in a VC fund unless you meet at least the accredited investor definition; many VC funds restrict their investors to the even higher, qualified investor standard.

There is an exception to these rules—the crowdfunding provisions that the US Congress created as part of the 2012 JOBS Act. Under these rules, companies are permitted to sell up to $1 million of stock annually to unaccredited investors. There are a number of other hoops that companies have to jump through to take advantage of these rules, including, for example, that the investment materials be posted on an investor portal. As a result, while this was intended to provide some level of democratization to the private fund-raising process, most companies that raise VC money do not avail themselves of the crowdfunding rules.

Thus, VC investing is undemocratic not only in the sense that the winners seem generally to just get richer, but also because a limited number of players are allowed to ultimately compete.

How Can We Measure Success for a Venture Capital Firm?

What are the implications of all this for investing in venture capital?

First, diversification is a bad strategy for investing in VC firms. If you are an institutional investor who is lucky enough to have built a roster of successful firms whose returns are not the median but in the high-return section of the power-law curve, you don't want to diversify. Returns in the top end of VC funds can often be as much as 3,000 basis points higher than at the bottom end; dispersion of returns is huge when you have power-law distributions. In general, diversification is likely to push you toward the median/low-return section of the power-law curve and thus be dilutive to overall returns. Thus, many institutional investors seek to have a concentrated venture portfolio—which, by the way, probably further exacerbates that power-law distribution of returns.

And that brings us to the second implication—it's very hard for new firms to break into the industry and be successful. Admittedly, that has changed a bit over the last decade—in part due to the changing nature of the financing environment, which we'll cover later—but it's still pretty tough. To become a top VC firm that institutional investors want to invest in, you have to get yourself into that good part of the power-law curve, but if you don't have the brand to create the positive signaling that attracts the best entrepreneurs, it's hard to generate the returns—you get the picture. It's a classic chicken-and-egg problem.

Forget the Batting Average

But here's the rub. VCs with the highest batting averages do not usually make the best VCs.

There's nothing like baseball to help us understand the venture business. For the baseball averse, let's start with defining "batting average." A player's batting average is the quotient obtained by dividing the number of hits a player gets by the number of times at bat the player has (I know that walks don't count in the denominator, but it doesn't matter for my analogy). So a player who has a .300 batting average—which over the course of a career will get him into the Hall of Fame—gets a hit three out of every ten times that he comes to the plate.

Good VCs get a hit about five times out of ten at bats (a .500 batting average). A VC "hit" means that the investment returns more than the original amount the VC invested in a company. At first blush, that may sound good. But it's not—and, more importantly, it doesn't really matter in determining success.

For most VCs, the distribution of at bats looks something like this:

- 50 percent of the investments are "impaired," which is a very polite way of saying they lose some or all of their investment. Think about that for a second—VCs are completely wrong about half the time and lose most or all of the money that their investors entrusted to them as a result. In probably any other professional endeavor (baseball maybe being the exception that proves the rule), if you scored 50 percent, you'd likely be looking for a new job. But, hey, we VCs celebrate failure—sort of.

- 20–30 percent of the investments are—to continue with the baseball analogy—"singles" or "doubles." You didn't lose all the money (congratulations on that), but instead you made a return of a few times your investment. That $5 million you invested in Cryptocurrency.com returned you $10–$20 million—not bad. However, if you include the 50 percent of the "impaired" investments, the VC is still in trouble—70–80 percent of its invested dollars have yielded a total return of about seventy-five to ninety cents on the dollar. That doesn't sound like a recipe for success.
- Luckily, we still have 10–20 percent of our investments left— and these are our home runs. These are the investments where the VC is expecting to return ten to one hundred times her money.

If you're paying attention, this distribution of returns should remind you of the power-law curve discussion from the last section. It turns out that not only does the performance of VC firms follow the power-law curve, but so does the distribution of deals within a given fund.

Over time, funds that generate two and a half to three times net returns to their investors will be in the good portion of the power-law curve distribution and continue to have access to institutional capital. We'll talk about fees later, but to achieve two and a half to three times net returns (after all fees), VCs probably need to generate three to four times gross returns. That means if a VC has a $100 million fund, she needs to realize a total of $300–$400 million in proceeds from her investments in order to give $250–$300 million in net returns to the institutional investors.

What this tells us is that a batting average isn't the right metric for measuring success for a venture capital firm. In fact, the data show that firms with a better batting average often don't outperform those with a lower one—how can that be?

Because what matters most is your "at bats per home run." In baseball, at bats per home run is the quotient obtained from dividing the number of times a player comes to bat by the total number of home runs achieved. Mark McGwire has the top stat here, with a lifetime at bats per home run of 10.61. That means that McGwire hit a home run roughly one out of every ten times that he came up to the plate.

In VC, all we really care about is the at bats per home run. That is, the frequency with which the VC gets a return of more than ten times her investment—which we consider a home run. If you do the math, you'll see that VCs can get a lot of things wrong. Their overall batting average can be even less than 50 percent, as long as their at bats per home run are 10–20 percent, better than the all-time best baseball players.

And, as noted above, that's in fact what we see in the industry. The difference between a top-performing venture fund and a poor-performing one is not the batting average, but rather the at bats per home run. In many cases, in fact, firms that do the best have a worse batting average than the firms that underperform: they're like a baseball slugger who either strikes out or hits a home run every time he comes to the plate. It turns out that you can't de-risk your way to a winning venture fund. If you want to be in this business, you have to have either a stomach made of steel or a lifetime supply of Maalox.

Accel Partners is famous for, among other things, investing in a very early round of Facebook. At the time, Facebook was valued at roughly $100 million. Assume that Accel held those shares until Facebook went public, which it did at a market capitalization of around $100 billion. (We're keeping the math here simple for illustrative purposes, so forget for now about whether Accel's initial investment was diluted by subsequent rounds of financing, and forget about those first few days or weeks of Facebook's trading in the public markets.)

Rough math says that Accel made one thousand times its money on that investment—that certainly puts it in the home-run category. What do you think Accel made on the other investments it made as part of that fund? It's a trick question. The answer is, "It doesn't matter!" If you make one thousand times your money on one investment, you could be wrong on everything else and still have a top-performing fund, which Accel has done. It turns out that Accel did in fact make other great investments in that same fund, including AdMob, XenSource, and Trulia, among others—a curtain call of epic proportions. But all of that was financial gravy after the power-law return of the Facebook investment.

The Venture Capital Industry Is Tiny but Punches Well Above Its Weight

If you live in California, Massachusetts, or New York and are part of the VC or technology startup ecosystem, you can't open your Twitter feed or even your local newspaper without being overwhelmed by news of the industry's happenings. And it might make you think that VC is a really big industry, or at least that the earth revolves around it.

In fact, venture capital is a really small business, particularly when you compare it with other financial asset classes. The year 2017 was big: investments in companies by VC firms topped $84 billion. That's the largest amount in a while, and the business bottomed out (in recent years) at just below $30 billion in 2009. If you look across the prior five years or so, US VC investments in portfolio companies tended to be around $60–$70 billion per year. Interestingly, the number of discrete investments has declined in recent years, as more of the dollars are being concentrated into the companies valued at greater than $1 billion; in 2017, $19 billion (nearly 25 percent of the total capital invested across all companies) went to a very small number of these greater than $1 billion valuation companies. There's the power law again at work.

The other size metric for the industry is the annual amount of dollars raised by VC firms from institutional investors. In 2017, US firms raised about $33 billion from investors. At the peak of the dot-com bubble in 2000, US VC firms raised about $100 billion from investors, so we are well off of the peak.

To give you some perspective on these numbers, the global buyout industry raised about $450 billion in 2017. The hedge fund industry manages north of $3 trillion. The US GDP is about $17 trillion. So, by any measure, the venture capital industry represents a tiny amount of capital at work in the broader financial system.

But the impact of venture-capital-funded businesses punches well above its weight.

As we've already talked about, the five largest US market capitalization companies are all venture backed—Apple, Facebook, Microsoft, Amazon, and Google.

Stanford University published a study in 2015 highlighting the concentration of venture-backed companies in the US public markets since 1974. Stanford picked this year because the VC industry dramatically expanded starting in 1979 with the passage of the "prudent man rule." Prior to 1979, investing in VC was not considered "prudent" for most institutional investors. Thus, the industry largely attracted money from family offices, university endowments, and philanthropic foundations. With the introduction of this rule, pension funds were now permitted to invest in the VC asset class, and thus assets under management grew significantly. Despite the introduction of the rule in 1979, Stanford went back to 1974 to capture one or two significant companies—e.g., Apple—that would have otherwise been missed.

Using the 1974 data cutoff, 42 percent of public companies are venture backed, representing 63 percent of total market capitalization. These companies account for 35 percent of total employment and 85 percent of total research and development spend.

That's pretty good for an industry that invests about 0.4 percent of the US GDP!

CHAPTER 3

How Do Early-Stage
VCs Decide Where to Invest?

Let's take a look at how VCs decide which companies they should invest in and why. In an investing world glamorized by *Shark Tank*, *Silicon Valley*, and "unicorns," there is not a whole lot of simple, straightforward communication about what drives VC decisions.

As I mentioned, at the early stage of venture investing, raw data is very hard to come by. Obviously! At that point, the company usually hasn't gone to market yet in any real way. So at the time when many VCs are evaluating a startup for possible investment, qualitative evaluations dwarf quantitative ones.

As we'll see later in the book, there are a lot of quantitative ways to model the potential future returns of an investment. These are great spreadsheet exercises when and if you have enough data to inform the assumptions in the spreadsheet.

But the old adage "garbage in, garbage out" is particularly apt for early-stage venture investing. There simply aren't enough financial metrics to meaningfully model future potential returns for a business that just doesn't exist beyond the PowerPoint slides the entrepreneur has put together (sometimes just hours in advance of the pitch meeting with a venture firm).

So what do you do? Well, it turns out that there are qualitative and high-level quantitative heuristics that VCs use to evaluate the prospects for an investment. And they generally fall into three categories: people, product, and market.

1. People and Team

Let's start with people, as this is by far the most qualitative and, for early-stage investing, likely the most important evaluation criterion. When the "business" is nothing more than a very small collection of individuals—in some cases only one or two founders—with an idea, much of the VCs' evaluation will focus on the team.

In particular, many VCs delve deeply into the backgrounds of the founders for clues about their effectiveness in executing this particular idea. The fundamental assumption here is that ideas are not proprietary. In fact, VCs assume the opposite—if an idea turns out to be a good one, assume there will be many other founders and companies that are created to pursue this idea.

So what matters most is, why do I as a VC want to back this particular team versus any of the x-number of other teams that might show up to execute this idea? The way to think about this is that the opportunity cost of investing in this particular team going after this particular idea is infinite; a decision to invest means that the VC cannot invest in a different team that may come along and ultimately be better equipped to pursue the opportunity.

John Doerr, a VC from the firm Kleiner Perkins, is famous for purportedly saying that a cardinal rule of venture capital is "No conflict, no interest," but the reality of modern VC is that conflict is king. Venture capitalists are de facto unable to invest in businesses pursuing the same opportunity, though of course the definition of conflict is always in the eye of the beholder.

Why is that? Because a VC's decision to invest in a company is effectively an endorsement of the company as the de facto winner

in the space. After all, why would I invest in Facebook instead of
Friendster if I felt as though Friendster were the likely company
to dominate the social networking market? Recall the earlier discussion about the positive signaling effect of a VC's brand on the
portfolio company's brand; they are deeply entangled as a result
of the investment, for better or for worse. Thus, every investment
decision has infinite opportunity cost in that it likely prevents you
as a VC from investing in a direct competitor in that space; you
have picked your horse to ride.

In light of this, among the cardinal sins of venture capital is
getting the category right (meaning that you correctly anticipated
that a big company could be built in a particular space) but getting the company wrong (meaning that you picked the wrong
horse to back). For example, you might have discerned in the
early 2000s that social networking was going to be big, but then
decided to invest in Friendster over Facebook. Or you might have
recognized that search was going to be a big business in the late
1990s but elected to invest in AltaReturn over Google.

So how do you evaluate a founding team? Different VCs of
course do things differently, but there are a few common areas of
investigation.

First, what is the unique skill set, background, or experience
that led this founding team to pursue this idea? My partners use
the concept of a "product-first company" versus a "company-first
company."

In the product-first company, the founder identified or experienced some particular problem that led her to develop a product
to solve that problem, which ultimately compelled her to build
a company as the vehicle by which to bring that product to the
market. A company-first company is one in which the founder
first decides that she wants to start a company and then brain-
storms products that might be interesting around which to build
one. Successful businesses can of course ultimately be created
from either mold, but the product-first company really speaks to

the organic nature of company formation. A real-world problem experienced by the founder becomes the inspiration to build a product (and ultimately a company); this organic pull is often very attractive to VCs.

Many people are undoubtedly familiar with the concept of product-market fit. Popularized by Steve Blank and Eric Ries, product-market fit speaks to a product being so attractive to customers in the marketplace that they recognize the problem it was intended to solve and feel compelled to purchase the product. Consumer "delight" and repeat purchasing are the classic hallmarks of product-market fit. Airbnb has this, as do Instacart, Pinterest, Lyft, Facebook, and Instagram, among others. As consumers, we almost can't imagine what we did before these products existed. Again, it is an organic pull on customers, resulting from the breakthrough nature of the product and its fitness to the market problem at which it is directed.

The equivalent in founder evaluation for VCs is founder-market fit. As a corollary to the product-first company, founder-market fit speaks to the unique characteristics of this founding team to pursue the instant opportunity. Perhaps the founder has a unique educational background best suited to the opportunity.

We at a16z saw this with Martin Casado and his decision to found Nicira, a company that created software-defined networking (SDN). Martin not only worked on early iterations of SDN for the intelligence community, but he also earned his PhD at Stanford in the area. His entire professional career effectively led him to the development of Nicira, which by the way was ultimately acquired by VMware for $1.25 billion.

Perhaps the founder had a unique experience that exposed her to the market problem in a way that provided unique insights into the solution for the problem. The founders of Airbnb fit this bill. They were struggling to make ends meet living in San Francisco and noticed that all the hotels were sold out locally whenever there was a major convention in town. What if, they thought, we could rent out a sleeping spot in our apartment to conference attendees to help them save money on accommodations and help us meet our rent obligations? And thus was born Airbnb.

Perhaps the founder has simply dedicated his life to the particular problem at hand. Orion Hindawi and his father, David, founded a company called BigFix in the late 1990s. BigFix was a security software company that focused on endpoint management—the process by which companies provided virtual security for their PCs, laptops, etc. After selling the company to IBM, Orion and David decided to found Tanium, essentially BigFix 2.0. Incorporating all the lessons learned from BigFix and, as important, the changes in technology infrastructure that occurred over the intervening ten-plus years, Tanium is today a world-class, modern endpoint security company. Tanium represents the culmination of a lifetime of living and breathing enterprise security challenges.

In a strange way, sometimes familiarity can breed contempt—and conversely, the distance from the problem that comes from having a completely different professional background might actually make one a better founder. Though not venture backed, Southwest Airlines was cofounded in 1967 by Herb Kelleher and of course has gone on to become a very successful business. When interviewed many years later about why, despite being a lawyer by training, he was the natural founder for an airline business, Kelleher quipped: "I knew nothing about airlines, which I think made me eminently qualified to start one, because what we tried to do at Southwest was get away from the traditional way that airlines had done business."

This has historically been less typical in the venture world, but, increasingly, as entrepreneurs take on more established industries—particularly those that are regulated—bringing a view of the market that is unconstrained by previous professional experiences may in fact be a plus. We often joke at a16z that there is a tendency to "fight the last battle" in an area in which one has long-standing professional exposure; the scars from previous mistakes run too deep and can make it harder for one to develop creative ways to address the business problem at hand. Perhaps had Kelleher known intimately of all the challenges of entering the airline business, he would have run screaming from the challenge versus deciding to take on the full set of risks.

Whatever the evidence, the fundamental question VCs are trying to answer is: Why back this founder against this problem set versus waiting to see who else may come along with a better organic understanding of the problem? Can I conceive of a team better equipped to address the market needs that might walk through our doors tomorrow? If the answer is no, then this is the team to back.

The third big area of team investigation for VCs focuses on the founder's leadership abilities. In particular, VCs are trying to determine whether this founder will be able to create a compelling story around the company mission in order to attract great engineers, executives, sales and marketing people, etc. In the same vein, the founder has to be able to attract customers to buy the product, partners to help distribute the product, and, eventually, other VCs to fund the business beyond the initial round of financing. Will the founder be able to explain her vision in a way that causes others to want to join her on this mission? And will she walk through walls when the going gets tough—which it inevitably will in nearly all startups—and simply refuse to even consider quitting?

When Marc and Ben first started Andreessen Horowitz, they described this founder leadership capability as "egomaniacal." Their theory—notwithstanding the choice of words—was that to make the decision to be a founder (a job fraught with likely failure), an individual needed to be so confident in her abilities to succeed that she would border on being so self-absorbed as to be truly egomaniacal. As you might imagine, the use of that term in our fund-raising deck for our first fund struck a chord with a number of our potential investors, who worried that we would back insufferable founders. We ultimately chose to abandon our word choice, but the principle remains today: you have to be partly delusional to start a company given the prospects of success and the need to keep pushing forward in the wake of the constant stream of doubters.

After all, nonobvious ideas that could in fact become big businesses are by definition nonobvious. My partner Chris Dixon describes our job as VCs as investing in good ideas that look like bad ideas. If you think about the spectrum of things in which you could invest, there are good ideas that look like good ideas. These are tempting, but likely can't generate outsize returns because they are simply too obvious and invite too much competition that squeezes out the economic rents. Bad ideas that look like bad ideas are also easily dismissed; as the description implies, they are simply bad and thus likely to be trapdoors through which your investment dollars will vanish. The tempting deals are the bad ideas that look like good ideas, yet they ultimately contain some hidden flaw that reveals their true "badness." This leaves good VCs to invest in good ideas that look like bad ideas—hidden gems that probably take a slightly delusional or unconventional founder to pursue. For if they were obviously good ideas, they would never produce venture returns.

Ultimately, what all these inquiries point to is the fundamental principle that most ideas are not proprietary, nor likely to determine success or failure in startup companies. Execution ultimately matters, and execution derives from a team's members being able to work in concert with one another toward a clearly articulated vision.

2. Product

We've hinted at many of the product issues already, but the fundamental question to be asked by early-stage VCs is, Will this product solve a fundamental need in the market (whether or not that need is known currently to customers) such that customers will pay real money to purchase it?

One of the first truisms of product evaluation is that the product is not static. In fact, most VCs assume that the product that is initially conceived of and pitched is not likely the product that will ultimately prevail. Why is that? Simply because until the startup builds a version of the product and gets it into market with early adopter customers, any notion that the company has about the fitness of the product to the market need is purely hypothetical. Only through iterative testing with real customers will the company get the feedback needed to build a truly break-through product.

Thus, much of what an early VC is evaluating at this stage is the founder's idea maze: How did she get to the current product idea, incorporating which insights and market data to help inform her opinions? Assuming that the product will in fact change many times over the course of discerning product-market fit, it's the process of the idea maze that is the better predictor of the founder's success than the actual product idea itself.

In fact, you'll often hear VCs say that they like founders who have strong opinions but ones that are weakly held, that is, the ability to incorporate compelling market data and allow it to evolve your product thinking. Have conviction and a well-vetted process, but allow yourself to "pivot" (to invoke one of the great euphemisms in venture capital speak) based on real-world feedback.

The other vector of product evaluation centers on the break-through nature of the product. Large companies have institutional inertia that makes it difficult for them to adopt new products; consumers have habits that also make change difficult. Max Planck, the German scientist who is credited with inventing modern quantum physics, said it most eloquently: Science advances one funeral at a time. Simply put, it's hard to get people to adopt new technologies.

So new products won't succeed if they are marginal improvements against the existing state of the art. They need to be ten times better or ten times cheaper than current best in class to compel companies and consumers to adopt. (Of course, "ten times" here is just a heuristic, but the point is that marginal differences won't get people off the couch.)

Ben Horowitz uses the difference between a vitamin and an aspirin to articulate this point. Vitamins are nice to have; they offer some potential health benefits, but you probably don't interrupt your commute when you are halfway to the office to return home for the vitamin you neglected to take before you left the house. It also takes a very, very long time to know if your vitamins are even working for you. If you have a headache, though, you'll do just about anything to get an aspirin! They solve your problem and they are fast acting. Similarly, products that often have massive advantages over the status quo are aspirins; VCs want to fund aspirins.

3. Market Size

"Market" is the third leg of the stool that VCs use to evaluate early-stage investment opportunities. It turns out that what matters most to VCs is the ultimate size of the market opportunity a founder is going after. If the adage in real estate is "Location, location, location," the saying in venture capital goes "Market size, market size, market size." Big markets are good; small markets are bad.

Why?

The big-market rule follows directly from the power-law curve and "at bats per home run" section we covered earlier. If VCs are wrong more often than they are right, and if success (or failure) as a VC is wholly a function of whether you get 10–20 percent of your investments to fall into the home-run category, then size of the winners is all that matters.

I noted before that a cardinal sin of venture investing is getting the category right but the company wrong. Well, there are a couple of other cardinal sins to supplement that one.

First, getting the company right but the market wrong, that is, investing in a company that turns out to be a nice, profitable business, with a great team and a great product, but in a market that just isn't that big. No matter how well the team executes, the business will never get to more than $50–$100 million in revenue, and thus the equity value of the business is capped.

Second, sins of omission are worse than sins of commission. It's okay for a VC to invest in a company that ultimately fails—as we've discussed, that's par for the course in this business. What's not okay is to fail to invest in a company that becomes the next Facebook. Remember, you can't risk-averse your way to success in this business.

All of this leads us to the truism that VCs must invest in big-market opportunities. Success against a small market just won't get a VC the type of returns she needs to generate to stay in business. Thus, VCs often think of market size as the "so what?" question in evaluating a startup's potential success. It's all well and good that the team is great and the product is great, but so what, if the market size isn't sufficient to sustain a large business. Andy Rachleff, a founder of Benchmark Capital, has said that companies can succeed in great markets even with mediocre teams but that great teams will always lose to a bad market.

Why is market size so challenging to get right? Because often it's unknowable at the time of investment how big a market actually is. Thus, VCs can fool themselves in multiple ways when evaluating markets.

Market size estimation is easiest when a new product is positioned as a direct substitute for an existing product.

Take databases as an example. We know that Oracle is a huge company in the database market, so we can fairly easily posit that a startup going after that market opportunity is playing in a big market—easy enough. But what we don't know is how the overall database market will play out over time. Will there be other new technologies that might supplant the functions of the database and thus hollow out the market? Or maybe the number of applications that require databases will grow exponentially as cloud computing dominates workflows, and thus the database market will become even bigger than it is today? Those are all good questions, but most

VCs would probably be fine assuming that a startup going after the database market, if successful, has a big enough market to build a big company and thus become an investment home run.

The more challenging aspects of market size estimation come from startups going after markets that do not exist currently or that are smaller markets today because they are constrained by the current state of technology.

Take Airbnb. When Airbnb first raised money, the use case was predominantly people sleeping on other people's couches. One could have asked the question of how many starving college students there were who would do such a thing, and have reasonably concluded—similar to the size of the mac and cheese and ramen markets, other products purchased by starving college students—that the market simply wasn't that big.

But what if the service expanded to other constituents over time? Maybe then the existing hotel market would be a good proxy for total market size. Okay, but what if the ease of booking reservations and the lower price points that Airbnb offered meant that people who never before traveled decided that they would now do so—what if in fact the market for travelers needing accommodations would expand as a result of the introduction of Airbnb?

As it turns out, the success of Airbnb to date seems to suggest that the market size has indeed expanded, owing to the existence of a new form of travel accommodations that never previously existed. Fortunes can be won or lost based on a VC's ability to understand market size and think creatively about the role of technology in developing new markets.

CHAPTER 4

What Are LPs and Why Should You Care?

There is a story that Queen Isabella of Spain was the first true VC. She "backed" an entrepreneur (Christopher Columbus) with capital (money, ships, supplies, crew) to do something that most people at the time thought was insane and certain to fail (a voyage) in exchange for a portion of the to-be-earned profits of the voyage that, while probabilistically unlikely, had an asymmetric payoff compared to her at-risk capital.

If you attended Harvard Business School, you may have read about a similar early VC-like tale here in the States in the 1800s— the whaling industry. Financing a whaling venture was expensive and fraught with risk but, when successful, highly profitable. In 1840s New Bedford, "agents" (today's VC equivalent) would raise capital from corporations and wealthy individuals (today's limited partners) to fund ship captains (entrepreneurs) to launch a whaling venture (startup company) in search of asymmetric returns that were heavily skewed to the top agents, yet often plagued with failure. Thirty percent of voyages lost money . . . .

Fewer than fifty years later, in 1878, J. P. Morgan would act as "venture capitalist" to Thomas Edison, financing the Edison General

Electric Company and becoming its first evangelist/beta tester by having Edison wire Morgan's New York City home. Rumor has it that not only did Morgan's house almost burn down from some of the early wiring mishaps, but his neighbors also threatened him as a result of the loud noise emanating from the generators required to sustain the illumination. Banks would continue to play a significant role in the direct financing of many startup businesses until the 1930s passage of the Glass-Steagall Act restricted these activities.

Today, VC firms exist by the grace of limited partners who invest some of their own funds into specific VC funds. Limited partners do this because, as part of their desire to maintain a diversified portfolio, venture capital is intended to produce what investment managers refer to as alpha—excess returns relative to a specific market index.

Though each LP may have its own benchmark to measure success, common benchmarks are the S&P 500, Nasdaq, or Russell 3000; many LPs will look to generate excess returns of 500–800 basis points relative to the index. That means that if the S&P 500 were to return 7 percent annualized over a ten-year period, LPs would expect to see at least 12–15 percent returns from their VC portfolio. As an example, the Yale endowment's venture capital portfolio has generated returns north of 18 percent per year for the past ten years versus an S&P 500 return of about 8 percent in the same time period.

Types of LPs

There are many categories of LPs, but most tend to fall into the following buckets:

- **University endowments** (e.g., Stanford, Yale, Princeton, MIT)— Nearly every university solicits donations from its alumni. Those donated funds need to earn a return on investment. Those returns are used to fund operating expenses and scholarships for the schools and, in some cases, to help fund capital expenditures, such as new buildings.

- **Foundations** (e.g., Ford Foundation, Hewlett Foundation)—Foundations are bequeathed money by their benefactors and are expected to exist in perpetuity on these funds. Foundations need to earn a return on their funds to make charitable grants. In the US, to maintain their tax-free status, foundations are required to pay out 5 percent of their funds each year in support of their mission. Thus, over the long term, real returns from venture capital and other investments need to exceed this 5 percent payout level to ensure a foundation's perpetual existence.

- **Corporate and state pension funds** (e.g., IBM pension, California State Teachers' Retirement System)—Some corporations (although many fewer these days), most states, and many countries provide pensions for their retirees, funded mostly by contributions from their current employees. Inflation (particularly in health-care costs) and demographics (more retirees than current employees) eat away at the value of these pensions, absent the ability to generate real investment returns.

- **Family offices** (e.g., U.S. Trust, myCFO)—These are investment managers who are investing on behalf of very-high-net-worth families. Their goals are set by the individual families but often include multigenerational wealth preservation and/or funding large charitable efforts. There are single-family offices (as the name suggests, they are managing the assets of a single family and its heirs) and multifamily offices (essentially, sophisticated money managers who aggregate the assets of multiple families and invest them across various asset classes).

- **Sovereign wealth funds** (e.g., Temasek, Korea Investment Corporation, Saudi Arabia's PIF)—These are organizations that manage the economic reserves of a country (often resulting from things that we US citizens know nothing about—government surpluses) to benefit current or future generations of their citizens. In the specific case of many Middle Eastern countries, the sovereign wealth funds are taking profits from

today's oil business and reinvesting in other non-oil assets, to
protect against long-term financial reliance on a finite asset.

- **Insurance companies** (e.g., MetLife, Nippon Life)—Insurance
companies earn premiums from their policyholders and invest
those premiums (known as "float") for when they are required
to pay out future benefits. The monies they earn from investing
these premiums are then available to pay out the insurance policies as they mature.
- **Funds of funds** (e.g., HarbourVest, Horsley Bridge)—These are
private firms that raise money from their own LPs and then
invest in venture capital or other financial managers. LPs of
fund of funds are typically smaller instances of direct venture
LPs and thus find it difficult or economically inefficient to invest
directly in VCs—e.g., they might be university endowments or
foundations with less than $1 billion in assets, such that hiring
an in-house team to cover venture capital relationships may
be prohibitively expensive. The fund of funds aggregate small
LP assets and deploy the capital into VCs. Unlike the other categories of LPs, fund of funds are not permanent capital; that
is, just as with venture capital funds, fund of funds need to go
raise money on a periodic basis from their LPs in order to have
money to invest in venture capital funds.

As noted above, while there are lots of potential LPs with
varying uses for their capital, the overarching goal of LPs is to earn
a return on their money that enables them to satisfy their mission.

The mission for a university endowment, for example, is to
be able to provide a predictable stream of revenue from which
to cover the many operating expenses associated with running a
modern university. In many cases, university endowments contribute between 30 and 50 percent of the annual operating expenses for a school.

Inflation (in its many forms) is the kryptonite to the long-term
success of LPs. University endowments worry most about inflation in their expense drivers (namely, salaries for professors and

administrators), which has outstripped regular inflation significantly over the years. Foundations worry about generalized inflation that eats away the purchasing power of its dollars (and thus its ability to make grants). Insurance providers, of course, worry about the same—if inflation exceeds the returns on their investments, the real purchasing power of their assets declines and can make it difficult for them to be able to pay out insurance claims in the future.

But in trying to increase the real value of their investments, LPs don't just invest in VCs; they construct a diversified portfolio around a defined asset allocation to try to achieve their return goals, but within a defined volatility (or risk) framework.

Where LPs Invest

Generally speaking, the types of investments to which LPs allocate capital fall into three big buckets:

- **Growth assets**—These are investments intended (as the name suggests) to earn returns in excess of what less risky assets (bonds and cash) are expected to earn. There are several subcategories of assets within growth:

  Public equities—Stocks that trade on public market exchanges. Most LPs typically have some allocation to US domestic equities, developed international country equities (e.g., Europe), emerging market equities (e.g., China, Brazil), and frontier market equities (e.g., Indonesia). Within these geographic areas of focus, some LPs will also have specific targets for types of equities—e.g., small cap versus large cap, and value versus growth.

  Private equities—Stocks that do not trade on public exchanges but are instead managed by funds that transact in privately held companies. Buyout firms are a big category of private equities; VC is in this category as well.

  Hedge funds—Funds that invest mostly in publicly traded equities but have the ability to take both long (i.e., buy a stock) and short (i.e., bet that a stock will decline in price) positions. There are lots of different types of hedge funds, to name a few: long-only funds, long/short funds, event driven (e.g., they invest in equities where the company might be going through an acquisition), macro (e.g., they are making an investment bet on a country's inflation outlook, currency movements, etc.), or absolute return (they aim to meet a defined return target independent of overall market movements). Some LPs have differing views on the role of hedge funds in the portfolio. In some cases they are thought of as regular growth assets—meaning that they should yield equity-like returns and thus provide asset appreciation to the portfolio. Other LPs think of hedge funds as closer to diversifying (or, as the name suggests, "hedging") assets; that is, they look for hedge funds whose returns are not correlated with the overall equity markets so as to provide a more balancing effect on overall returns depending on whether equity markets are up or down in a given year.

- **Inflation hedges**—These are investments meant to protect against the decreasing value of a currency. In other words, in an inflationary environment, they are expected to earn a rate of return in excess of inflation. There are several subcategories of assets within inflation hedges:

  Real estate—Rising inflation should increase the underlying value of a property holding and, in most cases, as inflation rises, the landlord can increase the rent she collects from tenants.

  Commodities—Gold, silver, and other precious metals tend to increase in value with inflation as people look to them as stores of value in an environment where currencies are inflating.

  Natural resources—Investments in oil and gas, timber resources, and agriculture also tend to be viewed as inflation-protecting assets. Inflation often accompanies economically expanding environments, driving demand for raw materials needed to sustain that growth; thus, natural resources pricing is expected to outpace inflation.

- **Deflationary hedges**—When prices drop (deflation), the purchasing power of currency actually increases. To take advantage of this, LPs often hold some portion of their assets in the following:

    Bonds—In general, interest rates fall with deflation and, because the value of a bond is inversely correlated with interest rates, bond prices increase.

    Cash—A dollar tomorrow in a deflationary environment is worth more than a dollar today. Thus, holding some assets in cash provides a hedge against unexpected deflation.

Depending on the overall return target an LP is trying to achieve, its willingness to accept volatility in investment returns, and the time horizon over which it is willing to tie up its capital, an LP will construct an asset allocation from the above mix that marries all these objectives.

And LPs will try to achieve some element of diversification, meaning that they don't have too many eggs in one basket and hold some combination of assets that might be uncorrelated with one another in case the overall investing environment moves wildly in one direction or the other. Of course, you know what they say about the best laid plans: as the 2008 global financial crisis illustrated, many assets that LPs had previously thought were uncorrelated turned out to all move in the same direction—down!

The Mighty Bulldog

One of the best examples of modern asset allocation is the Yale University endowment. Its current, and long-standing, chief investment officer is David Swensen, whom people credit with designing the allocation model that many leading institutional investors follow today. There are Yale acolytes who are now running a large number of other US-based endowments and foundations, thus helping to introduce the Yale endowment model to a variety of other institutions.

Interestingly enough, Yale came to its current asset allocation model on the heels of a disastrous run of investment returns. From the late 1930s until 1967, the Yale endowment was composed almost exclusively of bonds, specifically treasury bonds. The strategy proved costly, as the endowment missed out on one of the great equity bull markets in US history. To remedy this, the endowment (at the height of the equity bull market) invested heavily into small-cap stocks in 1967, ultimately liquidating this position at a material loss in the late 1970s.

Swensen joined the endowment in 1985, when the total assets were roughly $1 billion; more than thirty years later, the endowment tops $25 billion. Of course, alumni have donated money over time as well to help increase the size of the endowment, but over the last ten years, the Yale endowment has returned more than 8 percent net from its investment allocation, ranking it among the very top educational institutions.

The endowment's main purpose is to provide a steady source of funding to the university. In 2016, the endowment contributed $1.15 billion to the university, accounting for one-third of the institution's revenue. Maybe surprisingly (it was to me), tuition and room and board that Yale's student population paid amounted to only about $333 million that year, or about 10 percent of the total university budget.

Given the magnitude of the university's reliance on the endowment to keep the lights on, predictability of the endowment's contribution is pretty important to Yale. If the contribution were to swing wildly from one year to the next, for example, Yale, which has a high fixed expense base (mostly employee salaries), would be forced to hire or fire employees from one year to the next. Alternatively, Yale could significantly adjust the amount it takes from the endowment, but that would make it hard for the endowment to know how much of its assets it could hold in liquid versus illiquid investments, making longer-term asset allocation planning more difficult. Finally, since the goal of the endowment is to be perpetual and to grow its assets over time, if the endowment had to provide more cash to the university every time the stock market were down, the endowment returns would likely suffer as a result.

To address this challenge, Yale uses what's called a "smoothing model" to determine the amount of money it contributes each year to the university's budget. This enables the university to plan its expenses with more certainty and allows the endowment to plan its asset allocation model with more certainty as well. By definition, the smoothing model says that the endowment will give the university an amount equal to 80 percent of the prior year's spending rate plus the product of 20 percent of the board-determined spend rate and the value of the endowment from two years prior. Currently, this adds up to an overall spend rate of around 5.25 percent of the endowment's value, but it has ranged over time between 4 and 6.5 percent.

So what does that tell you about the kind of returns that the Yale endowment needs to achieve to sustain its financial commitment to the university and ultimately grow the value of its assets? At a high level, if inflation is currently running a little north of 2 percent, and if the endowment needs to contribute 5.25 percent of its assets every year to the university, then the endowment's investments need to earn at least 7.25 percent in gross returns to grow the asset base. Luckily, as we said above, the endowment has been generating just north of 8 percent annually over each of the last ten years. Mission accomplished.

Let's now turn to Yale's actual asset allocation to understand how it intends to keep achieving these results and ultimately the role that VC is playing in the endowment.

Here's how Yale is allocating its growth assets:

- **Domestic equities**—Yale has a 4 percent allocation to US publicly traded stocks; over the last twenty years, Yale's domestic equity portfolio has returned about 13 percent annually. Note that the average university endowment has about 20 percent of its portfolio in domestic equities. Yale's decision to invest materially less in these assets reflects a belief on its part that there are other assets that have higher return potential coupled with lower volatility. We'll see shortly where Yale's extra dollars are in fact going.

- **Foreign equities**—Yale has a 15 percent allocation to non-US publicly traded stocks, 6 percent to developed international markets and 9 percent to emerging international markets. As with its domestic equity allocation, Yale's foreign equity allocation trails the average university endowment by about 6 percentage points. Over the last twenty years, Yale's foreign equity portfolio has returned about 14 percent annually.

- **Hedge funds**—Yale calls its hedge fund strategy "absolute return," meaning that it is investing in this asset class largely to generate high long-term returns by exploiting market inefficiencies with relatively low correlation to broader equity market and fixed income returns. Yale's allocation of 22 percent to absolute return strategies is generally in line with other university endowments and has returned 9 percent annually over the last twenty years (with the expected low correlation to equities and bonds).

- **Buyout funds**—Yale has a 15 percent allocation to buyout funds; recall that these are private equity funds that typically buy controlling ownership stakes in existing businesses and seek to increase their value over time by improving their financial operations. At 15 percent, Yale's allocation to buyout funds well exceeds the 6 percent average among university endowments. Over the last twenty years, Yale's buyout portfolio has returned about 14 percent annually.

- **Venture capital**—Yale has a 16 percent allocation to our good old venture capital category, again way in excess of the 5 percent average among other university endowments. And, boy, has this paid off for the Yale endowment; over the last twenty years, Yale's venture capital portfolio has returned about 77 percent annually. No, that is not a typo—basically, that means that

Yale has been doubling its money in venture capital every year for the last twenty years!

If you add all of that up, the Yale endowment is allocating 72 percent of its endowment to growth assets. That makes sense when you think about the financial obligations the endowment has to the university and the need to keep pace with university inflation, which has been well in excess of more generalized price inflation.

Here's how Yale is allocating its inflation hedging assets—a total of 20 percent of its assets are geared toward protecting against unexpected inflation:

- **Natural resources**—Yale has a 7.5 percent allocation to oil and gas, timberland, mining, and agriculture assets, each of which is intended to protect against unexpected inflation and generate near-term cash flow. At 7.5 percent, Yale's allocation is generally in line with the average university endowment. Over the last twenty years, Yale's natural resources portfolio has returned about 16 percent annually.
- **Real estate**—Yale has a 12.5 percent allocation to real estate investments, well in excess of the 4 percent average at other university endowments. Over the last twenty years, Yale's real estate portfolio has returned about 11 percent annually.

The smallest portion of Yale's endowment is targeted to deflation hedging assets—7.2 percent, well below the 12.7 percent allocation of the average university endowment:

- **Fixed income**—Yale has a 4.9 percent allocation to bonds, which are intended to protect against unexpected deflation and to provide near-term cash flow. Over the last twenty years, Yale's bond portfolio has returned about 5 percent annually.
- **Cash**—Yale has about a 2 percent allocation to cash.

A couple of big-picture things stand out when looking at the Yale endowment portfolio.

Yale has a heavy concentration in illiquid assets—Yale targets to have about 50 percent of its endowment in illiquid assets (essentially funds where the money is tied up for longer periods of time). Yale's investments in VC, buyout, real estate, and natural resources fall into this category—as of 2016, they added up to about 51 percent, so pretty much on target. Swensen's view is that illiquid markets tend to have less efficiently priced assets; thus, there is more opportunity for smart asset managers to capture above-market returns.

Yale also relies heavily on external asset managers versus doing most of its investing directly in-house. Harvard most notably experimented with running much of its endowment in-house before abandoning that strategy, but Swensen has been a longtime proponent of external managers. In fact, most of the due diligence that the Yale team does in analyzing investment opportunities is to analyze what makes a manager unique and how appropriately aligned they are with the endowment's overall long-term financial goals.

Before we leave our friends in New Haven, let's take a final look at the role of VC in the Yale endowment.

As we noted, Yale has an outsize asset allocation to venture (at least relative to other university endowments) and has been paid handsomely over the last twenty years as a result. While I don't think the Yale team expects to earn 77 percent annually forever (in fact, their 2016 report mentions a target annualized return of 16 percent, and they have realized about 18 percent annually over the last ten years), regardless of the actual number, Yale is indeed looking for venture capital to be a high absolute and relative return driver to the portfolio.

Note the significant difference in Yale's VC returns over the twenty-year period (77 percent) compared with its returns over the last ten years (18 percent). The dot-com bubble that we talked about earlier in the book created an incredible return for VC firms and their LPs in a very concentrated period of time in the late 1990s. While 18 percent returns are nothing to sneeze at, Yale's experience gives you a good idea of how outsize venture returns can be in good vintages as well as the variance that can occur in less buoyant times. Most experienced institutional investors will tell you that this reinforces the need to "stay the course" in venture investing throughout stock market cycles. Missing a great vintage can be the difference between realizing long-term outsize returns in VC and not getting paid adequately for the risk and illiquidity of the asset class. Yet again, our friend the power-law curve enters the story.

And, no doubt, those high-return expectations will drive the behavior of VCs. Venture firms will continue to focus on the at-bats-per-home-run average and thus ultimately look for big enough markets that can sustain viable home-run companies. That's how the world turns.

Importantly, as well, because Yale has a lot of its assets tied up in illiquid categories such as venture capital, it does ultimately care a lot about eventually achieving liquidity. In other words, Yale wants to be able to realize its 18 percent annual return in VC by tying up its money for longer periods of time, but in order to keep funding the university and reinvesting in its venture managers, it needs to eventually get liquidity from its earlier venture investments. And, again, that drives corresponding behavior among the VC firms— they need to either sell or take the companies in their portfolio public at some point in time in order to realize cash to provide back to Yale.

Time Is of the Essence

Thus, as a potential entrepreneur and a consumer of VC dollars, you need to be aware of the time constraints ultimately imposed on you. At some point in your company's life cycle, the VCs will push for an exit to generate this type of liquidity. When that happens is a function of not only how the company is doing but also where a firm might be in its fund life cycle and how the rest of the companies in the fund are performing.

To this end, one thing for you as an entrepreneur to consider is how old the fund is from which you are receiving your investment. This is a perfectly fair question to ask of your potential VC partner at the time you are deciding whether you want to work with them.

We are going to cover the fund specifics in the coming chapters, but in choosing a firm to work with, it's reasonable to ask where the firm is in the life cycle of that particular fund. If they are early in the fund, then they should have less pressure to return capital to, say, Yale (or their other LPs) and thus should put less pressure on you as the CEO to generate a near-term exit. But if they are later in the fund cycle and haven't generated sufficient liquidity from other investments, the pressure for a more near-term exit could be more intense. While you may not be able to get all this information from a conversation with your prospective partner, there are some ways to get insight into these questions.

First, you should ask about the specific fund from which the VC is proposing to invest in your company—most funds are serially numbered with Roman numerals. You can then check the initiation of that fund to determine its age. As you'll see later, funds tend to be ten years in life and often can get extended for a few years beyond that. But VCs are generally limited in how late into the fund they can make new investments (often only through years five or six). So if you are taking money from a VC and they are in the first three or four years of the fund, they are more likely to have both time and available capital to live with you for many years hence. But if they are just investing in your company for the first time in year five or six, things may be different.

That's because—as we'll discuss in more detail shortly—VCs tend not only to invest capital in startups earlier in the life of a fund, they also generally set aside "reserves," expected monies that they anticipate they might invest in a startup over the course of its next several financing rounds. Thus, the later in a fund cycle your investment occurs, the greater the likelihood that the VC may also not have sufficient reserves to set aside for subsequent financing rounds.

It is true, by the way, that VCs can and often do invest in the same portfolio company in a subsequent fund, particularly if they run out of reserve capacity in the original fund that made the investment. However, this is not as easy as investing reserves out of the same fund as the original investment, in part because the mix of LPs could be different from one fund to the next and thus create potential conflicts between the funds.

For example, the VC may have invested originally in your company via its Fund I, a $300 million fund with twenty LPs who each invested $15 million in the fund. Several years later, your VC may have raised Fund II, a $500 million fund with fifty LPs (thirty of which were brand new to the VC), each investing $10 million.

In this case, if the VC proposes to invest additional monies into your company from its Fund II, the Fund I LPs might object because they feel as though they "own" that investment opportunity and will be receiving a smaller proportionate allocation of the investment if it goes into Fund II. By the same token, the Fund II LPs might object to the investment in their fund for fear that this new investment isn't a great opportunity for the fund relative to other investments you could make; that is, they might think you are just trying to save a poor investment from Fund I by investing additional dollars via Fund II.

The other thing to think about—now that you understand how LPs like Yale think about their venture investments—is how well the overall firm has done over the years, and if they are likely to be able to raise new funds in the future as a result. As you've (hopefully) seen from our discussion about Yale, venture firms need to be able to generate high absolute rates of return to their LPs and ultimately do so via cash (versus just marking up the value of the illiquid investments on their financial statements). So if you are thinking that you might need more capital from your venture firm in the future—and in particular if you are receiving an investment later in the life cycle of a fund—you'll want to assess the likelihood of the firm being able to raise its next fund.

This is admittedly a hard thing to dig into, in large part because the financial results of VC funds are generally not publicly available. In some cases, if the fund has public investors—e.g., public universities or state-run pension funds—these entities are required to disclose some level of financial performance on their websites or otherwise make it available to those who inquire. But in the vast majority of cases, your best bet here is to just do reference checks on your proposed VC partners with others in the community to at least get a sense, reputation-wise, for how the firm is doing.

Obviously, if all goes well and you never need to raise money again, none of these things may matter. But that's not likely the case—and that's not a statement of any entrepreneur's likelihood of success. Rather, most entrepreneurs tend to raise money at least once or twice after the initial funding round, because if they are doing well, they'll want to accelerate the growth and fuel that with additional capital, and if they are not doing well, they will need the capital to get to the next set of milestones. Thus, at least in the early years of a company's life, access to capital is critically important.

CHAPTER FIVE

The "Limited" Edition: How LPs Team Up with VCs

We've been talking a lot about LPs, and rightly so, because without LPs, venture funds would not exist. But it's the VCs who are on the hook to generate the high returns that LPs are looking for. So let's turn our attention to the venture funds themselves and explore the dynamic between the funds and the LPs.

You may wonder why you, as a busy entrepreneur, should care about the relationship between an LP and a VC. Well, because the LPs are the ones giving VCs the money to invest in you. They are also the ones that the VC needs to pay back, at huge multiples. So naturally how the VCs get paid, and with whose money, will have an impact on how they interact with their portfolio companies—you!

What Does "Limited Partner" Mean?

We've been using the term "limited partner" without any discussion of what this means. "Limited" is intended to describe the governance structure that exists between LPs and venture funds.

The LPs in fact have a "limited" role in the affairs of the fund in two important ways.

First, they have limited governance over the affairs of the fund. In the main, this means that LPs have no say over the investments that the fund chooses to make. As long as the fund invests in the set of things that are prescribed by the fund parameters, the LP is essentially investing in what's often called a blind pool—blind, that is, to the LP itself, which has no ability to weigh in on investment decisions. Similarly, the LP has limited ability to influence the decision to exit an investment and determine the manner and timing of whether to distribute the proceeds of that investment. As we'll explore in a little bit, there is a formal document that defines with more nuance some of the LPs' rights, but the fundamental way to think of LPs is as passive investors—they are along for the ride on which the venture fund decides to embark.

Second, as a result of their limited governance, LPs enjoy the protection of limited liability from a legal perspective if something goes wrong. For example, if a portfolio company or other investor sues the venture fund for some action it may have taken (or failed to take) to protect the interests of shareholders, the LPs are basically immune from any potential liability. Simply put, LP passivity is rewarded by also shielding them from any downstream liabilities to which the venture fund might be exposed.

If the LPs are by definition passive and shielded from liability, someone else must step into the fray—cue the VC fund. More specifically, cue the general partners (or GPs), the senior members of the fund who are responsible for finding investment opportunities, managing them during the lifetime of the opportunity, and ultimately generating a return of capital back to LPs to compensate them for the time and risk of being investors. And the GPs also take on all the liability if things go wrong.

This hardly sounds as though the LPs and GPs are partners, but this is legally what they in fact are. The legal entity that binds the LP and GP is a partnership—if you followed the 2017 tax reform discussion in DC, you'll know that partnerships (and other similar entities) are euphemistically referred to as "pass-through entities." That means that, unlike C corporations (which is what Amazon, Facebook, Apple, Google, and most other publicly traded companies are), partnerships don't pay taxes. Instead, the earnings of a partnership "pass through" to the underlying owners of the partnership, in our case the LPs and GPs. Each of the parties then reports the earnings on their respective tax filings.

Why is that a good thing? Well, first, it means that you avoid the dreaded double taxation of corporate earnings. If you own shares of Facebook and the company earns a dollar, it pays corporate taxes on that dollar (it used to be 35 percent and now is 21 percent after the 2017 tax reform bill); then, if Facebook decides to distribute some of its earnings to you as a shareholder, you pay tax a second time once you receive that distribution. In contrast, LPs and GPs pay tax only once on earnings.

Second, and of particular relevance to a number of LPs in VC funds, many LPs are tax-free entities. Specifically, university endowments and foundations are nonprofit entities that don't owe Uncle Sam any taxes on earnings. So passing through income to them means they avoid taxes altogether.

The LPA: The Rules of the Road

We said before that the LP invests into a blind pool and basically cedes control over that money to the GPs, but it's not quite that simple. LPs don't just part with billions of dollars without some say in the matter. The limited partnership agreement (or LPA) is the legal document that formally lays out the rules of the road— the economic relationship between the LP and the GP and the governance relationship between the LP and the GP.

Let's turn to the LPA and start with the economic terms. You care about this as an entrepreneur because financial incentives matter at all levels. Incentives drive behavior, and how a VC gets paid will affect how she interacts with your startup.

The Management Fee

A cornerstone of the economic relationship is the management fee that the GP charges the LP. Most GPs charge an annual management fee that is calculated as a percentage of the capital that the LP has committed to contribute to the GP over the life of the fund. Typical VC firms charge 2 percent annually, although some firms are able to charge as much as 3 percent.

Notice we said that the percentage amount is multiplied by the capital that the LP has committed to contribute over the life of the fund. We need to explain a new concept here to understand the economics, "calling capital."

When a GP closes a $100 million fund, it doesn't collect $100 million up front from LPs. Rather, the LPs make a financial commitment over the life of the fund to provide the capital when "called" by the GP. The reason for this practice is simple—keeping cash idle in the GP's bank account depresses the ultimate rate of return a GP can earn for its LPs. Just-in-time calling of capital eliminates this drag on returns. Typically most of the capital will be called over the first three to four years of the partnership, since that is when the lion's share of the investing is likely being done by the GP.

So even though the GP is not investing (and thus not calling) all of the $100 million up front, the GP is able to take a 2 percent management fee, or $2 million per year, on the full amount of the committed capital. (It's true that some VC funds charge the management fee on a pay-as-you-go basis, collecting the fee only against the actual monies invested. However, the typical pattern is to charge on committed capital.)

What is the management fee for? It's the pot of money from which the GP pays the bills necessary to keep the lights on in the VC fund—employee salaries, office space and supplies, travel, and any other day-to-day expenses of the fund. As you can imagine, LPs want to keep this fee as small as possible since it can be a drag on overall returns of the fund.

It is the case, by the way, that the fee sometimes changes as the fund ages. If most of the money is being invested in the first three to four years of the fund, it follows that the GP is spending more time at the beginning of the fund evaluating and selecting new investment opportunities. LPs thus are willing to fund this activity by paying the full management fee. As the fund ages and more of the GP's activity shifts to managing existing investments (versus finding new ones), many funds start to have a step-down in the fee.

The step-down is typically reflected in a few ways, sometimes in concert with one another. In the first instance, the 2 percent fee often gets reduced by 50–100 basis points in the later years of the partnership. The second mechanism to reduce fees is to change the application of the fee against committed capital to apply the fee only to the cost of the investments remaining in the portfolio. So, for example, if we were in year eight of our $100 million fund and all but one investment (for which we invested $10 million) had been sold off, the management fee might be applied only against the remaining $10 million versus the $100 million committed amount. Each of these bells and whistles is of course negotiated by the LPs and GPs at the time of the initial creation of the fund, so how they are resolved is often a function of the balance of power in the negotiation.

The final piece of the management fee puzzle comes in the form of ancillary fee waivers. It's pretty unusual in VC funds (although more common in buyout funds), but sometimes a GP gets compensated by a portfolio company for her engagement with the company.

Perhaps, for example, the company grants the GP some equity or cash incentive for being on the board of directors. The question then becomes: What does the GP do with that compensation? In most modern LPAs, the GP can keep the compensation if she wants, but she needs to credit that fee against the management fees otherwise being charged the LPs. In other words, no double-dipping; if you get paid by the company, you deduct that compensation from what you charge the LPs so that the GP ultimately has the same amount of disposable fee income in either case. This economic incentive drives the behavior on the part of the GP that we see in most portfolio companies; that is, paying a GP to sit on the board is very unusual (other than post-IPO, where compensation is par for the course).

Carried Interest

The heart of compensation for GPs (at least for those who are successful investors) is carried interest. It's rumored that the term "carried interest" derives from medieval traders who carried cargo on their ships that belonged to others. As financial compensation for the journey, the traders were entitled to 20 percent of the profits on the cargo. That sounds very civilized, if not rich. I've also heard—although my Google search is failing me now—that the carry portion of carried interest referred to the fact that the traders were allowed to keep as profit whatever portion of the cargo they could literally "carry" off the ship of their own volition. I prefer that story.

Regardless of its historical origins, *carried interest in the VC context refers to the portion of the profits that the GP generates on her investments and that she is entitled to keep.* As with the management fee, the actual amount of carried interest varies among venture funds but often ranges between 20 and 30 percent of the profits.

As it turns out, how we define "profits" and how and when the GP decides to distribute those profits to herself and her LPs is a matter for negotiation in the LPA.

Let's use a simple example to illustrate.

Go back to that $100 million venture fund we talked about before, and assume that we are in year three of the fund's existence. The GP invested $10 million in a portfolio company earlier in the fund's life, and now the company is sold for $60 million. So, on paper at least, the GP has generated a tidy profit of $50 million for that investment. She's also invested the rest of the $90 million in other companies, but none of those has yet been sold or gone public. Ah, she can taste the carry check already!

But how does the money get divvied up between the LPs and the GP? Let's assume that the GP has a 20 percent carried interest; in simple terms that means that when the fund earns a profit, 20 percent of that goes to the GP.

So, in our example, the GP is sitting on a $60 million check, of which $50 million represents profit, and wants to give 80 percent of the profit (or $40 million) to the fund's LPs and keep 20 percent (or $10 million) for herself. The other $10 million in this example will go back to the LPs as a return of their original capital. We'll come back to this later in this chapter and add some additional complexity.

But wait a second. Is there really a profit on which the GP is entitled to take her 20 percent? The answer is maybe. We need to take a little detour to introduce two other important concepts before we can conclusively answer that question.

As with fine wine, VC funds should get better with age. In fact, that's why people in the industry refer to funds by their "vintage year" (or birth year), just as winemakers date mark their wines based on the year of the grape harvest.

As we discussed earlier, in the early years of a fund, VCs are calling capital from LPs and investing that capital in companies. This is a decidedly negative cash flow motion—money is going out with (likely) no near-term prospect of money coming in. That's an expected effect, but eventually a VC must harvest some of those investments in the form of those companies going public or being sold.

The effect of calling capital from LPs in the early years coupled with the long gestation cycles for companies to grow and ulti-mately exit—in many cases it takes ten or more years for com-panies to be sold or go public—creates what is known as the "J curve." As you see in the figure on the next page, the LP has neg-ative cash flow (from the capital it's giving to the venture firm for

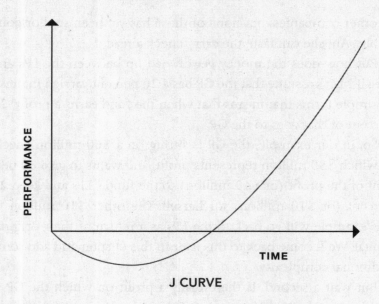

J CURVE

investment) in the early years of a fund and (hopefully) positive cash flow in the later years of the fund, a combination both of the capital having already been called and invested and the portfolio companies being sold or going public.

Venture capital is truly a long-term game. But, as explained in our discussion of the Yale endowment in chapter 4, cash does eventually need to come out the other end. Successful GPs will manage their portfolios to drive to this outcome, which can affect how they interact with entrepreneurs on this topic.

One phrase you often hear in the hallowed halls of VC firms is "lemons ripen early." That is, the nonperforming companies tend to manifest themselves close in time to the initial investment. Interestingly, this exacerbates the J-curve problem in that not only are VCs investing cash in the early years of a fund, but the nonperforming assets are certainly not helping the GP return money to the LPs.

Understanding Valuation Marks

Venture firms (as is the case for other financial companies) are required under generally accepted accounting principles (GAAP) to "mark to market" the value of their underlying company holdings on a quarterly basis. But, unlike a hedge fund, for example, where the mark is based on the actual, marketable value of a public security, VC marks vary highly based on multiple valuation methods prescribed by different accounting firms, as well as a VC firm's qualitative assessment of the likely future prospects for that business.

That means that for every company in a GP's portfolio, there is likely another VC invested in the same company that marks it at a different valuation than she does.

These are the primary methods used by venture firms:

- **Last round valuation/waterfall**—Some firms value their companies by taking the last round valuation in the private market and assigning that value to the firm's ownership in that company. For example, if a firm owned 10 percent of a company and the last round valuation was $200 million, a firm that utilized the last round/waterfall method would report the value of its holdings as $20 million (0.10 × $200 million).

- **Comparable company analysis**—Other firms, particularly for companies that have substantive revenue and/or profits, will use a public company comparables analysis. In this method, the firm will devise a set of public "comparables"—companies that have a similar business model or are in a similar industry—and pick a valuation metric (often a revenue multiple) to reflect how the broader public market values this set of companies. That metric is then assigned to the financials of the portfolio's companies. For example, if a portfolio company is generating $100 million of revenue and its "comparable" set of companies are valued in the public markets at five times the revenue, a venture firm would then value the company at $500 million ($100 million × 5). The firm would then multiply this company value by its percentage ownership in the company to reflect its holdings based on whatever percentage of the company the firm owned. Often, a firm will then also apply what's affectionately known as a "DLOM" (a discount for lack of marketability) to reduce the carrying value of the company—basically, this discount says that because the stock is private and can't be freely traded, it's worth less than that set of comparable public companies.

- **Option pricing model**—The newest (at least to VC firms) tool in the valuation tool set is what's called an "option pricing model" (OPM). This one is the most complicated mathematically and uses the Black-Scholes option model to value a portfolio company as a set of call options whose strike prices are the different valuation points at which employee options and preferred shares convert into common stock. Perfectly clear, right? Here's a quick example: If our hypothetical company raises a Series C financing at five dollars per share, the OPM says that all we know for certain is that anyone who holds Series C shares should value them at five dollars—simple enough. But if you own a Series B or a Series A share, the OPM says those are worth some fraction of five dollars—why? Well, to really answer that question you'd need to have a Nobel Prize in economics (as does Myron Scholes, the co-inventor of Black-Scholes), but the not-too-mathematical answer the OPM generates is that those Series A or B shares could be worth many different values based on a series of probabilistic outcomes if/when the company ultimately gets sold or goes public. So the OPM will assign a value to the Series A and B that is a substantial discount to the price of five dollars per share that is assigned to the Series C.

Let's look at an example to see how all this influences valuation marks.

Assume that our GP owns 10 percent of a company for which she paid $10 million. Lucky for our GP, the company just raised new money at a $3.8 billion valuation.

How would our GP "mark" the valuation of the company based on the differing methods we described above?

- **Last round valuation/waterfall**—Under this method, the value of the company would be $380 million (0.10 × $3.8 billion).

So, on the initial investment of $10 million, that is a hypothetical return of thirty-eight times.

- **Comparable company analysis**—Assume our company is forecast to generate $130 million of revenue in the coming year. Looking at high-growth multiples for comparable companies in the public markets, investors might assign a multiple of ten on that revenue, resulting in a $1.3 billion value for the company. So the GP might value the company at $130 million (0.10 × $1.3 billion) and then assign a 30 percent DLOM to that, resulting in a $91 million valuation ([1 − 0.30] × $130 million). That's a hypothetical return of nine times—not bad, but quite different from the thirty-eight times above.
- **OPM**—You'll have to trust me on this one, since the math does not easily lend itself to a paragraph summary! But an OPM with reasonable assumptions on time to exit and volatility would yield about a $160 million valuation for the GP's holding, or a sixteen-times hypothetical return.

So which accounting methodology is right? Well, the answer is that they are all theoretically "right" in that different accounting firms would likely sign off on these as consistent with GAAP. But, at the same time, they are all "wrong" in that none of them actually tells an LP anything about what the company might ultimately be worth to the fund when and if it ultimately goes public or gets sold and the proceeds of those events are distributed back to LPs.

Now that all that is as clear as mud, let's return to where we started.

As a reminder, our GP is in year three of her fund. She's invested $100 million and has just received a check for $60 million from selling one of her companies (in which she invested $10 million). She was planning to keep 20 percent of the profit for herself and give 80 percent back to her LPs. What do you think?

Well, if all the other investments in the fund have gone to zero (in other words, bankrupt), then she invested $100 million and has only returned (and will only ever return) $60 million. In that case, the answer is pretty simple: no. There are no profits, and all $60 million goes to the LPs—and our GP not only earns no carry on this fund, but she will also have a hard time raising her next fund!

But what if, instead of every other company in the fund going kaput, the other companies are valued based on interim valuation marks at $140 million? Forget about which combination of the valuation methods we talked about is being used; it doesn't matter as long as the GP's accounting firm is willing to sign off that the other $90 million she invested in other portfolio companies is worth $140 million. Again, these are marks because we are not talking hard cash here, but rather just an accounting of how much we think we could generate if we were to sell all these companies today.

In this case, the fund has $60 million of actual cash and $140 million of hypothetical value in the form of marks, for a total of $200 million in current value. The fund only raised $100 million from its LPs, so there is $100 million ($200 million in current value—$100 million invested) of theoretical total profit. So, since the theoretical profit exists, our GP can now keep 20 percent of the $50 million in cash profit as her carried interest. So 80 percent ($40 million) goes to the LPs and 20 percent ($10 million) goes to the GP.

Let's now assume that the fund has reached its time limit and is over. Most venture funds have a ten-year life with two or three one-year extension periods.

What happens if that $140 million in interim marks we booked in year three were ephemeral and all the companies comprising those marks proved to be worth no more than the paper this book was written on?

So, in reality, the fund generated only $60 million in total returns on a fund of $100 million; all those other profits disappeared. But the GP distributed $10 million to herself back when the prospects for the fund were looking up. What do we do now?

Unfortunately for our GP, she overdistributed profits to herself and is now subject to what's called a clawback—the money needs to be returned by the GP to the LPs. That sucks, but it is fair in that the GP never would have been entitled to that money had she waited to distribute the $60 million until the fund was over. She didn't, after all, really generate any profits on the $100 million of capital the LPs gave her to invest. (To avoid this problem, some LPAs restrict the GP's ability from being able to take any carry until she has returned the full $100 million in LP commitments back to the LP in cash. Admittedly, this is pretty rare.)

While it may not seem this way, we simplified things quite a bit in our example. There are a few other nuances to the economic terms of the LPA that are worth reviewing (and unfortunately complicate our example a bit).

First, what about those pesky management fees we talked about earlier? In our $100 million fund, the GP is of course supposed to use that money to make venture investments, but she'd also like to be able to use her annual management fee to pay the basic expenses of the business.

If the fund lasts for ten years and she is entitled to an annual fee of 2 percent on the $100 million committed amount of capital, then the total fees over the life of the fund will be $20 million (10 years × 0.02 × $100 million). If the GP collects all these fees, however, she will not be able to invest the full $100 million fund into companies; there's only $80 million left to invest.

Some GPs may decide to do this. But, as you might imagine, the LPs don't really love this approach because for their $100 million in committed capital, they'd like to have as many portfolio company investments as possible. And so would most GPs. After all, the more at-bats you have (hopefully), the more likely you are to improve your at-bats-per-home-run average.

The way to satisfy the desires of both the GP and LP is to "recycle": most LPAs have a provision that allows the GP to reinvest, or recycle, some portion of her interim winnings into other companies.

So in our example above, when our GP got that $60 million in year three from the sale of her company, she could have elected to recycle some of that money. If she wanted to cover her full $20 million in expected lifetime fees, our GP could have held back $20 million from the proceeds and then distributed the remaining $40 million based on her $10 million return of capital and then a split of 20 percent (GP) and 80 percent (LP) on the remaining $30 million of profit.

Our second simplification is how the capital gets contributed to the fund. Recall that we talked about how the GP calls capital from the LP as she makes investments. But we had simplified things by assuming that all $100 million came from the LP. In reality, the GP also has to have some skin in the game; the more the better (from the LP's perspective). After all, nothing sharpens the mind like managing your own money alongside your LPs' money. As a result, most GPs contribute 1 percent of the fund's capital, and many times they will contribute 2–5 percent of the capital. Thus, over the life of a $100 million fund, between $95 million and $99 million will be contributed by the LPs, and between $1 million and $5 million will come from the GP.

If we return to our carried interest problem from before, we need to add this to the equation.

Let's look again at the good scenario—the fund has returned $200 million in actual cash at end of life. How do we distribute that money? Keep in mind that $100 million is the return of capital invested, and the extra $100 million is the profit generated by the investments.

If the GP contributed 2 percent of the capital, this means that $2 million came from her and $98 million came from the LPs. So, logically (and this is how most LPAs read), we should return the capital to the parties in the same way that it came in: $2 million to the GP and $98 million to the LPs. Then we distribute the profits 20 percent ($20 million) to the GP and 80 percent ($80 million) to the LPs. Not much different from what we talked about before, but it's important to note that capital generally first gets paid back in the same way that it came in.

The final complexity that we ignored—and rightly so, because it is not that common among VC funds (though much more so in buyout funds)—involves the opportunity cost of money. Because LPs have a choice of asset classes in which to invest, they naturally want to know that investing in VC funds will pay them a premium compared to other asset classes. After all, venture capital is risky and has long time horizons during which the LP's capital is tied up. Instead of investing in a VC fund, an LP could choose to invest in the S&P 500 or some other asset class.

To account for this, some LPAs introduce the concept of a "hurdle rate" into the profits calculations. A hurdle rate says that unless the fund generates a return in excess of the hurdle rate (this is a negotiated number, but often around 8 percent), the GP is not entitled to take her carried interest on the profits. If the fund exceeds the hurdle rate, then the GP can start collecting her carried interest as if the hurdle rate didn't exist. So, as long as you clear the bar, you are good; fall short and you get nothing.

A "preferred return" is another mechanism to accomplish this, but it is more LP favorable. Unlike the "clear the bar and take the money" aspect of a hurdle rate, a preferred return doesn't just fall away when you clear it. Rather, if the preferred return were 8 percent, the LPs would get 100 percent of the money back until the preferred return is met, and then the GP participates in any profits *above* the preferred return. In our ten-year, $100 million fund, an 8 percent preferred return would amount to about $216 million [$100 million$/(1.08)^{10}$] at the end of ten years; thus, a $200 million total fund return would garner our GP a big fat zero in profits!

Caring About How the Money Flows

As an entrepreneur, nobody expects you to ask your prospective VC funder to see all their documents and review them in detail. And I highly doubt any VC would hand them over to you even if you were to ask politely. But because economic incentives do matter, you should have an appreciation for how the money flows inside of a venture fund. After all, depending on how well the GP is doing converting her other portfolio companies into profit, she might think differently about liquidity with respect to your company.

How the fund is doing may also influence your GP's willingness to invest additional money in your startup or her desire to seek an exit. If the fund is doing well—meaning the GP is on her way to her desired rate of return and thus likely to be able to raise a next fund from her LPs—she might be more interested in taking a gamble on your fund-raising and see whether you can help her generate even more profits for the fund.

But if your company is the lone shining star in an otherwise poor portfolio and you receive an acquisition offer that would meaningfully help the GP to get cash back to her LPs (and therefore increase the likelihood of her being able to raise a next fund), she might be more inclined to push you to take that deal, even if you think there is still more upside to come from running the business. Or if your GP is close to being in a clawback situation and you receive an acquisition offer that, while not that exciting for you, might give the GP just enough money to get herself out of that pickle, she might think differently about the offer.

And as we'll learn later in the book, the GP is going to be an integral part of this decision-making process. In many cases, she will be a member of the board of directors and thus have a formal say in the vote on whether to accept an acquisition offer. There are of course legal issues that the GP needs to think about in her capacity as a board member that could limit her actions here. None of this is to suggest that GPs necessarily want what you might rightly consider a bad outcome for your company, but we are influenced by the incentive structures under which we operate. Even if she is not on the board, the GP will be a shareholder in the company, likely with special voting rights that attach to acquisition decisions. Better, therefore, to be informed.

Governance: How Is the GP-LP Relationship Managed?

Now that we've covered the big-picture economic issues that the LPA is intended to address, let's shift to some of the governance issues. That is, how is the relationship between the LPs and the GP managed?

We've already noted above that the LPs' engagement is by definition limited—to preserve their lack of legal liability, they need to have a pretty light hand on the levers of the fund management. But, understandably so, LPs don't want to just hand over the money with no strings attached.

So the LPA does put in place a few guardrails. These are as follows.

1. Investment Domain

This may sound obvious, but the LPA will define the areas of investment for the GP and any hard-line restrictions on that. For example, is this a life sciences fund or a generalized information technology fund? Are there restrictions on stage—i.e., can the GP invest in seed- versus early-stage venture companies versus later-stage companies? Although most venture firms by definition invest in private companies, some LPAs will allow the GP to invest a portion of the funds in publicly traded securities. What about geographic restrictions—can the GP invest in China-domiciled companies from this fund? The type of investment can also be defined—is the GP allowed to invest in equities only, or can she also invest in debt or debt-like securities?

In general, the GP wants to leave the definitions as broad as possible—and most LPs in fact want to do the same. After all, what LPs really want is the GP's best investment ideas, period, so the restrictions are mostly intended to prevent too much style drift and to keep the GP focused on her best ideas in the domains in which she is supposed to be an expert.

As an entrepreneur, when you investigate whether a particular GP is appropriate for your business, you'll want to understand whether you fit into their investment domain. There's no sense in your wasting your time pitching your life sciences company to a firm that simply can't (by virtue of its LPA) or won't invest in you, regardless of how exciting your company may be.

2. Best Ideas

Speaking of "best ideas," how do we make sure the GP's best ideas go into the fund itself versus her taking them directly for her own benefit? In some cases, GPs have either invested their own money alongside a fund investment or declined to make the investment via the fund and instead invested personally in the company. Most of the time there is nothing nefarious going on here, but it raises the question of conflicts—how do I as an LP know that I am getting the GP's best ideas in the fund versus the GP potentially cherry-picking her best deals to invest in with her own money outside of the fund? So, many firms have a restriction in their LPA that limits this activity or, at a minimum, requires disclosure to the LPs at the time of the investment.

We talked earlier about Accel Partners and their tremendous success in early-stage investing at Facebook. Well, alongside that fund investment, the firm's managing partner at the time, Jim Breyer, invested about $1 million of his own money for a 1 percent stake in the company. We know how that turned out: a return on the investment of about one thousand times for Jim, depending on when he sold it. Understandably, some of Accel's LPs were concerned about this investment in that it presumably meant that, absent Jim's decision to invest personally, $1 million could have been invested by the Accel venture fund into Facebook, the value of which would have accrued to the fund's LPs. Facebook of course turned out to be such a hit for Accel and its LPs that I suspect any hurt feelings were quickly forgotten, but nonetheless, LPs have become more sensitized to this issue of GP co-investments along-side fund investments.

3. I Work Hard for the Money

This, of course, is what the LPs want their GP to do for them. But just in case, the LPs have a few mechanisms to hold the GP's feet to the fire.

First, the LPA generally says that the GP has to devote "substantially all" of her efforts to running the firm. Go coach your kid's soccer team on the weekends or sit on a nonprofit board here and there, but otherwise direct your energies full-time to investing on behalf of the LPs. This seems pretty noncontroversial (although sometimes you might be surprised). Being a GP should be a full-time job.

What happens if either the GP is no longer satisfying this obligation or the LPs collectively decide that the GP has lost her mind and is no longer a good steward of their capital? Well, just as in any good relationship, separation and divorce are always options.

In VC land, "suspension" is our version of separation. Suspension comes into play if any or some combination of the GPs are no longer devoting substantially all their time to the affairs of the fund. We call these GPs (or combination of GPs) the "key men" (and, yes, I realize that is not gender neutral, but old habits die slowly in the private equity world). If this happens, most LPAs will have a defined voting threshold by which some set of LPs (often at least one-half or two-thirds) can invoke a suspension. During a suspension period, the key men need to present a plan to the LPs for how they are going to remedy the situation or, if they are unable to do so, the LPs can initiate divorce proceedings. This often requires some even higher supermajority of the LPs to vote to dissolve the fund.

Most states have what are called no-fault proceedings for married couples looking to get divorced. In essence, this means you don't have to come up with a specific reason for the divorce; one party can simply decide they are done with the marriage and begin the legal proceedings to dissolve the marriage. Just as with most real marriages, we also have "no-fault" divorce provisions in the LPA. Obviously, the threshold for voting among the LPs is pretty high here (often more than 80 percent), but there often is a mechanism by which the LPs can just say to the GP: "Thanks for playing, but we want out."

The LPA often runs over one hundred pages, so I haven't done full justice to it by simply giving you a few-page rundown. Nonetheless, this is sufficient for informing one factor that you as an entrepreneur need to think about when choosing your venture partner.

GP-to-GP Relationships: The Equity Partners Agreement

We've spent a lot of time talking about the relationship between LPs and GPs, and rightly so, as they are codependents. However, equally important is the way that GPs within a firm interact with one another: they are, after all, partners. Conveniently, the legal document that governs their relationship is often called the equity partners agreement.

But not all partners are created equal. Some partners may have only an economic interest in the fund but not have any other governance rights. This means that they cannot legally bind the fund to make an investment (or get rid of it), nor be involved in hiring or firing other partners. Some may have full economic and governance rights and some may be in between.

You, as an entrepreneur, are unlikely to know any of this since these agreements are not publicly filed, but it's an important thing for you to understand. Being aware of this will help you understand the decision-making process inside a firm.

This is no different from what you would want to know if you were selling software to an enterprise customer—Who are the economic buyers, the champions within the account, etc.? Organizational dynamics matter in decision-making, so at least ask the question of how a venture firm makes a decision if you are going down a funding path with that firm.

The equity partners agreement also spells out the economics of the partnership; that is, how does the carried interest pie get split? There are a ton of flavors here, but they range from fully equal partnerships (where everyone has the same share of carry) to multitiered partnerships (where longevity or performance might dictate differing shares of the pie).

Just as is the case with founders and employees of startup companies (more on this later), most GPs have to vest their share of the carry pool over time. "Vesting" means that you accrue ownership over a specific period of time, such that if you leave the firm before that time expires, you would have earned only that proportion of the carry that equates to your time at the firm. Recall that the life of most of the funds is ten years, so naturally some venture firms want to ensure that GPs are financially incented over the life of the fund by having a ten-year vesting period. But, again, different firms handle this differently.

While most venture firms expect GPs to make a long-term commitment when they decide to join the firm, it does happen that GPs sometimes turn over during the life of a fund. In addition to the vesting issues noted earlier, you as an entrepreneur may be affected if the partner who sits on your board (or sponsored your investment) leaves the firm. In some cases, GPs retain their existing board seats in exchange for the firm's agreement to continue vesting their economic interests in the funds in which they participated. Other times, the GP takes on a new full-time role that may require a time commitment from her that is inconsistent with retaining her board seats. In that case, you may have a new GP assigned to your board to take the place of the former GP.

The final piece of the GP puzzle is "indemnification." Remember that in the GP-LP relationship, the GP has legal liability if things go south. To incent people to want to be VCs (just as we do with boards of directors), GPs can be indemnified from legal liability, meaning that they do not have to worry that their personal financial resources could be called upon to satisfy financial liabilities of the fund. We'll come back to this later when we talk about the fiduciary duties of a GP—both to the fund and to the shareholders of the companies on whose boards they sit—and dive deeper into what this actually means in practice for GPs.

We've spent enough time for now talking about LPs and GPs. Time to move to what I'm sure you've been waiting for, and the most important part of the venture capital ecosystem—the startup!

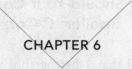

CHAPTER 6

Forming Your Startup

Starting a company comes with no shortage of poetic adjectives. Great founders are innovative, brave, inspiring, and visionary. Their ideas are groundbreaking and world changing.

So I'm sorry to throw a wet blanket on the heroic journey of starting a new company by kicking it off with a visit to your lawyer's office, and by talking about things like tax and governance.

But it's critical to the health of your future company to understand how to set up your business. So let's eat our broccoli together.

The first part of this chapter is going to focus on some of the tax and corporate governance implications of how many entrepreneurs choose to set up their businesses. It is admittedly a US-centric view of these issues, so, in the interest of transparency for any non-US readers, you may want to consider whether this first section is relevant to your entrepreneurial journey. For the US audience, I offer no such hall pass.

What Form Should Your Company Take?
Spoiler: C Corp

GPs and LPs decided that a partnership was the best corporate structure for their relationship, so why are most startup companies formed as traditional C corporations?

There are lots of reasons, but probably the most fundamental is that the C corp is a good vehicle for companies that are focused on building long-term equity value in the business versus distributing profits directly to shareholders. Remember that when we talked about a partnership, one of the features was that the earnings of the company are passed through to the company's owners. This makes partnerships a very tax-efficient way to distribute profits to their owners—the cash can flow through, along with the tax liability, so there is no second-level corporate tax. That's a good thing.

With a startup, though, in most cases we don't really want to distribute profits to the owners, at least not in the early days. Rather, if we have profits (and, of course, most startups have losses in the early years), we would likely choose to reinvest those profits in the business to continue to grow its value. So, if we were lucky enough to generate profits but did not pass that cash through to the owners, we'd be creating a tax liability for the owners without the cash to pay Uncle Sam. That's not a good thing.

Because most startups do in fact have losses in the early years, some entrepreneurs rightly wonder whether a pass-through structure, at least initially, would make more sense. With losses, a pass-through provides the owners an economic benefit, in that you can deduct those losses from other income on your tax returns. Theoretically, you could start life as a pass-through and later convert to a C corp once you are generating profits that you want to retain in the business, but in practice I have never really seen anyone do this. It's a nontrivial thing to do the conversion from pass-through to C corp, and it creates all kinds of other issues when you are trying to allow equity participation for other employees.

The cost of course of being a C corp is that, when profits do get distributed from the C corp, we have to deal with the double taxation problem: profits are taxed first at the corporate level and then a second time at the individual owner's level when paid out.

The non-pass-through nature of a C corp also lends itself well to the fact that many startup companies grant equity in the business to their employees—more on this later. A startup could issue partnership interests to employees, but it just makes things more complicated from a tax perspective (in large part because of the pass-through nature of partnerships).

A C corp is just a simpler mechanism through which to provide broad equity ownership to a startup's employees. And a C corp does not have any limits on the number of shareholders that can be part of the organization; thus, as a startup hopefully grows, later employees can also benefit from potential equity ownership.

C corps also have several advantages for the VC firms that might invest in them.

First, C corps allow you to have different classes of shareholders with different rights. (Truth be told, as we talked about earlier, partnerships can have different types of partners with different rights as well, but the C corp structure has other advantages.) This is important because, as we'll talk about later in our discussion on term sheets, VCs like to invest in what is called "preferred stock," whereas most founders and employees hold "common stock." Basically this allows different rights to be assigned to the different classes of shareholders; C corps permit and facilitate this.

The second advantage for VC firms comes back to tax—I know you never thought you were signing up to master the tax code when you picked up this book! Recall that many LPs of venture firms are tax-free (e.g., endowments and foundations). They enjoy the benefits of this tax-free status and don't look favorably on GPs who threaten to interfere with this. Under US tax laws, pass-through entities (e.g., partnerships or limited liability companies) can cause even tax-free entities to have to pay tax on what is called "unrelated business income." ("UBIT" is what the cool kids say.) If GPs invest in pass-through entities, they can therefore create this potential tax risk for LPs; investing in C corps raises no such issues. Thus, most GPs will avoid investing in pass-throughs as much as possible.

Carving Up the Ownership Pie

Okay, so we've got an entity—check! What else needs to happen as part of the company formation process?

Well, next up is how we divide ownership of the company. Most companies have more than one founder. And when you start a company, it's you and your cofounder against the world. You will both sacrifice everything to build your vision. Sleepless nights, forgoing a social life, letting your health go to crap, and even neglecting your own family are all on the table to achieve your dreams, but it's going to be okay, because you are in it together. Together forever.

But what if it's not forever? What if you sacrifice everything and in two years your cofounder decides to quit to go find herself? What if her ego gets bruised, because you are the CEO and, as the company grows, she becomes less important? What if she develops a serious drug problem? What if she turns out to be not quite as talented as you thought?

Well, it can be okay. Or it can destroy your company. It all depends on how realistic you are when you set things up.

Yes, breaking up is hard to do—whether in love or in business—but at least in business, there are some things founders can do proactively to lessen the pain. Think of it as a common-sense prenup to protect your company.

So what can you do to help ensure that founder breakups don't end your startup dreams?

As with most things in life, a little planning between founders can go a long way toward ensuring that a breakup doesn't crater your dreams of world domination.

And, from a more positive point of view, what can you do to encourage each other to do your best to make the company as successful as possible?

Founder Stock Vesting

The basic purpose of founder equity is to create long-term incentives. That's the whole idea of vesting: you contribute to the success of the company by helping to grow the business, and you are rewarded over time with an increasing ownership position in the equity you helped create.

Founder stock (or equity) vesting differs in several ways from the GP vesting scenario we discussed in chapter 5 but is identical in its purpose. The rationale for vesting is to tie the founder to some defined term of employment before she can exit the firm and take 100 percent of her equity with her. Think of it as providing a long-term financial incentive for founders to behave as equity owners and do their best to increase the value of the firm for all shareholders.

In most founder cases (and for most employees who receive stock option grants as part of their compensation package—more to come on this later), full vesting is often achieved at the end of four years from the date of the option grant. We'll talk more about the origin of that four-year practice and why it may no longer make the most sense.

When we say a founder is half-vested in her shares, whether or not she is employed by the firm, that means that she has the rights to the economic interest of only 50 percent of her shares. If she wants to sell the shares to someone else and monetize their value, then she can only sell what is in fact vested.

As a result of this in particular, founders understandably want to get full credit toward vesting of their founder shares from the first conceivable time they began working on the new idea. It is often the case that by the time founders raise their first institutional financing round, they may be as much as 50 percent vested, assuming that they have been working on the company for at least two years prior to the time they raised financing. However, with companies staying private demonstrably longer these days, the work required to build the business into a successful venture has really just begun.

Unfortunately, we often see cases where a cofounder leaves—whether voluntarily or otherwise—once she has fully vested, leaving the other cofounder to bear the brunt of managing the business and building long-term shareholder value for many years to come. And, although the remaining cofounder may receive incremental equity grants from the board over time for her continued service, the likely financial value of her new equity pales in comparison to the value of the fully vested equity the former cofounder has realized.

The conversation with the remaining cofounder is the same each time: "I'm here every day working hard trying to build long-term equity value for my employees and investors while Joan [names have been changed to protect the innocent] is living the celebrity party scene."

So what can you do?

More about Vesting

At a minimum, most founders vest their shares over a four-year period. But given the much longer runway most private companies will have before they get to their public market debut, founders should think about whether four years is enough time. Equity is intended to provide long-term incentives, so the question is whether the definition of "long-term" needs to change. Admittedly, this is a hard thing to change because most companies want to have consistent vesting policies for both their founders and the rest of the employee base. And the market for employee vesting largely remains at four years. But as a founder, it's worth considering whether you should have longer vesting periods for founders given the likely longer time period which it may take to build value and get to a liquidity event.

Leaving the Business

Think about the circumstances under which you and your cofounder can be removed from the business. In many cases, founders control the board of directors, meaning that they have a majority of the seats on the board and thus can be removed only with the agreement of the other cofounder. That is, the VCs or other board members do not have sufficient votes to remove the founders from their roles. Given that, in most cases the only way a cofounder can be removed from her role in the business is if she voluntarily decides to leave. But that's not likely a good position to find yourself in if one cofounder is not performing at the level required to make the business a success. So you may want to consider at the time of founding the company how you and your cofounders will govern such situations.

Removing a cofounder from her executive role is one thing; removing her from the board is another. Often we see companies where the cofounders have what are called "hardwired" board seats. This means that each cofounder has the right to be on the board, regardless of the function she is performing in the company and, often, regardless of whether she is still even employed by the company. The genesis of this is understandable: founders are often worried about VCs amassing a majority of the seats on the board and potentially voting to remove one or more cofounders from the board.

However, in doing so, cofounders are creating a risk of "ruling from the grave"—having a cofounder who is no longer employed by the company remaining on the board and potentially interfering with the company's ability to move forward. To deal with this situation, you will want to make sure that board seats are conditioned upon continued service to the company as an employee, not simply granted to someone as a function of having been a cofounder. This is a simple thing to implement as of the founding of the company, but an often overlooked one.

Ultimately, this is about making sure that founder equity serves its purpose—to create long-term incentives—and that the economic rewards of success accrue to those who are remaining with the company over the long term to help increase shareholder value. And incentives are perfectly aligned here between you (as the remaining cofounder) and your VCs: the company retains valuable stock to grant the remaining employees who are actually contributing to the growth of the business.

Transfer Restrictions

Imagine that your cofounder has not only left but is now sitting on hundreds of millions of dollars in vested stock and wants to sell the stock privately. Plus, you're in the middle of trying to raise money for your business—and your cofounder's secondary stock is competing for that demand.

What do you do?

The right answer is to have instituted blanket transfer restrictions on stock sales from the founding of the company. A blanket transfer restriction means that shareholders cannot sell without some form of company consent—often the board's consent is required to do so. And since founders control the board in many cases of venture-financed companies today, this is a relatively innocuous provision to implement: if the remaining cofounder wants to permit her former cofounder to sell, she will often have sufficient board votes to do so. Transfer restrictions are designed to be permanent, but, as with most governance provisions in private companies, they can be removed by the company with a majority board vote and shareholder vote.

Once the genie is out of the bottle on this one, it's very hard to put it back—why? Because you can't just implement it at a later date and impose it on all existing shareholders. To implement transfer restrictions post hoc requires consent of the shareholder; you're unlikely to get that because you are asking her to give up a valuable right that she already has.

While most companies we see have not instituted blanket transfer restrictions, it is the case that most companies have a right-of-first-refusal (ROFR) agreement. The ROFR agreement means that if someone (in this case, a cofounder) is trying to sell her stock, the company has a right to match any offers received and effect the purchase. This is a good right to have, but it is often insufficient because this alone does not prevent cofounders from selling stock. Rather, it gives the company an option to buy the shares itself, but doing so requires that the company utilize its existing cash to do so. In most startups, this is not the highest and best use of cash, and as a result, most companies waive this right and permit the third-party sale to go through.

Acceleration of Vesting

In most cases, of course, founder stock vesting is tied to continued employment with the company. Remember, the whole idea of vesting is that you want your team to contribute to the success of the company by helping to grow the business, and you are all rewarded over time with increasing ownership positions in the equity you helped create.

But what happens when your cofounder leaves? Should she continue to vest her stock or get her vesting accelerated? "Accelerated" means that you elect to increase her vesting of stock beyond the point at which the time-based vesting would otherwise permit. What if you sell the company while your cofounder is still there, but she refuses to join the acquirer—should her vesting accelerate?

As long as you and your cofounder have agreed on the circumstances under which either of you can be removed (and you are comfortable that the decision to do so is governed by a fair and deliberate process), you may not want to provide for accelerated vesting on termination of employment. You are likely better off being able to use any unvested equity to incent other employees who are still contributing to the long-term success of the business.

How does this work? Equity that is unvested at the time a co-founder or employee leaves essentially expires. However, that expired equity can be returned to the company in a manner that permits shares to be reissued to someone else who is currently employed by the company. For example, if your cofounder leaves when she is 50 percent vested and therefore surrenders her remaining 50 percent of shares—assume for the sake of this conversation that there are one million surrendered shares—those one million shares can now be regranted by the company to another current employee of the company, thus providing her an economic incentive to increase shareholder value.

However, in the acquisition scenario, founders will often have single-trigger or double-trigger acceleration provisions. In a single-trigger provision, the founder's stock is accelerated upon the closing of an M&A event; in a double trigger, both the closing of the deal and the acquirer's decision not to retain the founder in the new entity are required for acceleration.

A single trigger is suboptimal for the company for the same reasons that accelerating vesting post-employment without an M&A event is: you are consuming equity for an individual who is no longer contributing to the success of the company. And in the event that your cofounder elects to stay with the acquiring company as an employee, the single trigger is equally problematic. The acquirer will of course want to have an economic incentive in the form of equity to entice your cofounder to stay with the new company, but because her original stock vesting was accelerated, creating this incentive will require the issuance of additional shares. This has an economic cost to the acquiring company that they would rather not incur. If your cofounder has the option to accelerate on a single trigger, the acquirer will need to offer additional cash/equity incentives to retain your cofounder. There are no free lunches: that additional consideration must come from somewhere when the purchase-price pot is fixed.

A double trigger solves that problem. If the acquirer wants to retain your cofounder, they can just continue the vesting of her original shares as a condition of her continued employment. And, if the acquirer decides not to extend an offer to your cofounder to be part of the post-acquisition team, the double trigger will protect the cofounder by fully accelerating her stock vesting. It's only fair in this case that she not be penalized by losing unvested equity since she was not given the option to stay on as an employee with the acquiring company.

Intellectual Property

Before your head starts spinning, let's take a break from talking about equity for a second to talk about intellectual property. (We'll come back to employee equity in a minute.)

Intellectual property is the lifeblood of most startup companies, so we need to protect it carefully.

Since many startup founders are coming from an existing job, we need to make sure that there is no entanglement of the intellectual property with the previous employer and that the startup owns all the inventions. Mechanically, we do this by having founders sign what's called an invention and assignment agreement. Basically, this agreement says that the founder is assigning to the company the creations that she has invented, other than an enumerated list of prior inventions that the founder claims for her own.

But how do we know that our founder didn't start working on these inventions while she was still at her prior employer, and thus we might find ourselves fighting an intellectual property lawsuit five years down the road when our technology gets bought by Google for $2 billion? This is part of the due diligence process that good lawyers will do when they form the startup and that venture capitalists will do when they invest in the company.

VCs will ask whether you developed the technology during work hours at your last employer, whether you used company property (e.g., your company-issued laptop) to develop the technology, and whether you downloaded anything from your employer (documents or source code) that may have influenced your startup's technology. So the best thing you can do if you are thinking about starting a company is to invest in a real "clean room" in which to develop your foundational intellectual property.

The recent Uber case brought these hazards to light. Anthony Levandowski was an employee of Google working on its autonomous driving initiative (Waymo). In 2016, Anthony left Google to start a company called Otto, which was intending to build an autonomous trucking company. Shortly after its founding, Otto was acquired by Uber to help expand its own autonomous driving initiatives.

But Waymo alleged that Anthony had downloaded a large volume of proprietary documents before leaving the employ of the company and that those documents had found their way into Uber. More specifically, Waymo alleged that the Uber CEO had conspired with Anthony to induce him to steal the intellectual property and provide it to Uber and, in effect, that the creation of the separate Otto company was largely a sham to enable Uber to acquire Waymo's intellectual property. The case dragged on for a while and was eventually settled for $245 million in Uber equity paid to Waymo.

The central question in the case was less about whether Anthony had downloaded the documents—that seemed largely agreed upon by both sides—but whether the documents had in fact found their way to Uber. This was a tough case for Uber to prove: they were in the position of trying to prove a negative, which is generally not a good place to be when fighting a lawsuit.

However, the key lesson for entrepreneurs is to really be careful when starting a new company on the heels of just having left your former employer. What may look like an innocuous downloading of documents that you just want to have because they represent work you did at your prior employer can quickly turn into an allegation of theft of intellectual property.

And in most cases, these claims coincide with a good event—likely an acquisition. That is, your prior employer might not notice or even care too much about this when you are just starting your company, but when there is potential money to be had, these claims can often be raised many years in the future. Careful planning up front can save you a lot of headaches, even heartache, down the line.

Employee Option Pools

Okay, back to equity! The final piece to consider about company formation is the creation of the equity compensation model the startup wants to pursue. As we discussed, in most cases startups want to have their employees incented in the form of equity stock options. That way, if the employees do great work that increases the value of the company, the employees participate in that upside. Incentives align.

The way startups do this is to create an "employee option pool." Assume the founders of our company have decided that they each want to own 50 percent of the company. At the outset, then, the equity is owned fifty-fifty between the two cofounders. They then realize that they want to be able to hire employees to whom they want to grant equity.

To do this, the founders put in place an employee option pool equal to 15 percent of the company. (I somewhat arbitrarily picked 15 percent, but this does tend to be the standard size of an initial employee option pool in a startup.) As a result, the ownership of the company has changed: the two cofounders are splitting 85 percent of the equity, and the employee option pool comprises the final 15 percent. This is just simple math.

But let's start at the beginning—what are "stock options"?

Stock options are a contract that gives the option holder the right, but not the obligation, to purchase the stock at a future date, at a specified price. That price is called the "exercise price." So, if a startup gives you an option to purchase one hundred shares of stock at an exercise price of one dollar per share and that option is valid for ten years, that means that any time over the next ten years, you can pay the company one dollar per share of stock (or one hundred dollars for the full option exercise) and therefore own the stock.

So why would you do this?

Well, if you joined the company when the stock was actually worth one dollar per share and, say, four years later the price of the stock has increased to five dollars per share, you are "in the money." That is, you can pay only one dollar per share for stock that is worth five dollars per share—that's a deal you want to do all day, every day. The act of buying the stock at the exercise price is called "exercising" the option. If, however, the stock is worth only fifty cents per share, you would never pay one dollar to buy the stock and then lose money by selling it at fifty cents per share. Thus the "option" gives you the choice to not buy the shares as well.

There are two types of stock options that startups can issue.

One is called an "incentive stock option," or ISO. In general, ISOs are the most favorable type of options. With an ISO, the employee does not have to pay taxes at the time of exercise on the difference between the exercise price of the option and the fair market value of the stock (though there are cases sometimes where the alternative minimum tax can come into play). This means that an employee can defer those taxes until she sells the underlying stock. If she chooses to hold the stock for one year from the exercise date (and at least two years from the date on which she was granted the option), the gains on the stock qualify for capital gains tax treatment, which is significantly lower than the tax rate on ordinary income.

"Non-qualified options," or NQOs, are less favorable in that the employee must pay taxes at the time of exercise, regardless of whether she chooses to hold the stock longer term. And the amount of those taxes is calculated on the date of the exercise, so that if the stock price were to later fall in value, the employee would still owe taxes based on the historic, higher price of the stock.

So why don't all companies issue ISOs only?

Well, there are a few restrictions on ISOs, including the fact that there is a limit of $100,000 of market value that can be issued to any employee within a single year. Of course, it is a good "problem" for an employee to have such a highly valued option grant.

ISOs also have to be exercised by the employee within ninety days of the employee's leaving the company. As companies are staying private longer, this can create challenges for departing employees. They may have ISOs that have appreciated, meaning that the value of the stock is much higher than the exercise price, but to exercise the stock requires that the option holder pay out of pocket for the exercise price. This can prove to be cost prohibitive to many employees and thus they could be confronted with the need to let the options expire unexercised, leaving a bunch of money on the table.

As a result, more companies have been extending the post-termination option exercise period from ninety days to a longer period of time, often as long as seven to ten years. This has the negative effect of automatically converting ISOs into NQOs (because it violates the ninety-day post-termination rule that is required of ISOs), but still gives employees a much longer window in which to exercise their stock options post-employment.

We talked about vesting of stock options in the context of founders, but it's equally applicable to the broader employee base. Remember after all that stock options are intended to be long-term incentives for employees to remain at the company, different from the short-term nature of a base salary or cash bonus.

Most startup stock options vest over a four-year period. There are various bells and whistles that can apply to stock options, but the most common we see is a one-year cliff vest—meaning that if the employee leaves before the first anniversary of her employment, she vests nothing—followed by monthly vesting over the next three years at a rate of one thirty-sixth per month. Thus, at the end of a four-year period, the employee is free to leave and take her vested stock options with her.

The New Normal for Longer IPOs

But why four years, and what do we do after that, presuming we want the employee to stick around? Well, four years is really an anachronism from the days in which companies went public in about four to six years from founding. The theory was that the average employee might join the company somewhere in the first few years post-founding, and she would have the ability to sell her shares in the public market as the options vested; with a shorter time to IPO, most employee options fit into this paradigm.

But as we talked about earlier, the time to IPO for most startups has substantially elongated, in many cases ten or more years from founding. So this introduces complexities with vesting that modern entrepreneurs need to grapple with.

So what happened along the way to getting to a much longer time to IPO for venture-backed companies?

First, the facts: About two decades ago (from 1998 to 2000), we used to have around three hundred IPOs per year. Since then, that average has fallen by more than half, to a little more than one hundred per year. As a result, the number of publicly listed stocks in the US has declined by 50 percent over the last twenty years.

In addition to the total number of IPOs declining, the type of IPO candidates has changed as well. "Small-cap IPOs"—companies with less than $50 million in annual revenue at the time of initial public offering—have declined over this same twenty-year period from more than half to just a quarter of all IPOs; more money is being raised for bigger versus smaller companies.

While the trend is clear, how we got here isn't. Experts and those who study this sort of thing actually have differing opinions about why the dearth of IPOs, with theories ranging widely, as follows.

1. It Costs Too Much Money to Go Public

Post the dot-com bubble, the US Congress passed in 2002 the Sarbanes-Oxley Act. This legislation was designed to increase the robustness of financial disclosures from public companies to ensure that shareholders were well-informed about the true financial state of public companies. Sarbanes-Oxley was well-intended legislation but also had the effect of increasing the costs of going public and being public, mostly through additional internal financial controls and reporting required under the legislation.

Thus, the argument goes, fewer companies choose to go public because of the increased costs of regulatory compliance. And those that do go public wait until they are much larger so that they can amortize these costs over a much higher base of earnings. More importantly, dollars spent on regulatory compliance are dollars that could have been devoted to early research and development investment. This is particularly relevant for venture-backed companies, as they spend a significant amount of their expenditures on engineering development.

2. Efficiency Rules Disproportionately Affect Smaller Companies

In 1997, the SEC began promulgating various rules—Regulation ATS (Alternative Trading System), Decimalization and Regulation NMS (National Market System), etc.—designed to increase the trading efficiency of stocks. The goals were laudable: basically, the SEC wanted to increase the overall efficiency of the stock market by creating more competition and thereby reducing the costs of buying and selling stocks. And it worked: the US equities market, as a whole, is highly efficient and liquid.

But this very efficiency has disproportionately affected the trading dynamics for companies that have smaller capitalizations and therefore lower trading volume. The various rules made it cost prohibitive for those who play an important role in facilitating trading of small-cap stocks—these players include research analysts who publish information about the companies, traders who take positions in the stock, and salespeople who market the stock to institutional investors—by reducing the profits associated with those activities. As a result, the small-cap trading market is anything but liquid. And small-cap companies are loath to go public for fear of being stuck in an illiquid trading environment where it's very difficult to raise additional capital in the public markets to grow their businesses.

3. Mutual Funds Are Bigger, and Therefore Like Bigger Companies

Mutual funds, such as Fidelity and Vanguard, are the major way that most people access public stocks. The funds get paid based on the total amount of assets they are managing, so the larger the asset base, the more money they get. And the amount of assets being managed by the mutual fund industry has indeed grown: sixteen times from 1990 to 2000 (reaching $3.4 trillion in assets) and another five times since 2000 (topping $16 trillion in assets in 2016).

Why does this matter? When mutual funds get big, they are motivated to focus on large-cap, highly liquid stocks because they need to be able to put large amounts of money to work in individual stocks. Doing so in smaller capitalization stocks just doesn't scale very well. As a result, mutual fund holdings tend to be concentrated in large-cap companies at the expense of small-cap ones.

4. There Are Alternative Forms of Private Financing Out There

We've of course been talking in this book all about venture funds as the primary funders of startup companies. And that is true. Over the last five years, though, as startups have been staying private longer, the landscape of private investors that now invest at the later stages of a private company's development has increased to include public mutual funds, hedge funds, private equity buyout firms, sovereign wealth funds, family offices, and even traditional endowments and foundations. This availability of private capital, some argue, has supplanted the need for companies to go public.

The phenomenon is real, but it doesn't answer the question of cause and effect—that is, have public market investors entered the private markets because companies are choosing to stay private longer and delay entering the public markets? Or, if going public were more palatable to private companies, would they in fact choose to go public and obviate the need for these large, private rounds? While it seems to be a bit of a chicken-and-egg question, the data point toward the former, as the average age of companies from founding to IPO started increasing (from six and a half to ten and a half years) and the annual number of IPOs started decreasing years before robust late-stage private financing became available.

5. There's Too Much Pressure on Public Companies These Days

The lack of IPOs has also been partly blamed on the rise of activist investors. These are investors who purchase stock in a public company and try to agitate for change designed to increase the value of the stock. Such changes often include introducing new board members, who in turn can make changes to the leadership of the company. So why navigate these public company pressures if there's enough capital available in the private markets to stay private longer?

Staying Private and Staying Motivated

Regardless of how we got here, the critical thing for you as a founder to think about is that it's likely that you will be a private company for substantially longer than you might anticipate. As noted above, it's likely that you will be private for ten or more years.

So if it takes that long to get the company public, we presumably want good employees to stick around longer to help get the company to that milestone. Thus, the whole idea of whether a four-year vest still makes sense is up for debate. But knowing that it's hard in a competitive employment market for startups to be out of market by introducing longer vest periods, we don't often see companies extending the vest period.

In lieu of longer vest periods, however, most companies utilize some form of refresher option grants for high-performing employees. That is, perhaps at the end of year two (when half of the employee's original stock option grant has vested), the company may award her a new option grant that will vest over a four-year period from the new grant date. Thus, good employees may often have some amount of options always continuing to vest, providing a greater economic incentive for longer-term retention.

While the "refresher" grants are often smaller than the initial grants, Tesla has been rumored to have turned this a bit on its head. Tesla's view is that we know least about an employee's capabilities when she is first hired; after all, most companies rely on interviews, which research has shown to be largely not predictive of an employee's ultimate success in a company. We know a lot more about the employee once she has actually started working in the company, producing (or not) value to the organization. Thus, Tesla generally provides smaller stock option grants to its employees upon hiring and, for top-performing employees, grants increasingly larger amounts of options as part of their refresher program.

All right, we've now formed our C corp and have figured out the initial allocation of equity among our cofounders and the employee option pool. Time to raise money from a venture capitalist. For half of you reading this, that phrase gets you fired up and excited. For the other half of you, you just broke out in a nervous sweat. Don't worry—I'll walk you through it and offer up truth, transparency, and insight that, I hope, will help your next meeting with a VC go smoothly.

CHAPTER 7

Raising Money from a VC

Before you get too excited thinking this is where I give you Marc Andreessen's secret email address, this chapter simply asks the fundamental questions: Should you raise venture capital? If so, how much? And at what valuation?

Once we've covered that, in chapter 8 we will get into the more prescriptive (and, for some, sexier) *how-to* approach of pitching to a VC.

But you're not ready for your pitch until you know what you want, how much, and why.

At first blush, the answer to these questions seems fairly obvious—raise as much money as you possibly can at the highest possible valuation in order to grow your business. John Doerr famously compared fund-raising to attending a cocktail party. When the waiter comes around with the tray of mini hot dogs, you should always take one. The reason being that you never know when in the course of the remainder of the cocktail party the waiter will make it back to you. In similar fashion, the right time to raise capital is when the capital is available; who knows if the fund-raising waiter will ever make it back to you when you decide you are in fact ready to raise money.

But let's talk first to see if you're even at the right cocktail party . . .

Is Venture Capital Right for You?

Let's start with the decision to raise money in the first instance, and specifically, since you're reading this book, the decision to raise from VCs. Hopefully you now have a better sense of the "company–venture capital fit" for your business. Just as with product-market fit—where we care about how well your product satisfies a specific market need—you need to determine whether your company is appropriate for venture capital.

We talked earlier about the cardinal rule of VC investing: everything starts and ends with market size. No matter how interesting or intellectually stimulating your business, if the ultimate size of the opportunity isn't big enough to create a stand-alone, self-sustaining business of sufficient scale, it may not be a candidate for venture financing.

Rules of thumb are overgeneralizations and crude ways to simplify complex topics, I admit. But, as a general rule of thumb, you should be able to credibly convince yourself (and your potential VC partners) that the market opportunity for your business is sufficiently large to be able to generate a profitable, high-growth, several-hundred-million-dollar-revenue business over a seven-to-ten-year period.

There is no magic to any of these numbers, but if you think about what it takes to become a public company, these financial characteristics (at least in today's market) could support a public market capitalization of several billion dollars. Depending on the VC's ultimate ownership level of the company at this time, the returns to the VC on this investment should be meaningful enough to move the needle on the fund's overall economics.

What If Your Market Isn't Huge?

So, what if the market opportunity just isn't of that scale? That doesn't make you a bad person or your business a bad business. It's unfortunate how many founders can feel that way. You could be running a multimillion-dollar business with great profits and be living a happy, wealthy, influential life. Your business might be helping people, enriching lives or even saving them, and still not be the right fit for raising VC. All that means is that you might need to think differently about where and how to raise capital, and come up with a different approach.

For example, there are smaller VC funds (often with less than $100 million fund sizes) that do invest very early in companies and for which the business model is to exit companies largely through acquisitions at lower ultimate end valuations. That type of firm might be more appropriate for your opportunity if the market size can't support a stand-alone business. Not every small fund adopts this strategy; there are many angel and seed investors who, despite their smaller investment amounts, are also playing the at-bats-per-home-run game. So make sure you understand the core strategy of your potential partner up front. And we talked earlier in the book about debt financing from banks as well as another potential source of capital in such situations.

The point is simply that venture capital may not in all cases be the right source of capital for you. It might not be the right tool for the job.

What does that mean? Well, as you've hopefully learned from reading this book so far, VCs are people, too, and they respond to the incentives that are created for them. Those incentives, simply put (and boiled down to financial ones only), are:

1. To build a portfolio of investments, with the understanding that many will not work (either at all, or will work only with

constrained upside) and a small number will generate the lion's share of the financial returns for a given fund; and

2. To further turn those large financial returners into cash within a ten-to-twelve-year period so that the cash can be paid back to their limited partners, with the hope that the limited partners will then give that cash back to the VCs to play the game again in the form of a new fund.

That's the venture cycle of life we discussed earlier.

And even if your business is appropriate for VC (because of the ultimate market size opportunity and other factors), you still need to decide whether you want to play by the rules of the road that venture capital entails. That means sharing equity ownership with a VC, sharing board control and governance, and ultimately entering into a marriage that is likely to last for about the same time as the average "real" marriage. (It turns out that eight to ten years is about the average length of real marriages in the US . . . make of that what you will.)

How Much Money Should You Raise?

Now, assuming you made the decision to raise venture capital in the first place, how much money should you raise? The answer is *to raise as much money as you can that enables you to safely achieve the key milestones you will need for the next fund-raising.*

In other words, the advice we often give to entrepreneurs is to think about your next round of financing when you are raising the current round of financing. What will you need to demonstrate to the next round investor that shows how you have sufficiently de-risked the business, such that that investor is willing to put new money into the company at a price that appropriately reflects the progress you have made since your last round of financing?

That's a lot of words, so let's unpack it a bit.

In general, most entrepreneurs at the early stages of their business raise new capital every twelve to twenty-four months. Those time frames are not sacrosanct, but they do reflect the general convention in the startup world and also reflect reasonable time periods during which meaningful business progress can be made.

Thus, if you are raising your first round of financing (typically called the Series A round), you will want to raise an amount of money that gives you enough runway to get to the milestones you will need to hit to be able to successfully raise the next round of financing (the Series B) at (hopefully) a higher valuation than the A round.

What are those milestones? Well, it varies significantly by the type of company, but for purposes of our example, let's assume you are building an enterprise software application. The Series B investor is likely to want to see that at least the initial version of the product is built (not the beta version, but the first commercially available product, even though the feature set will of course be incomplete). They will want to see that you have some demonstrated proof in the form of customer engagement and contracts that companies are in fact willing to pay money for the product you have built. You probably don't need to have $10 million in customer business, but something more like $3 million to $5 million is likely sufficient to get a Series B investor interested in providing new financing.

If you posit that set of facts, then the decision you need to make at the A round is how much money you will need to raise to give yourself a realistic chance of hitting those milestones over the one-to-two-year period before you try to raise the B round. This, of course, is partly a spreadsheet exercise, but also includes a gut check from you as CEO to build in some cushion for things that just might not go according to plan (because nothing *ever* goes exactly to plan).

A fair question to ask here is why not just raise all the money you need for the company, all at once, and forget this idea of staging out capital raises by round? Well, first, a successful enterprise software company that makes it to an IPO is probably going to raise at least $100 million (and, in some cases, a few multiples of that), so there aren't too many VCs who are going to write that size check up front.

More likely, even if you could raise that amount of money, the terms on which you would raise it—in particular, the valuation you would receive and thus the amount of the company you would need to sell—would be prohibitively expensive. Spreading out your capital raises allows you, as the entrepreneur, the ability to get the benefit of increases in the valuation of the company as you de-risk the opportunity, and provides the VC the ability to rightsize her total capital exposure to the business based on the achievement of these milestones.

In other words, if you accomplish the objectives that you laid out at the time of your A round, your B round investor will pay you for that success in the form of a higher valuation. This means that you will have to sell less of the company per dollar of capital you raise. In that case, you and your employees are all better off—you have the capital you need to grow the business, and the cost of that capital is less than it would have been had you raised more money than needed at an earlier stage.

The other consideration regarding the amount of capital to raise is the desire to maintain focus for the company by forcing real economic trade-offs during the most formative stages of company development. Scarcity is indeed the mother of invention. Believe it or not, having too much money can be the death knell for early-stage startups.

As a CEO, you may be tempted to green-light projects that might be of marginal value to your company's development, and explaining to your team members why they can't build something, or hire that next person, when they know you don't have financial constraints is harder than it may seem.

Nobody is suggesting that everyone live on ramen and sleep on the floor, but having a finite amount of resources helps to refine what are in fact the critical milestones for a business and ensures that every investment gets weighed against its ultimate opportunity cost.

. . . And at What Valuation?

We're going to talk a lot more about valuation when we get into the mechanics of the term sheet, but I'd be remiss if I didn't touch on valuation in this section, because it's a key part of the question: "How much money should I raise (and at what valuation)?" Of course, you might say, I should raise the money at the highest valuation at which I can get a VC to invest. But that's not always the right answer.

This might be what you'd expect a VC to say—after all, a venture capitalist benefits economically from paying a lower valuation—but bear with me, as there are important considerations here.

Recall the discussion we just had—that the current round of financing should be driven by the milestones needed to achieve the next round of financing *at a higher valuation that reflects the progress (and de-risking) of the business*. If you allow yourself or a VC to overvalue the company at the current round, then you have just raised the stakes for what it will take to clear that valuation bar for the next round and get paid for the progress you have made. After all, you might be able to get away with overvaluation at one round (or possibly more than one), but at some point in time, your valuation needs to reflect the actual progress of the business.

I've had the following conversation with many founders over the years: "I've more than doubled my business since the last fund-raising, but the valuation I am receiving in the current round is way less than double the last round valuation. What gives?"

Well, what gives is that your next round valuation is not a function of your last round valuation. Rather, it reflects the current state of business as valued within the current state of the financing world.

So a few things could have happened. First, the valuation metrics by which the business is being judged could have changed. For example, if the public stock markets have dropped since your last financing round and thus the public markets value a mature company using a lower valuation metric than before, your valuation may be affected as well. In other words, the market environment will undoubtedly have an impact on valuation for your startup.

Second, although you may have doubled your business, the new investor may look at your last valuation and feel as though you had been given forward credit for that type of success. As a result, that new investor might decide that tripling is the new doubling; in other words, the new investor is not that impressed that you only doubled the business coming off of the previous round's valuation and capital resources; they expected more.

As a result, one very important thing to do as an entrepreneur—assuming you do decide to optimize for valuation—is to make sure that you raise a sufficient amount of money to give you plenty of time to achieve the now-higher expectations that the next round of investors may have. One big mistake we at a16z have seen entrepreneurs make is to raise too small an amount of money at an aggressive valuation, which is precisely the thing you don't want to do. This establishes the high-watermark valuation, but without the financial resources to be able to achieve the business goals required to safely raise your next round well above the current round's valuation.

Third, competition drives valuation. Whether we like to admit it or not, valuation is more art than science, and "deal heat" can drive VCs to pay more than they might otherwise think is appropriate for a company at a particular stage. And a higher valuation hurdle from the last round may scare away competition. The potential B round investor might like the business but see what valuation you achieved at the last round and fear that she will not be able to match your expectations for the current round. Much of this unfortunately goes unsaid and is a result of people interpreting others' expectations without engaging in a full dialogue, but this happens nonetheless.

And, if you have enough investors who refuse to bid on your B round because they are afraid to offend you by not being able to match your business progress with a commensurate increase in valuation, you will fail to generate competition for the round. That is generally not a good place to be.

An obvious objection to what I'm saying—if you aren't already objecting to my arguments against stretching too much on valuation as being self-serving—is that all of this is interesting, but it doesn't matter. That is, if I get the benefit of overvaluation in one round and then I pay the price for that in the next round by getting undervalued, am I not still better off?

When you raise money from a VC, the transaction goes as follows: the VC gives you cold hard cash, and you issue her an amount of equity that corresponds to whatever valuation terms the two of you agreed upon. For example, if the VC agreed to invest $5 million in the company in exchange for owning 20 percent of the equity, she would give the company the $5 million, and the company would issue her shares equal to 20 percent of the total equity. Thus, when we talk about dilution, in this example, you, your employees, and any other existing shareholders in the company are being "diluted" by 20 percent; that is, if you owned 10 percent of the company before this financing round, you will own 8 percent after this round.

In most cases, of course, companies go on to raise subsequent rounds of financing, often with increasingly larger amounts of capital being raised and (hopefully) at materially higher valuations. So if you were to later raise $20 million in exchange for 10 percent of the company's equity, everyone would have their ownership diluted by an additional 10 percent. Your 8 percent stake is now about 7.2 percent.

So the logical objection to my above comments regarding valuation is: If I overvalue the company at the first financing and thus get diluted by less than 20 percent, who cares if I have to pay the piper with an undervalued price at the second financing, as long as I still end up with 7.2 percent in either case?

Let's concede for a second that in the theoretical sense your math is right; there's something deeper at work that is critical. Employee expectations and sentiment matter a lot to a company's development. Great employees who have lots of job opportunities want to work for great companies where they can achieve their personal growth goals. When a company is doing well in all respects—employee hiring and development, customer goals, product goals, financing goals—it's easy to retain and motivate employees. After all, who doesn't love being on a winning team where the growth of the company can translate into personal career growth for the employees?

However, if the company is in fact on track to achieve its goals but then faces a disappointment in fund-raising, things can get tougher. In particular, the company's valuation is the one highly visible external benchmark that every employee often seizes on (whether you want them to or not) as a measure of interim success. Momentum can appear to be stalling and employees may start to wonder whether everything you have told them as CEO about how much progress the company is making is in fact true. At a minimum, you now have to explain why your financing partners value your progress differently than do you or the others in your company.

I've been there. When I joined LoudCloud in 2000, things couldn't have been any rosier. We were in the height of what turned out to be the dot-com mania, and the business was on fire. We were hiring employees quickly, growing our customer base, expanding our office footprint—everything was exceeding plan.

My first job when I started was to raise more capital to allow us to continue on our growth path. Working with the other members of the executive team, we were able to raise $120 million at an $820 million valuation in June 2000. This, by the way, was for a company that was nine months old! Our prior round of financing in September 1999 was $21 million at a $66 million valuation. We were feeling pretty good about this as our CEO (Ben Horowitz) and I were preparing to host an all-hands meeting to discuss the results of the raise.

But rather than ride off into the sunset to a standing ovation, the first question we got was: "How come you didn't get a $1 billion valuation?" It turned out that a company in our same cohort of startups (StorageNetworks) had raised money a month before at a $1 billion valuation. So the heart of the question was "If you're so smart, how come you aren't as rich as the next guy?"

Now, keep in mind, none of us had set the expectation that we would be able to raise at a $1 billion valuation. But it didn't matter. Our employees had a data point that caused at least some of them to think that we had fallen short of what defined world-class in this financing environment.

We recovered from this—and granted, the dot-com bubble was a crazy time—but nonetheless it served to remind us of three very important lessons. First, employees do often judge the success of the business at least in part on the external measure of valuation in a financing round. Second, even if that valuation looks great in the absolute sense (or in the relative sense, compared with your previous round of financing), employees are likely to compare it to other companies that have raised money recently, in many cases independent of whether those companies are relevant benchmarks. Third, never underestimate the value of always maintaining momentum in the business, one measure of which may be a successful financing round. And, in the LoudCloud case, we were not even talking about a lower valuation than the prior round, nor a modest step-up in valuation; those things can be debilitating for companies and often hard to recover from.

Ultimately, the best story for you as a CEO is to be able to point to the proverbial "up and to the right" valuation graph. If your financing valuation is inconsistent with the success story you've been telling about the company, you've likely got some explaining to do. And even if the explanation is honest and truthful, it's far better to never have to explain it in the first place.

We've been talking so far about suboptimal, but still reasonable, situations whereby you are raising capital at a higher price than the last round, just less so than you or others might have anticipated. Where the wheels can really come off of the bus is either if you end up not being able to raise money at all or if you have to raise at a valuation below the last round's valuation. We'll talk more about the implications of that when we cover the economics of the term sheet. I keep punting on this because we have a lot to cover, but it's coming up soon. When you see chapters 9 and 10 you'll know what I mean. (Grab your coffee in advance!)

CHAPTER 8

The Art of the Pitch

For many entrepreneurs, the act of pitching their business to a venture capitalist can be a harrowing experience. After all, you are at your most vulnerable place in your professional career. You've probably just quit a job that provided a steady income and had to convince your spouse or significant other that all of this would eventually work out in the form of greater financial security for your family. But, in the meantime (i.e., the next ten or more years), you are going to live cheaply, take no vacations, work longer hours that you ever have before, sleep fitfully (my partner Ben remarked in his book about his experience as a startup CEO that he slept like a baby every night—waking up every few hours crying), and, on top of all that, beg VCs to finance this glamorous lifestyle. Sounds like fun, right?

I'm assuming that since you've read this far, you're all in, so here we go.

Foot in the Door

Let's start by talking about how you get the opportunity to pitch. Most VCs have websites that provide an email address for you to contact if you have a business idea. But, as with a lot of businesses, that's not the recommended path to get in front of a decision-maker.

Unlike regular jobs that have job listings and application processes, VCs don't have such a formal structure. But there are informal structures that provide a similar function.

Angel or seed investors are often an important source of referrals for VCs. It helps that they are upstream from the VCs in that they are typically investing at an earlier stage in the company's development than might a traditional VC. As a result, many VCs develop relationships with angel and seed investors, with whom they live in a symbiotic relationship in the venture world. Angel and seed investors have a direct interest in seeing the companies in which they have invested raise additional (and usually bigger) capital downstream from VCs, and the VCs are interested in a curated pipeline of interesting opportunities in which to invest.

Law firms also tend to be important avenues into venture firms. As we talked about earlier, often the first stop along the entrepreneurial journey is at your lawyer's office to form the company itself. Thus, as with seed and angel investors, lawyers are often upstream of the VCs and in a position to see opportunities at their most nascent state. Lawyers, too, are motivated to introduce their best startup clients to VCs, as more institutional funding for these clients means that they can become long-term business clients of the law firm.

If neither of these routes is available to you, get crafty. (Please also consider the difference between crafty and invasive.) You should be industrious enough to find someone who knows someone who has some relation to a VC. While I recognize in some cases this can be challenging, it's a great test of your mettle as a startup CEO. If you can't find a creative way to get to a VC, then, for example, how are you going to find a way to get to the senior executive at a potential customer prospect of yours?

Your ability to find a warm introduction to a VC, while not a requirement, is often a screening heuristic that VCs use as a gauge on your grit, creativity, and determination, each of which might be an important characteristic of a successful founder.

It's important to note here that there are *hundreds* of fantastic blog posts, books, podcasts, and conferences about networking, being generous, enchanting people, and getting your foot in the door. It's part likability, networking, hustle, showing up, following up, persistence, salesmanship, confidence, experience, storytelling, and yes—sheer dumb luck.

For the sake of keeping this book focused on understanding how venture capital works, we are going to assume you have what it takes to get a meeting with a VC who invests in your market. So let's time travel a little and cut straight to the scene where your first meeting with a VC is booked.

What Goes into the Pitch?

Before you show up for your meeting, let's demystify the pitch process by remembering and applying some of the things that we've talked about already in this book. Recall that we talked about what motivates VCs and how they evaluate investment opportunities (not the least of which is remembering that they are humans, a lot like you, and they are looking for a good financial outcome).

On the motivation front, VCs are incented by their LPs to produce outsize returns ("alpha" in the finance world) relative to the alternative uses for which LPs might invest that capital. The implicit bargain between the LP and the GP (the VC) is that LPs will lock up their capital for ten or more years to give the GP the time to realize those returns in the form of acquisitions or IPOs of portfolio companies. And remember our batting average analogy—most of what VCs invest in will not yield much, if at all, in the way of financial returns. It is those few home runs that return ten to twenty-five times, or more, of the VCs' invested capital that will make or break their business.

So your job as an entrepreneur is simple: Convince a VC that your company has the potential to be one of those outliers. That's it. Piece of cake, right? Okay, so, how can you do that? Go back to the first principles we discussed earlier about the evaluation criteria VCs are likely to apply to early-stage investment opportunities.

Pitch Essential #1: Market Sizing

Let's start with market sizing, because it's really the first and biggest factor that you need to help a VC understand. It is your job to lead the VC to the water. It's your job to be a patient and inspiring teacher here. Don't assume the VC understands the market or its potential size. You need to paint the picture for them that enables them to answer the "so what?" question. That is, if I invest in this company, and the CEO and her team do everything they say they are going to do and build a nice business, can that business be big enough to really drive an outsize return to my fund? Will it ultimately be big enough and material to accomplishing my objectives as a VC?

We mentioned Airbnb earlier in the context of discussing market size to illustrate that the answer to this question might not always be obvious. Now let's look at Lyft as a way to show how you can best position market size as an entrepreneur.

When Lyft was getting started (Lyft actually started as another company called Zimride, a long-distance ride-sharing company), it wasn't obvious how big the market for ride-sharing could be. A lot of people evaluating the financing opportunity started with the existing taxi market as a proxy for market size and made some assumptions about what percentage of that market a ride-sharing service could reasonably capture. That line of thinking was perfectly logical, but the entrepreneurs didn't stop there.

Rather, they made the case—convincingly at least to us at Andreessen Horowitz—that that line of reasoning was too myopic.

Instead, Lyft argued that the taxi market was too limiting because people made assumptions about the availability of taxis, the security of taxis, and the convenience of hailing taxis in choosing whether to in fact order a taxi. If you closed your eyes for a moment and imagined a world in which everyone was walking around with a fully networked supercomputer in their pockets with GPS tracking, which is exactly what a smartphone is, then the market size for on-demand car sharing could be much larger. After all, drivers who couldn't afford to purchase a taxi medallion could just use their own cars to increase the supply of available drivers, and this increase in supply would therefore dramatically increase the convenience of utilizing the service for consumers. Increased supply would drive increased demand, which would in turn drive more supply into the market. You get the picture—a true network-effects business.

Network effects of course don't exist in every market, but this line of reasoning could be (and has been) applied to lots of pitches to VCs. For example, if cancer screening techniques improved to the point that they are materially less invasive and have a higher predictive value relative to current screening modalities, people might get cancer screenings as part of their annual physical exams, and the market for early-stage cancer screening could become orders of magnitude bigger than it is today. That was a key part of the investment thesis when we invested in a company called Freenome, which is using machine-learning technologies to identify early-stage cancers from blood tests.

Many startups are going after existing markets, which may themselves already be quite large. In that case, your job as an entrepreneur is to fit yourself into that market and explain what macro trends are evolving in that market that create an opportunity for you to own it.

An example from our portfolio is Okta, which is a now-public company that we first invested in back in 2009. Okta is an enterprise software company that provides a way for companies to consolidate log-in credentials for their many software-as-a-service

(SAAS) applications. For example, many modern companies use Gmail, Salesforce, and a variety of other internet-based SAAS applications, each of which has its own method of logging in and authenticating users into the applications. Okta provides a unified portal whereby a user needs only to log in to Okta once, and then Okta passes those credentials through to all the SAAS applications for which an employee is granted access.

When we invested in Okta in 2009, such a solution already existed. Microsoft had developed a software package called Active Directory that did what Okta was proposing to do, but for traditional applications that were managed and maintained inside the IT environments of most major companies. And they were by far the market leader.

But what Okta convinced us of was that there was a change in the existing market landscape that created an opportunity for a new company to take over. Traditionally, the number of applications that an enterprise could deploy was limited by the amount of available IT staff in the enterprise; every application had to be implemented and supported by the internal IT staff of the organization. What the advent of SAAS applications enabled was the lifting of this constraint and thus the potential for a proliferation of applications within the enterprise. The marketing department could now use applications that were different from those used by sales or engineering or HR, precisely because these were SAAS applications that were managed by the SAAS vendors themselves versus by the enterprise's internal IT staff.

This proliferation of disparate applications, Okta suggested, would give rise to the need for a new way to manage access to and security for these applications. And thus a new company could be created to take advantage of this market opportunity. We bought the argument and invested in Okta. It's now a more than $5 billion market capitalization public company because their vision of how the market would develop was in fact correct.

Sometimes as an entrepreneur you have the hard job of positing the creation of a market that develops as a result of a new technology. For example, we were seed investors in 2010 in a company called Burbn—that is the correct spelling, and they were not creating a new adult beverage. Burbn originally started with a different product focus but ultimately developed into a photo-sharing application for the iPhone. The iPhone, of course, had been invented only three years prior, and the smartphone category was not nearly the size that it would ultimately become.

So the market-size challenge in this case was to build your argument on two assumptions: (1) this iPhone thing would really become a dominant global computing platform, and (2) photo-sharing would be a killer app for the platform. People of course had shared photos before the advent of the iPhone, but that market size would never get a VC excited about this investment. So for a VC to make the investment decision, she would need to forecast that iPhones would be big and that photo-sharing would be enabled in a way by this new technology platform so as to create its own big, new market. And then you'd have to assume that there would be some way to monetize photo-sharing. This last piece, I think—if most VCs are being honest—was a complete unknown at the time, but it was not a crazy hypothesis that if you can amass billions of photos that are being shared among millions of people, there ought to be some way to make money from that.

Lucky for us at Andreessen Horowitz, we took the leap on market size and invested in Burbn. Two years after we invested, Facebook acquired the company—now named Instagram—for $1 billion.

Pitch Essential #2: Team

Next up in your pitch, and what matters to the VC, is team. Once you've established that the market opportunity is in fact big, the real question for a VC now becomes "Why you?" That is, "Why do I want to back this set of entrepreneurs versus waiting for the next set that might walk into my office tomorrow tackling the same idea?" After all, ideas are a dime a dozen; execution is what sets the winners apart from the pretenders.

Recall that there's not a lot for a VC to diligence at any early stage; much of the analysis is qualitative. But team is one area where VCs can truly dig in.

As uncomfortable as it may be, you need to spend a significant amount of time in your pitch talking about you as the CEO and the rest of your team. In particular, what makes *you* as a person uniquely qualified to win the market? Some entrepreneurs are hesitant to do this, and believe that touting one's own abilities is a form of self-aggrandizement. But VCs don't see it that way; rather, they view this as a way to learn about the unique set of skills you have that will make you best suited for the opportunity at hand.

It's not an exercise in boasting but rather an exercise in helping the VCs assess your fitness for the role you are proposing to take on. Thus, you should relate your prior accomplishments or experiences to the current business you are pitching—what do they say about your likelihood of success in the current venture? Don't be shy to talk about your failures—after all, experience is what you get when you don't accomplish what you set out to do—and relate what you learned. VCs love infinite learners.

In 2010, we invested in the Series A round of financing for a new startup called Nicira. The company was a pioneer in the area of software-defined networking—essentially the idea that much of what hardware had traditionally done in networking (dominated largely by Cisco) could be done via software. We believed in the market opportunity, so the logical question to be addressed was whether this team was the right one. After all, we knew that, given the size of the opportunity, the market would attract multiple companies into the space.

Martin Casado was the consummate founder for this business. He had spent his early career at the CIA building out the foundations for software-defined networking and then went to Stanford to earn his PhD in the same area. His doctoral thesis was the seminal paper on the topic. There couldn't have been better founder-market fit. And so we invested in Nicira, which was ultimately acquired by VMware for $1.25 billion. And then after spending several years at VMware running the business division into which he was acquired, Martin joined Andreessen Horowitz as a general partner.

We talked earlier about Okta in the context of our market size discussion. In addition to going after a great market, Okta was founded by two individuals with a perfect fit to their market opportunity. Todd McKinnon, the founding CEO, had spent most of his professional career running engineering at Salesforce, the pioneer in the SAAS market. Through this role, he experienced firsthand the challenges that many of Salesforce's customers were having in managing the various SAAS applications they were using. His partner and founding COO, Frederic Kerrest, was also a Salesforce alumnus, having spent his career there learning how to sell the SAAS value proposition to potential customers. The combination of these two skill sets—a deep technical understanding of the problem to be solved, coupled with the knowledge of how best to develop the right sales and marketing strategy (we often call this strategy "go-to-market") in a still nascent SAAS market—made Todd and Frederic the ideal founders to back in this space.

Understandably, not everyone is going to have a PhD in the area in which they want to start a company, but you do need a convincing story as to why you are the best fit to start a company in a competitive market. Perhaps the business requires a certain skill set in sales and marketing that you have mastered in a previous role. Perhaps you encountered the very market problem you are endeavoring to solve organically through your own experiences and felt compelled to build a company around this idea. Or maybe you have a special skill that enables you to tell stories in a compelling way—not tall tales, but a way to articulate a vision that is likely to lead employees, customers, and financiers to want to come along for the ride.

We were fortunate enough to see the pitch for the Series A

round of Square, a financial services payment company that has gone on to become a $25 billion public company. Unfortunately, we were not lucky enough to make the decision to invest in that round. What did we miss?

Well, at the time of the A round, Jack Dorsey, the cofounder of Twitter, was not the CEO of Square. Instead, his cofounder Jim McKelvey was the CEO. Jim was a friend of Jack's from his hometown of Missouri and had previously been a professional glass blower. Jim was frustrated by the fact that he could sell his wares by accepting cash only at the country fairs where his finished products were featured. Jim and Jack thought there should be a way to enable credit card transactions for small, often sole proprietor, merchants. Thus, the idea for Square.

Great organic founder-market fit: the solution was derived from a personal experience of hardship, around which the entrepreneur felt compelled to build a company. However, we didn't know Jim nor did we have a good way to evaluate his skills as a CEO for the company, and we wondered whether Jack might prove to be a better long-term CEO for the business. And so we passed on the A round.

But we failed to appreciate two things.

The first was that Jack would realize that the best way to maximize success of the business was for him to become the CEO, something he effected a few short months after the Series A fund-raising. The second was that the star power that Jack possessed could provide the company unfair advantages in the marketplace. For example, Jack was so well-known that he was able to secure a spot on The Oprah Winfrey Show and use that as a way to tell his story to a broader audience; essentially, it was free marketing available only to someone with his brand appeal. He also was able to get directly to Jamie Dimon, CEO of J.P. Morgan, and convince Jamie to bundle the Square dongle with the J.P. Morgan credit card business in a way that generated tons of Square customers at very low cost. Again, not everyone is Jack Dorsey, but think about what skills, and advantages, you uniquely possess that will prove valuable to the ultimate development of your business.

Once you've successfully convinced the VCs of your fitness to the market opportunity, you still need to help them understand how you are going to build the right team around you. No matter how great a product genius any founder may be, she can't build a large business without employees and other business partners.

So what makes you a natural-born leader, or a learned leader, that will cause people to quit their jobs and come work for you; cause customers to be willing to buy your products or services when there are many safer, established choices available to them; cause business development partners to want to help you sell your wares and penetrate new markets; and, of course, cause funding partners to want to provide you the capital to do all of the above? Maybe you're a repeat entrepreneur and thus can point to having done all of the above before. But many entrepreneurs are doing so for the first time, so think about other leadership-like opportunities you've experienced before that might be good indicia of your ability to be a CEO-leader.

We talk a lot at Andreessen Horowitz about storytelling skills as a good indicator of potential success in an entrepreneur. And to be clear, we are using the word "story" in its purest sense; that is, the ability to captivate an audience (whether that audience is employees, customers, partners, financiers, etc.) and take them along for the proverbial ride. We are not talking about the negative connotation of storytelling, taking people on a proverbial ride because you're hoodwinking them.

True storytelling is a remarkable talent in so many endeavors, but particularly in a startup, where you have so little actual proof of success in the early years on which people can base their decision to join the company. Great CEOs find a way to paint a vision for the opportunity that simply makes people want to be a part of the company-building process. These same skills will help you land your first (and future) VC financing partners.

Pitch Essential #3: Product

Your product plan comes next in pitching the business opportunity. We mentioned earlier that no VC expects you to be clairvoyant about the precise needs of the market, but they are evaluating the *process* by which you came to your initial product plan. VCs are fascinated to learn how your brain works. We want to see the idea maze. What data have you incorporated from the market; how is it more aspirin than vitamin; how is this product ten times better or cheaper than existing alternatives?

VCs understand that your product plan is likely to pivot as you get into market and test a real product offering against real market needs, but they want to be comfortable that your process of evaluating the market needs to date is robust enough to enable you to adapt appropriately to changing market demands. Walk them through your thought process and demonstrate that you have strong beliefs, weakly held; that is, that you will adapt to the changing needs of the market but remain informed by your depth of product development experience.

Pitch Essential #4: Go-to-Market

The go-to-market section is often the most underdeveloped section of the pitch for an early-stage company. That is, how will you acquire customers, and does the business model support customer acquisition profitably?

Many entrepreneurs make the mistake of skipping over this at the early stage because the current funding round is not likely to get them meaningfully into market. But it's important to include this in your pitch, even if just at a high level, as it is foundational to the long-run viability of the business.

Are you planning to build a direct, outside sales force, and can the average selling price of your product support this go-to-market? Or are you planning to acquire customers through brand marketing or other online forms of acquisition? If so, how do you think about the costs of such activities relative to the lifetime value of a customer?

You don't need to have robust financial models at this stage of your company's development, but you ought to have a framework that gives a VC enough fodder to understand your thinking around customer acquisition.

As with the product section, walking VCs through your go-to-market strategy is a great way to show them how your mind works and how deeply you understand your audience.

Returning to our friends at Okta, the original go-to-market for the business was to sell to small and medium-size businesses (SMBs). The theory was that SMBs were more likely to be forward thinking about adopting new technologies and that the SAAS model lent itself better to this market. That is, because SMBs likely had smaller IT teams and budgets than did large companies, the ability to rent software and outsource the running and maintenance of the software to a third-party vendor would be a compelling sales proposition.

Yet as the company began to execute against this plan, they learned that selling into the large enterprise market was actually a better place to start. Why was that? It turned out that the larger a company was, the more likely it was to have lots of individual SAAS applications being utilized across disparate departments, and thus the value proposition of the Okta software resonated best with these companies. At this earlier stage of development of the SAAS market, the SMBs just hadn't deployed enough SAAS applications to take advantage of the automation the Okta software provided. As the SAAS market began to mature and the SMBs started to invest in more SAAS applications, the SMBs also ultimately became good customer prospects for Okta.

You are not expected as an entrepreneur to have all the correct answers figured out, but you do need to have theories grounded in reasonable assumptions against which you can then apply real-world experience. Again, strong opinions, weakly held.

One side note on the context of adaptability: A hallmark of startup companies is that they often "pivot"—this is a euphemistic way of saying that the original product, go-to-market, etc., didn't quite work in the way you expected, so you decide to change that aspect of the business and try again. Some pivots can be minor adjustments, while others might be wholesale changes of direction.

One of the most amazing pivots of all time comes courtesy of Stewart Butterfield. Andreessen Horowitz invested in 2010 in a gaming company called Tiny Speck, run by a great entrepreneur by the name of Stewart Butterfield. Tiny Speck set out to build—and ultimately did build—a massively multiplayer online game called *Speck*. It was a great game in many respects, but Stewart later concluded that it couldn't sustain itself as a long-term business.

With a few months of cash remaining from our original investment, Stewart approached the board (Accel Partners was also an investor in the company and represented on the board) with an idea: in developing *Speck*, the company had built an internal communications and workflow tool that they found significantly increased the efficiency of their engineering development processes. Stewart wondered whether other organizations could also benefit from this product, so he sought permission from the board to "pivot" into this business with the remaining cash on the balance sheet.

I'm happy that we were smart enough to say yes to Stewart's request. That pivot is now Slack, an enterprise collaboration software company that is valued in the billions of dollars.

I can assure you that not all pivots work out this way, but I mention this story in the context of the VC pitch to underscore a few important points. First, VCs understand that, despite the best intentions, most businesses go through some set of pivots along the way, whether small tweaks or almost complete restarts. So, as you pitch, you are not expected to be clairvoyant, nor do VCs expect that everything you say in the pitch will materialize as you have forecast.

Second, though—and this is really important—you do need to demonstrate to the VCs that you are the master of the domain you are proposing to attack and that you have thought about every important detail of your business in a way that shows depth of preparation and conviction.

For example, if you are pitching a VC and she suggests that your go-to-market plans are all wrong and should instead be done differently from how you have pitched, the wrong reaction is to immediately abandon your plan. While that may ultimately be the right path to take, the fact that you could be so easily convinced in a meeting, where the VC has spent a total of one hour hearing about your business while you supposedly have spent nearly a lifetime doing so, would raise some serious questions about your preparedness and fitness to be a CEO. A thoughtful, engaged discussion on how you came to the conclusions that you did and a willingness to listen to the feedback and incorporate it into your thinking, as appropriate, would be a far better response than pivoting on the fly.

Pitch Essential #5: Planning for the Next Round of Fund-Raising

For the final part of your pitch to VCs, you should clearly articulate the milestones you intend to accomplish with the money you are raising at this round. Remember that a VC is likely projecting ahead to the next round of financing to gauge the level of market risk she is taking by funding you at this stage. Are you raising enough money to accomplish the milestones you set out such that the next investor will be willing to invest new money at a substantially higher valuation than the current round? "Substantially higher" is very market dependent, but in general you want to aim toward a valuation that is roughly double your prior round. That momentum will be well received by both your current investors and your employees.

If, at the time you present the milestones, you or your VC feels as though the milestones are too much at risk, you're likely to have a discussion about raising more capital at the current round, lowering the current valuation, or finding other ways to increase the confidence interval around your forecast progress.

Remember that most VCs are building a portfolio of companies as part of a fund, and thus they are looking for some level of diversification across a number of investments. Thus, while they may be investing $10 million in your current round and reserving some additional dollars to support future rounds of financing, they are not assuming that they will be the only investor throughout your company's life cycle.

This is why VCs care about the achievability of the milestones you are laying out; in most cases, they don't want to be, or can't afford to be, the only capital provider at the next round of financing, so they are trying to estimate the risk of you (and them) getting stranded at the next round.

If all else fails and you forget everything we just talked about in the heat of the moment, remember to go back to first principles: How do I convince a VC that my business has a chance to be one of those outsize winners that can make her look like a hero in front of her LPs?

CHAPTER 9

The Alphabet Soup
of Term Sheets: Part One
(Economics)

Now, let's assume your startup story is compelling enough that you receive a term sheet from a VC. This is an exciting moment for many founders . . . and then their eyes start to cross. What do all those terms mean? How do you evaluate them? What's standard, what's not; what's a good deal versus a bad deal?

As I mentioned at the beginning of this book, the term sheet is where information asymmetry between VCs and founders comes into play the most, and often at the expense of the founder. This is because VCs have been through this process many times and have negotiated hundreds of term sheets. By contrast, founders only get a few shots on goal in a lifetime and likely can count the number of term sheets they have negotiated on one hand. This is normal, but it puts the founder at a disadvantage that I would very much like to correct. It is my goal in this chapter and the next to unpack the term sheet, including some explanation of how VCs think about various terms so that entrepreneurs can be informed and clear about what their term sheets mean for them and their business.

The term sheet is a magnum opus, by any measure, and there are a lot of mechanics to understand. I'm going to simplify the very long term sheet into two big buckets—economics and governance.

This chapter, the economics bucket, includes the sections that talk about the size of the investment, valuation, antidilution treatment, liquidation preference, the size of the employee option pool, and vesting of options and founder shares. Not surprisingly, these items occupy a lot of the attention of both parties in the negotiation. And they are certainly important. But the other big bucket probably has much greater long-term ramifications for the success of the company.

Chapter 10 details the governance bucket. This addresses who gets a say in what happens in the company.

One more note before we dig into the term sheet. I created a standard example of a term sheet for you, which you will find on page 277. It's a sample term sheet for a Series A financing for hypothetical XYZ Company to be led by Venture Capital Fund I (VCF1.) Please reference it as we go through chapters 9 and 10.

Now, just as a Broadway playbill gives you a cast of characters and a short description of each role, let's go through the various terms of a deal. We're starting with the economics section of a term sheet—the money decisions.

Security: Preferred Shares

We mentioned earlier that one of the benefits of a C corp is that we can have different classes of shareholders with different rights. Well, here it is: VCF1 is going to purchase Series A *preferred shares* of the company. These are distinct from common shares (which is what the founders and employees typically hold) and they are also different from potential future series of preferred stock (that will likely be labeled "Series B," "Series C," ad infinitum). As you'll see as we progress further in the term sheet, the whole reason for creating a new class of stock is to give it "preferred" economic and governance rights relative to those enjoyed by the common shareholders.

Aggregate Proceeds

This one's pretty easy—the term sheet says that VCF1 is going to invest $10 million into the company in exchange for a 20 percent ownership interest. The second part of the section is intended to make sure that, to the extent the company has any other debt outstanding, in connection with this investment, all those notes will convert into equity under the terms of this financing. The reason VCs care about this is that notes (or debt) are generally senior to equity; that is, if the company were to go out of business, the notes would get paid back out of any remaining proceeds before the equity. So, if a VC is going to invest in the company, she doesn't want other monies to be ahead of her in the event of a potential liquidation. By forcing all the notes to convert into equity in this round, the VC ensures that everyone is in the same position with respect to the distribution of proceeds in the event of an exit (at least until we start talking about liquidation preferences shortly!).

We touched briefly at the beginning of the book on debt and mentioned that many startups raise convertible debt in connection with their initial seed financing. Recall that convertible debt means that the instrument starts out as debt but can be converted into equity based on the occurrence of certain events. In most cases, the debt will convert into equity in connection with an equity financing round, typically in a Series A financing like the one we are discussing here.

More about Convertible Debt

There are several flavors of convertible debt. In its most basic form, the debt converts into equity at the same price at which the Series

A investors purchase equity. This is referred to as an "uncapped" note, meaning that the valuation at which the note converts is not restricted and will be determined based upon the Series A equity price. Investors, understandably so, are often hesitant to purchase this debt because they are investing at one of the riskiest stages of the company's life cycle—companies generally are using this seed capital to begin building their first product—and are not getting paid adequately for this risk. Rather, they are paying the same price ultimately as the Series A investors, who have the benefit of putting their capital at risk at a slightly later stage of maturity of the company.

As a result, most convertible debt has one or both of the following features. "Capped" notes establish a ceiling on the maximum price at which the debt will convert into equity. For example, a convertible note with a $5 million valuation cap means that in no case will the debt convert into equity at a price higher than $5 million. If the Series A round valuation comes in below the cap—say $4 million—then the debt holder gets the benefit of that lower valuation. And if the Series A valuation exceeds the cap—say $10 million—then the debt holder converts at the $5 million cap, in this case a full 50 percent discount to the Series A investor.

The second feature is a conversion discount, with or without a cap. For example, the convertible note may provide that it converts at a 10 percent discount to the Series A financing valuation. In the case of an uncapped note with a 10 percent discount, the nominal conversion price will move up or down with the Series A price but always remains at a 10 percent discount to that price. If you coupled a cap with a 10 percent discount, then the conversion would follow the same principles as the capped note above: the note holder would get the benefit of the discount up to the point at which the cap provides a more favorable conversion price.

Why do entrepreneurs choose to issue convertible debt at the seed stage of financing versus raising traditional equity? Oftentimes, entrepreneurs do this for cost and simplicity reasons; the standard convertible debt documents are pretty simple and don't require much legal time and expense. The other benefit of convertible debt is that it allows both the entrepreneur and the seed investor to punt on the question of valuation at this early stage of company development. Rather than having a big negotiation around pricing at the seed round, the parties essentially defer that discussion until the Series A financing. However, once you start to introduce the cap concept into a convertible debt round, it's no longer the case that you are truly deferring that valuation discussion. In effect, you are agreeing on the maximum valuation at which the debt will convert into equity; this sounds awfully similar to agreeing on a valuation!

One very common mistake that we see entrepreneurs make is to raise too much convertible debt in the early days of the company such that they end up giving away too much of the company to outside investors. Why does this happen? For a couple of reasons.

First, as noted above, the main feature of convertible debt is that it allows an entrepreneur to raise money quickly and with much less legal expense than would be typically associated with an equity financing. This is because the legal instrument is very simple to document and is often set up to allow the company to raise additional capital relatively easily beyond the current investment. In contrast, equity financings typically require execution of a myriad of documents, and amendments to those documents typically require consent of the existing equity holders.

As a result, convertible debt financings can often have multiple, rolling closings, whereas an equity financing typically has only one closing. While this distinction may sound trivial in theory, in practice it has real consequences. We see many entrepreneurs who decide to raise $1 million in a convertible note and close on that money very quickly. But commonly some other investors will come along a few months later and indicate that they, too, would like to join in the financing. Most entrepreneurs acquiesce to this, since more money is typically better than less. And then the process has a way of repeating itself a few more times, each in relatively small dollar increments, but with the end result of the entrepreneur finding that she has over time raised $2.5–$3 million on the same financial terms on which she set out originally to raise $1 million. Depending on the way the note was written, each new financing round might require the new investors to execute a separate note, but this is a relatively trivial process and does not create an obstacle to these rolling closings.

The second feature of the note then becomes more apparent to the entrepreneur when she decides to raise a regular equity round of financing from a venture capitalist—her Series A financing. Although the notes may have a valuation cap or specify that the notes will convert at some fixed discount to the Series A equity, because the actual conversion price is not known until the Series A financing price is agreed upon (which of course occurs sometime in the future when the Series A investor agrees to a deal), the actual effect of the notes on the company's equity capitalization is also not determined until such time as the Series A financing happens. In contrast, when an entrepreneur does a regular equity financing, the actual dilutive effect of the transaction is made clear at the closing of the financing when the new shares have to be issued to the new investor; thus, the entrepreneur knows exactly how much of the company she ultimately still owns.

As a result, a fact pattern we see very often at the time of a Series A financing is that the entrepreneur is surprised to learn that she has sold much more of the equity than she anticipated through a series of these convertible notes. Not only can this be upsetting to the entrepreneur, but it also can be problematic for the Series A investor. After all, the new investor wants the entrepreneur to be highly motivated in the form of owning a lot of the equity of the company—what better way to align incentives than to have the entrepreneur get rich alongside a great investment return to the venture capitalist? But if the entrepreneur owns too little of the company at such an early stage of the company's life, the likelihood is that either she will become demotivated over the coming years or the VCs will need to grant her more equity down the road to maintain her economic interest.

But that additional equity that may be granted to the founder doesn't just get created out of thin air. Rather, doing so requires that the company increase the total amount of equity and issue those new shares to the founder. But that means that everyone else who did not receive that additional equity (including both other employees and investors) will have their ownership interest in the company "diluted," or reduced by the amount of the new equity issuance. Thus, creating the right incentives comes with a cost.

Let's look at a simple example. Imagine that you are the founder and own 70 shares of equity out of a total of 100 shares in the company; you have a 70 percent ownership interest in the company. For sake of simplicity, let's assume that the other 30 shares are owned by the company's other employees. As a result of debt converting into equity, assume that we had to issue 20 additional shares of equity to the debt holders. Your ownership in the company has now been reduced—you still own 70 shares in total, but the total number of shares has increased to 120. As a result, your 70 percent ownership has been diluted to 58 percent (70/120).

If the Series A investors are worried that this dilution may disincent you from working hard to increase the equity value of the company, they may not want to invest in the Series A without increasing your ownership back to, say, 65 percent. How can they do that? Again, by having the company create additional shares and issue them to you. If you do the math, you would need to receive an additional 23 shares (to get you to a total of 93 shares), and the creation of those shares would increase the total shares in the company to 143. Thus, 93/143 = 65 percent. But notice that our poor employees still own 30 shares and have seen their ownership in the company reduced from 30 percent to 21 percent (30/143).

This dance between these two competing interests—properly incenting an entrepreneur and minimizing the dilution for other shareholders—is a carefully choreographed one that recurs many times throughout the life cycle of a company. So encountering it early on can be a tough way to get a relationship started.

What often happens to resolve this tension? One option is just to kick the can down the road. That is, the investor invests at the Series A round, the entrepreneur gets what she gets, and everyone agrees that we just might need to solve this dilution problem sometime into the future. While we've seen this happen many times, it's really not the best solution; unlike whiskey, most problems don't in fact age well.

The second option is to address it up front. While better to confront these issues head-on, this is a tough one to navigate. Why? Because the new investor coming into the Series A round will want to solve this by having the company issue more stock to the entrepreneur to offset the dilution she has suffered from the convertible debt offerings. But of course those debt investors don't want to do that because that dilution will come largely out of their ownership stake. And so the dance continues until the parties can come to some compromise that works for all involved.

The bottom line is that this problem can be avoided easily by just being mindful as an entrepreneur of this constant trade-off between raising the capital you need to grow your business and minimizing the dilution to yourself and other employees and investors who are coming along the journey with you. For every dollar of VC you take, do the calculation to figure out what that means for your existing crew of people involved.

Price per Share

Our sample term sheet says two important things about the price that the VCs are willing to pay for the $10 million investment.

First, the valuation is $50 million "post-money"—what does that mean?

"Post-money" means exactly what is sounds like: the valuation of the company once the VC has invested her $10 million. You'll often hear VCs use the term "pre-money" as well; this is the valuation of the company before the VC makes her investment. So, mathematically, pre-money + amount of investment = post-money (in our example, since VCF1 is investing $10 million and has said that the post-money valuation is $50 million, the pre-money must be $40 million).

You'll see that VCF1 says in the first section of the term sheet that it wants 20 percent ownership of the company for its $10 million investment. Hopefully, you can see that the math makes sense here—if I put in $10 million and the post-money valuation is $50 million, then I should own 20 percent of the company ($10 million investment divided by $50 million post-money valuation). So far, so good.

Note also that the term sheet says that the post-money valuation includes two important elements.

First, any shares that convert as a result of prior convertible debt (called "notes" in the term sheet) have to be included in this valuation. Recall our discussion about the use of convertible debt by many entrepreneurs, particularly in the early stages of company financing. We said at the time that a common mistake we see is the aggregation of quite a bit of convertible debt as a result of the rolling closes that debt permits. Here is where the sins of the past can come back to bite us, as that debt is now being taken into account as part of the valuation the VC is willing to pay. We now for the first time get the full accounting of just how much dilution has been created by the issuing of this debt, and this bill often catches entrepreneurs by surprise.

Second, and we'll talk about this more below, the valuation also includes the employee option pool (this is the stock set aside to incent employees of the company). This is important, because it means that when we add up all these shares, they can't exceed the $50 million post-money valuation for the company.

The VC could have said—and the founders would have preferred this—that the valuation is $50 million after it puts its money into the company, but that the conversion of the notes and the employee option pool would be additive to the post-money valuation. But, in that case, the VC wouldn't really own 20 percent of the company when all is said and done. She would own that amount for a fraction of a second and then get diluted by the additional shares issued for the note conversions and the employee option pool.

This is why the VC wrote the term sheet to hard-code the post-money valuation at $50 million. She wanted to be clear that whatever the existing capital structure of the company and however big an employee option pool the founders wanted to create, the VC would not be diluted by those.

So how did VCF1 come up with the $50 million post-money valuation in the first place? Let's take a short diversion to explore valuation in a bit more detail. If you have a background in investment banking, you'll be familiar with how banks tend to value companies. This is similar.

Comparable Company Analysis

We covered this briefly in chapter 5, but the comparable company analysis method of valuation requires that we find other publicly traded companies (or companies whose valuation and financial metrics are publicly known) that look and feel like the startup we are trying to value—so-called comparable companies.

Oversimplified, it's like looking at comp prices in your neighborhood when you are trying to buy or sell your house as a way to help set the price of your house or your offer.

As a better example, if we were trying to value Facebook in early 2012 (while it was still private), we might choose a set of other high-growth internet companies as comparables—e.g., Yahoo, Google. We would then look at how those companies are valued as a function of certain financial metrics: for example, Yahoo might have been valued at five times its revenue, while Google might have been valued at eight times its revenue. We then apply these revenue multiples to Facebook's revenue to arrive at an estimate of how the public markets would value Facebook.

Easy math, hard comparison. Maybe Facebook has a higher growth rate than these companies. Maybe Facebook has a higher margin structure. Maybe Facebook has a larger market opportunity to go after. Maybe Yahoo just missed its Wall Street estimates last quarter and thus investors have put it in the penalty box by selling the stock and thereby depressing the valuation. Or maybe the US is on the verge of World War III (we all hope not!) and thus equity market valuations as a class are at a local minimum. None of these questions is insurmountable, but they do go to the heart of whether "comparables" are in fact comparable.

This analysis is doubly hard as applied to startups because (we hope) startups are by definition unique, and the ability to forecast revenue is inherently unpredictable. So even if we get the comparables right, who knows if we will get our revenue forecast right—garbage in, garbage out.

Discounted Cash Flow Analysis

Financial theory says—and who are we to argue with it—that over the long run, the value of a company equals the present value of its future cash flows. That is, whatever annual cash a company can generate in the future, if we discount that cash to present-day values, an investor should be willing to pay no more than the current value of that stream of future cash.

How do we do this in practice? Well, it requires that you build out a financial forecast for your company, estimating how much cash flow the company will generate in each future year. Keep in mind that cash flow means "cash"—so we need to estimate not just what the accounting income will be for the company but also how capital expenditures will affect cash and how the timing of collecting cash from customers and paying cash to vendors and employees (otherwise known as "working capital") works. Once we know that, we then need to discount those cash flows back to present day using what's called a "discount rate." The simple way to think about discount rate is that it is the opportunity cost for a company's investments—so, if the company could earn 10 percent on alternative investments, then we should discount the future cash flows at least at that rate.

As you are probably noticing, this analysis makes sense for mature companies that have more predictable future financial results based on the history of their existing financial results. It's really tough to do this for an early-stage startup given that the financial forecasts for the business are probably not worth more than the Excel spreadsheet on which they were created. VCs often joke that "we can make the spreadsheet say whatever we want."

More significantly for startups—for those of you familiar with discounted cash flow models—because they tend to consume cash in the early years and (hopefully) generate cash in the mature years, most of the value in a discounted cash flow model will come from the far-out years, where the certainty of forecasts gets even more fuzzy.

In addition to all these challenges, the comparable company and discounted cash flow analyses also suffer from the fact that they don't account for dilution in the VCs' equity holdings resulting from future financings. Huh?

When a VC invests in a startup company, she hopes that maybe the last money the company ever needs to raise, but knows in her heart that that is highly unlikely. Most companies that are successful (and unfortunately many of those that are not) end up raising multiple rounds of financing. In fact, given that companies are staying private for a longer time, they are more likely to raise funding across several different rounds of financing.

To plan for this, when a VC invests in the first round of a company, she "reserves" additional monies beyond that which she invests in the A round to be able to participate in future financing rounds and preserve her ownership.

How does this work? Going back to our sample term sheet, if VCF1 invests $10 million to own 20 percent of the company, assuming that the company continues to do well, VCF1 will want to maintain that ownership level. But if the company raises another round of financing, the company will need to issue more shares to that next round investor. As a result, the total share count of the company increases, so by simple math, the shares that VCF1 holds represent a smaller proportion of the total company than the 20 percent it originally held.

To compensate for this, VCF1 may want to invest more money in this next round, likely in an amount equal to that required to maintain its 20 percent ownership in the company. Thus, at the time it makes the initial $10 million investment, VCF1 will reserve, or put aside for future use, some amount of additional dollars for subsequent financing rounds. To be clear, this is just an accounting fiction in that the money hasn't been invested, but VCF1 is earmarking this money for the time being so that it doesn't deploy that capital into another investment.

Recall that in chapter 4 we talked about getting to know your VC firm and, in particular, getting to know where it is in the investment life cycle of the fund from which the firm is investing into your company. This discussion of reserves helps articulate why that matters—if a firm is early in its life cycle, it probably has the ability to reserve additional dollars to participate in subsequent rounds of financing for your company. If it is later in the fund life and thus the firm needs to start thinking more about distributing cash back to its LPs, it may be less willing to set aside reserves.

You of course don't care about whether the firm is able to maintain its full ownership by investing in subsequent rounds, but you do care about whether the fund has cash at all to be able to invest in you. Why? Because often when you raise a new round of financing, the new investor will want to see that earlier investors still have faith in you and that they are willing to demonstrate that by putting new, additional capital at risk. If the fund is later in its life cycle and short on reserves, the fund's inability to participate in the new round of financing could affect the willingness of new investors to fund the business. Similarly, if the firm has not raised (or doesn't seem likely to be able to raise) a new fund, there may not be another source of capital it can tap to invest in your new financing round.

VC Valuation

So what do VCs actually do to value early-stage startups?

Wait for it—it's called the "what do I need to believe analysis."

I haven't trademarked this and, to be fair, some VCs might disagree with me on this, but in my experience, it's true. If VCF1 invests $10 million in XYZ Company and owns 20 percent of the company, what does the company need to look like in five to ten years to be a meaningful return driver, or winner, for its fund?

Let's assume a "winner" means a return of ten times (or $100 million) VCF1's investment. If VCF1 owns 20 percent (and let's ignore for now the reserves we talked about), then to earn $100 million on the investment, XYZ Company needs to be sold (or go public) for at least $500 million (0.20 × $500 million = $100 million).

Borrowing from our comparable company analysis above, let's assume that mature comparable companies trade at a revenue multiple of five. So to achieve our $500 million valuation goal for XYZ Company, it needs to be generating $100 million in revenue.

So what would have to go right with the business for that to happen? Is the market size they are going after big enough to support a company with $100 million in revenue? What are all the things that could cause the company to fail? How do I assess the probability of each of those nodes on the decision tree toward success or failure? This is in practice the valuation idea maze that VCs go through.

To be clear, we are talking here about very-early-stage investments where there are no real financial metrics with which to value a company. As startups get more mature and have financial statements that are more reliable, of course later-stage venture capital deals will adopt more of the traditional valuation metrics we've outlined above.

Now, back to our term sheet.

Capitalization

Notice here that VCF1 says that the valuation of the company includes the unallocated employee option pool—in this case, 15 percent. As we talked about before, VCF1 wants to make sure that it gets its 20 percent ownership after all is said and done, so it doesn't want the creation of the option pool to dilute its ownership.

How did VCF1 come up with 15 percent as the right pool size? Honestly, this is just a negotiation between the VC and the company CEO, but a good rule of thumb is that the option pool should be sufficient to handle the expected employee hiring until the next round of financing. So the VCs often ask the CEO to generate a head-count growth plan for the next twelve to eighteen months (the likely time frame until the company pursues another financing round) and estimate how much stock is required to grant to those planned hires.

The CEO would like to keep the pool size as low as possible because increasing the pool size before the current financing round dilutes her (and other existing common shareholders). The VC wants to make the pool size as large as possible because if the company needs to increase the pool after she has invested her money, she will also share in the dilution. This is the dance.

Dividends

I am not going to waste too many words on this section because it's generally meaningless, since startups can't afford to dividend out their cash to shareholders.

All this section says is that if and when the company's board decides to dividend out cash to shareholders—which it will likely never do—the dividend will be equal to 6 percent and will go to the preferred shareholders (i.e., the VCs) first before going to the common shareholders (i.e., founders and employees). The whole reason for this section—at least in my humble opinion—is to prevent the founders from dividending out money to themselves at the expense of the preferred shareholders. So if the founders want to pillage the company's cash, they have to pay the VCs first. Enough said.

Liquidation Preference

Now we are getting to the good stuff.

Liquidation preference is a fancy way of saying who gets their money back under certain circumstances. Those circumstances are called a "liquidation event," which basically means the company gets sold or is being wound down. It's true that there are corner cases where the company could have a change of control (i.e., selling more than 50 percent of its stock) that doesn't involve an acquisition, but most of the time we are talking about a company sale.

The specific type of liquidation preference in our sample term sheet is called "1x nonparticipating." Let's break that down.

It's "1x" because VCF1 gets its original investment amount back first, but no more. Liquidation preferences can be structured to be 1.5x, 2x or any "x" the company and VC agree upon. In those cases, the VC would be entitled to that multiple of its original investment off the top of any sale proceeds. Having a liquidation preference greater than 1x can be a big hurdle for startups, because it increases the acquisition price by that multiple of the monies invested by the VCs. As a result, 1x is the predominant form of liquidation preference for early-stage venture financings.

It is the case, however, that VCs that invest at later stages of a company's development may demand more than a 1x preference. Why is that? The idea is that if a VC is investing at a much later stage, she might be worried that there will not be enough upside on the investment if the company were to sell itself in close proximity to the financing, before the business has had a chance to grow to a point where its value is some greater multiple of the valuation paid in the financing round.

This can be particularly worrisome for a later-stage investor if there are a lot of other investors who invested in the company at much earlier stages and therefore much lower valuations. Those early investors may have very different economic incentives from this later round investor and be motivated financially to sell the company at a more modest increase in valuation relative to the later-stage investor's entry valuation. Thus, a greater than 1x liquidation preference can be a way of aligning interests more closely among investors (and employees) who have a much lower entry valuation into the company with those who are just entering the company for the first time at a significantly higher valuation.

"Nonparticipating" means that the VC doesn't get to double dip. Rather, she gets a choice: take her liquidation preference off the top or convert her preferred shares into common shares and take the equity value of her percentage ownership of the company. "Participating" is the opposite flavor—not only does the VC get her liquidation preference first (her original investment back), but then she also gets to convert her shares into common and participate in any leftover proceeds as with any other shareholder. Double-dipping is pretty unusual in the standard venture capital financing.

Let's do a quick example to illustrate the difference.

Assume that VCF1 has invested its $10 million (for which we said it owns 20 percent of the company) and a year later the company gets sold for $40 million. Because we have a 1x nonparticipating liquidation preference, VCF1 has to choose between taking its 1x off the top or converting into common. Which does she choose? The answer is the liquidation preference, because that nets her $10 million, whereas if she were to convert into common, she would receive only $8 million (0.20 × $40 million). That will leave $30 million for the common shareholders to take from the acquisition.

Hopefully you can see that her indifference point is at a $50 million acquisition—she would get $10 million in liquidation preference or $10 million from converting into common and getting her 20 percent of the $50 million acquisition price. This makes sense because she invested at a $50 million valuation, so we would expect that to be the indifference point.

Last example. Assume VCF1 successfully negotiated for a 1x participating liquidation preference. How does that change the math? Well, in the $40 million acquisition scenario, VCF1 would first get its $10 million liquidation preference, and then it would convert into common. As part of the common shareholder base, VCF1 will get an additional $6 million (0.20 × the remaining $30 million in proceeds). So you can see how the rest of the common shareholders are affected in this scenario—they get to share only the $24 million remaining after VCF1's double-dipping versus the $30 million in the nonparticipating example.

One other nuance to liquidation preference that we don't see in the sample term sheet—because it's for the first institutional financing round of the company—is the order of preference among the various parties who enjoy the liquidation preference. Recall that as a company goes through its life cycle, it will often raise multiple subsequent rounds of financing, each with a new series of preferred stock (Series B, Series C, etc.).

The question then becomes, do all the various series of preferred stock holders share equally in the liquidation preference, or do some have preference over the others? This preference is known as "seniority," which means that someone has a preference to acquisition or liquidation proceeds ahead of the other preferred holders. The opposite of seniority is pari passu, which is a fancy Latin saying that means we are all treated the same. Seniority typically only gets introduced into the term sheet negotiations at a later stage of financing when there are at least two classes of preferred stock who might want to fight over this right; that's why we don't see the discussion in this current term sheet.

At first blush as an entrepreneur, you might rightly think, "Who cares? If I've agreed to a liquidation preference overall, do I really care whether the VCs have decided among themselves to split it pari passu or to introduce some element of seniority?" You're right in one respect, in that the ultimate amount of money that you and your other common shareholders (mostly your employees) will receive in an acquisition or liquidation is not changed by seniority—no matter how the preference gets divided, it's still a finite amount of money that will go to the VCs. In practice, though, this term does matter in that it can create different incentives for your various VCs and thus cause them to think differently about an acquisition offer.

For example, assume you have a total of $30 million in liquidation preference and two different series of preferred stock (A and B) representing two different venture capital firms. Assume also that each firm has invested $15 million in its respective class of preferred stock. If you receive an acquisition offer for $25 million, all those proceeds would go to the preferred holders because the acquisition price is less than the $30 million in preferences. If the preference were pari passu, the VCs would split it fifty-fifty, each getting $12.5 million back on their original investments of $15 million. If the B shares were senior to the A shares, though, the B holders would receive their full $15 million back and the A holders would then get only the remaining $10 million.

In either case, you as a common holder are likely to get nothing because there simply isn't any money left over after satisfying the liquidation preferences. But the decision to vote for or against the acquisition could be influenced by the presence of a senior preference. As you see, the A holders lose money on the deal as a result of a senior preference in favor of the B holders, so they might be inclined to vote against the deal if they think there is some prospect of getting a better deal down the road that would make them whole. And even though you and your employees might not be getting paid on your common stock in the current deal, you might be getting employment offers with the acquiring company that could be attractive, and you may also believe that being part of the acquiring company is the best way for your original product vision to be realized. Not being able to realize these opportunities as a result of a competing set of incentives among your VCs would be a bad outcome.

Redemption

This explanation might even be shorter than the dividends one—no redemption! Think about it—the whole idea behind selling equity to a VC is that you want the money to be permanent so you can use it to build your company. If you had wanted to pay it back on some schedule, you would have raised debt instead. Thus, redemption is extremely unusual in VC. But, for completeness, if it existed in the term sheet, it would basically allow VCF1 to give back its stock to XYZ Company at some future time period in exchange for getting its money back (and sometimes with interest).

Redemption rights, if they exist, are likely to come into play at precisely the worst time for the company. Why would a VC, who is playing for home runs, want to redeem? Only if she felt as though the company were walking dead, and thus getting her money back was a better option than watching it slowly being vaporized. However, this is exactly when the company would not likely have sufficient cash to be able to give the money back. As a result, most state laws restrict the ability of investors to exercise their redemption rights if doing so would put the company in a dire financial situation. Thankfully, most venture deals keep things simple by just stipulating that the investment is in fact not redeemable.

Conversion/Auto-Conversion

Let's take these two together.

Recall that VCF1 is investing in a different security (Preferred Series A) than the founders/other employees likely have (common shares). So, at some point, VCF1 might want to convert its shares from preferred into common and, at other points, the founders (and maybe other later venture investors) might want to force VCF1 to convert into common.

Why would a VC ever want to do this (and why would the company/others ever want to force you to do this), given that the preferred shares have so many more rights and privileges than do common?

In the former case, a VC might want to do this as part of the IPO of the company. To take a company public, you will want to clean up the capital structure of the company by having everyone convert into common shares. It's not impossible to have multiple types of shares as a public company—in fact, more recently we have seen many technology companies implement "dual-class stock" as part of their IPO, which often splits common stock into a high-voting class and a low-voting class. For example, Google and Facebook each have dual-class voting structures, and Snap actually has a tri-class structure. This notwithstanding, preferred shares generally need to go away at the time of the IPO.

In most cases, an IPO is a good thing, and most VCs are more than happy to convert their shares into common in connection with the process of going public. But, as our term sheet reflects, VCF1 wants to make sure that the IPO is of sufficient size—both as a way to ensure that the valuation is attractive relative to their initial investment valuation and that the company will have sufficient market capitalization for enough trading liquidity (so VCF1 can at some point in time sell its shares in the public market).

Recall that we talked earlier about the reduction in the overall number of IPOs in the last twenty years and, in particular, the decline in the number of smaller-capitalization IPOs. Among the reasons for this are that smaller-cap public companies don't have great trading liquidity. This means that the volume of shares traded on any given day is small, making it hard for a shareholder who has a lot of shares to be able to sell that stock without moving down the price of the stock. To combat this, the IPO conversion term often includes a provision that the IPO be of a specific minimum size, which equates to a minimum expected market capitalization of the company intended to avoid being stuck in a low-trading-volume, small-cap stock.

In our term sheet, VCF1 agrees to be converted (we call this "auto-conversion") into common in connection with an IPO, as long as the proceeds from the IPO are at least $50 million. If you assume that most companies sell between 10 and 20 percent of the company at an IPO, this would imply a market capitalization of $250–$500 million. In today's market, however, this would be a very-small-cap IPO that would be likely to have little trading volume. But at the Series A stage of investing, it would be hard for VCF1 to argue for a significantly higher initial IPO market capitalization. Presumably, as there are other, later financing rounds, this minimum IPO threshold will increase.

Another flavor of the IPO auto-convert is to put in place a specific per-share price or a return on investment threshold to force conversion. For example, VCF1 could have said that it would only auto-convert on an IPO where the return on its $10 million investment was at least 3x. You sometimes see these return-based terms in later-stage venture financings where a new investor might be coming in close in time to an IPO and worries that the company might go public too soon before it has seen enough appreciation on its investment.

The other mechanism to convert shares from preferred to common that the term sheet stipulates is a voluntary conversion. In this case, the term sheet says that a vote of a majority of the preferred stock is another way to convert preferred into common.

When would a VC ever want to do this? Mostly, in a bad situation.

We are going to talk later about recapitalizations of companies, but for now let's just agree that oftentimes things don't go as planned in the startup world. Believe it or not, every now and then the company raises a lot of money and needs to effectively restart the company many years in. At that point in time, the company may have raised several different rounds of venture capital and thus has different investors who've invested different amounts and at different valuations. As a result there might be $30 million or $50 million or more in combined liquidation preference on the company.

Often, in order to restart the company, you want to clean up the capitalization table by getting rid of some or all of that liquidation preference. Doing so may make the company more attractive to a new investor and provide capital for the restart. For a new investor, having too much liquidation preference simply means that the valuation the company needs to achieve in a sale for the VC to make money on the deal may be prohibitively high. It also helps reincent the employees who otherwise have a very high bar to clear before they can earn any money on their common equity. Recall that employees hold common stock, so they don't get any proceeds from an acquisition until the full liquidation preferences of the VCs have been satisfied. Thus, employees can be financially disincented to stay at the company if they don't think there is a reasonable prospect of an acquisition clearing the liquidation preferences. So if the VCs believe in the go-forward prospects for the company, they might want to volunteer to give up liquidation preference to provide the company a fresh start.

How would a VC eliminate liquidation preference if she were so inclined? Precisely through this conversion mechanism. Remember that the liquidation preference attaches to the special type of shares that the VC holds—preferred stock. If the VC were to convert her preferred shares into common shares, the bells and whistles that she enjoyed as a preferred shareholder would simply disappear.

And this takes us to a very clever item in our term sheet that we've overlooked so far but now comes into play. Not clever as in "sneaky," but clever as in "smart." Who gets to vote on whether the preferred convert into common and thus give up liquidation preference?

Notice that the term sheet is very specific in using capital "P" Preferred Stock as the group that has to get to a majority vote as part of the voluntary conversion mechanism.

And who is that Preferred Stock? Go back to the dividends section of the term sheet and you'll see that "Preferred Stock" is defined as "any prior series of preferred stock, Series A Preferred Stock, and all future series of preferred stock." This means that no matter how many different classes of preferred stock may exist over the life of the company, they all vote together as a single group in determining whether a majority of them wants to voluntarily convert into common.

This is important, particularly in the case where the company turns south after having raised many different rounds of capital, as the alternative to this definition could have been to give each individual series of preferred stock its own majority vote. In that case, if any one of the different classes of stock refused to go along with the conversion, the whole deal would grind to a halt.

This, unfortunately, is not just a theoretical risk. We've seen it many times in our short history at Andreessen Horowitz, and it can create real issues. For example, we had a portfolio company that had raised about seven different rounds of financing in a series of ever-escalating prices. But when the business struggled later on and was in need of a capital infusion at a price materially lower than most of the previous rounds, the terms from the prior rounds came back to bite everyone. That's because each class of preferred stock (representing each of the previous rounds of financing) had its own conversion vote specific to its class only. There was no majority of "Preferred" vote, but rather a series of individual votes by each of the preferred series independently. As if that weren't tough enough already, each class of preferred was controlled by a separate VC firm.

Any new investor coming into the company at this point in time was unwilling to invest new money without converting at least some, if not all, of the existing series of preferred stock into common. Why? Because recall that one of the rights of a preferred shareholder is often liquidation preference, and the simplest way to get rid of liquidation preference is to convert shares from preferred into common. Having been through seven rounds of prior financing, the liquidation preference was sufficiently high that the return prospects for any new investor would be materially dampened without some abatement of the preference.

There is of course another alternative to help this new investor get comfortable with the size of the existing preference stack— allow that new investor to have a senior liquidation preference. Recall from our earlier discussion that this would mean that the new investor gets her money out first, ahead of all the other preferred investors, therefore protecting her investment much more than if she were to be pari passu (or even) with the other existing preferred investors.

But, as we saw before, that introduces other potential complexities. It creates very different financial incentives between the various classes of preferred investors in the event of an acquisition where the price does not exceed the full amount of preferences. Also, as a common shareholder, you would certainly prefer to have the total amount of the liquidation stack reduced to create a greater likelihood that you and your employees will be able to receive some proceeds from an eventual acquisition offer. This new investor likely wants this, too, as she wants the employees motivated to work hard toward a good financial outcome, rather than everyone feeling as though they are working with no prospect of ever realizing a financial return.

As you can imagine, this made it extremely difficult to get a new investor comfortable with even issuing a term sheet and nearly killed the company's financing prospects. The various investors eventually worked it out, but it took months of back-and-forth negotiations, all while the company remained idle without the needed cash infusion to continue building its business.

There may be times when giving different classes of preferred stock makes sense—and you do see this oftentimes as companies get more mature and raise larger amounts of capital at higher prices. But, doing so for XYZ Company at such an early stage is generally not recommended. Once you set the precedent of giving individual series of preferred stock their own votes, it's very hard to take that back. So for a Series A term sheet like we have here for XYZ Company, having the capital "P" Preferred vote on voluntary conversion is a smarter path to pursue.

Antidilution Provisions

Whenever VCs invest in a company, they hope that the valuation of the company keeps increasing at every round. If that happens, there is no need to worry about antidilution protection. But hope is not a strategy, so better to be safe than sorry.

Antidilution protection provides some element of safety in the event that the company raises money at a valuation below that at which a VC invested. We call this a "down round," since the valuation is in fact down from the prior round. That's not a fun place to be for either the VC or the founder/employees since the effect of a down round can be highly dilutive to everyone's ownership stake. This is because the company will need to issue a significant number of shares per dollar of capital it seeks to raise, and the addition of those shares to the company's capital stock means that all existing shareholders will own proportionately less of the company than they did prior to the down round.

Every new financing of course has some element of dilution, since in all cases—whether the price is high or low—the company has to issue new shares. But down rounds are particularly painful for two reasons. First, the lower price means that more shares need to be issued to raise a fixed amount of capital than if the price were higher. Second, in the case of an "up round," even though new shares are being issued, everyone is generally happy, notwithstanding the dilution, because the value of the company has increased. So while you may have been diluted by 10 percent as a result of the issuance of new shares, the value of your ownership position in the company should be much higher as a result of the higher valuation assigned to the company.

So the VCs have engineered what might be safely regarded as "schmuck insurance"—we think the company is worth five dollars per share on the day we invest in the company, but if, in the future, the valuation turns out to be two dollars per share, the insurance provides a price adjustment to minimize the otherwise dilutive effect of the two-dollars-per-share financing round.

The extent of the price adjustment depends on the precise type of antidilution protection.

In our VCF1 term sheet we have broad-based weighted average antidilution protection. That's a mouthful, and the formula, which I am not going to print here (you can Google it), is equally daunting. In simple terms, think of the broad-based weighted average as an intermediate form of antidilution protection. VCF1 does not get to reset its original purchase price fully to the new, lower purchase price, but it does get a blended price in between these two that is weighted by the amount of capital raised in the different financing rounds.

Contrast that with the true insurance policy that provides the VC a complete price reset—that's called a "full ratchet." In a full ratchet, using our five-dollars-per-share/two-dollars-per-share example from above, our VC would essentially ignore its original five-dollar price and reset its stock holdings based upon the two-dollar price. Mathematically, this means the number of shares that the VC will now hold based on its original investment in the company increases by roughly two and a half times (5/2). As you can see, the full ratchet therefore protects the VC from getting diluted by this down round of financing.

But what about the founder and employees? Tough luck—they don't have such a mechanism, so in effect they are subsidizing the VCs' antidilution protection by eating the dilution on their end. Before you get too worked up over this, as a practical matter, many VCs when faced with a situation where the antidilution protection will kick in may be willing to offset some of that founder/employee dilution by increasing the option pool and granting additional options to these folks. It won't solve the problem completely, but will put a dent in the dilution suffered by the common shareholders.

If you take this to its logical extreme, you get into a circular problem: the more the VCs get antidilution protection, the more the common shareholders get diluted, and thus the more the VCs are inclined to increase the option pool and grant them more shares, and the more in turn this dilutes the VCs. There is no perfect equilibrium for this problem, but sometimes the VCs will waive or modify their antidilution protection to prevent this circular spiral.

We talked earlier about whether you should always maximize valuation in a given round, and here is where the rubber really meets the road—in the context of a down round. Not only do you have to deal with the lack of momentum and upset feelings of your employee base, but down rounds have real economic consequences in the form of antidilution protection for the VCs.

This is largely avoidable if you try to structure your current financing to maximize the likelihood of success for your next round of financing.

Voting Rights

This section doesn't really say too much, as the meat of the voting is going to come in the protective provisions section below. Important to note here, though, is that each share—both common and preferred—has one vote. As we briefly discussed above, when some startup companies go public, they have different classes of shares with different voting rights. While it is not unheard of when the companies are still private, it's pretty unusual. In our term sheet, the voting follows the normal convention of one person, one vote.

As dual-class stock has started to proliferate among some public technology companies (e.g., Facebook, Google, Snap), some startups have been thinking about whether to adopt these structures as a private company.

There are two flavors of this that we've been seeing of late. First, some founders would like to have a high-vote stock that applies to their shares only. The theory is that, in addition to likely controlling the board, as we'll talk about in the next section, they also want to ensure that any time a corporate matter requires a shareholder vote, they have enough voting power to retain control over those actions. For example, if the company were to be acquired and a shareholder vote was required to approve the transaction, if the founders have, say, ten times the number of votes per share relative to any other shareholder, they are likely to be able to control the outcome of that vote. There are not any instances of this type of voting structure that I am aware of having actually been implemented in startup companies.

What has happened in a very small number of cases is that some founders have asked certain investors to enter into what's called a "voting proxy" in connection with their investment. This means that the investor hands the voting authority for her shares to the founders, such that the founders get to execute that voting authority in favor of whatever corporate actions come to a vote. While this is also very unusual, we do sometimes see this with very-late-stage, passive investors who are interested in the financial investment opportunity only and not in participating in the governance of the company.

The second variety of dual-class structures, which is more common than the first (although still in a minority of deals), is to put in place what's known as a springing dual-class structure in anticipation of an IPO. This means that we keep the one person, one vote construct while the company is private, but that immediately prior to an IPO, the dual class springs into being. The usual implementation of this is to have all existing shares at the time of the IPO convert into supervoting shares, including both common and preferred shares. Then the shares that are issued in the IPO have the regular one person, one vote. The theory here is that over time the venture investors will exit the company by selling their stock in the public markets and, when they do so, the supervoting attached to those shares disappears. Thus, likely within the first few years of the company's being public, the founders are left with significant governance control because they still have their supervoting shares, while the general public holds shares with only the single-vote structure.

CHAPTER 10

The Alphabet Soup of Term Sheets: Part Two (Governance)

Now we are starting to get to the heart of the governance structure of our company. This basically means: who gets a say in what happens in the company? Nobody likes to focus on these sections very much, but they turn out to be very important. For example, the board composition matters a lot. After all, the board gets to hire or fire the CEO and vote on major corporate actions—raising money, selling the company, etc.

And the protective provisions, which also determine what corporate actions the preferred shareholders (i.e., the VCs) get to have a say in, matter a lot. Ultimately, these are checks on the CEO's ability to undertake significant corporate actions. The auto-convert, drag-along, and voting sections are also part of this governance bucket.

So although these are less sexy to talk about, if you are a founder, make sure you don't just ignore these and focus exclusively on the economic issues. They can definitely come back to haunt you later in your company's life!

Let's make sure that doesn't happen to you.

The Board of Directors

We'll talk more about the role of the board of directors, but probably the most foundational thing that a board does is to hire (or fire) the CEO. Understandably so, many founder CEOs have been paying much more attention to the composition of the board of directors given historical concerns over VCs being quick to replace the founder CEO.

In our term sheet, we have a three-person board. (There are no requirements for an odd-size board, but many people prefer this to avoid situations where the board vote may be deadlocked.) One person is appointed by the holders of the Series A preferred (this is VCF1); it is pretty typical for the major investor in an early-stage financing to have a board seat.

We simplified our term sheet by having only one venture investor in this round of financing, but it is often the case that there are multiple investors. In that case, there is typically what's known as one "lead" investor who is driving the negotiation of the term sheet with the CEO and, as a result, is typically investing at least half of the total amount of the round. Given this lead position, that investor will likely be the board representative for that set of preferred investors.

The second seat is reserved for the common shareholders and designated to be the CEO. Note that the seat is reserved for the CEO, not for the founder per se. This means that whoever is sitting in that CEO seat at the time is entitled to the board seat. Sometimes the founder CEO herself asks to have the board seat designated to her directly (versus to the then-existing CEO).

At the beginning, this seems like a benign request, since she is in fact the CEO. But what happens if the founder gets removed as CEO or decides to quit the company of her own volition? If we hadn't written the board provision the way it is in the term sheet, the founder would continue to hold the board seat. We call this "ruling from the grave" (or sometimes "dead hand control"), neither of which is a good position for the company to be in.

It doesn't make a lot of sense for a founder who is no longer with the company to be sitting on the board. In cases, therefore, where the founder wants the seat designated directly to her, the VCs will often insist on some service requirement attached to her continued occupation of the board seat. That is, she can keep the board seat for as long as she is CEO (or maybe some other senior officer in the company), but she loses the seat when she ceases to hold one of those positions.

The third seat is reserved for an independent; that is, someone not otherwise affiliated with the company by virtue of being an investor or officer. The selection process here calls for the independent to be approved by the other two board directors.

If you take a step back, this is a pretty fair and even configuration of the board—the common shareholders are represented by the CEO, the preferred are represented by VCF1, and we have an ostensibly neutral third party who has no pecuniary interests in the company. Most corporate governance experts would view this as a balanced board.

But this isn't what the boards always look like. In more recent times, some founders have insisted on having what's called a "common-controlled" board, meaning that there are more board members representing the common shareholders than other classes of shareholders.

The reason for this is obvious: If common controls the board, then the VCs can't really fire the founder CEO, because they likely don't have the votes to do so. They would of course need to convince at least some of the common directors to go along with them, but in most cases the common board seats are controlled by the founders (since they have the most stock and therefore the most votes). Thus, removing a founder CEO will prove difficult. Some have argued that these board structures are at the heart of why there have been some high-profile CEO-board governance challenges of late in Silicon Valley.

The Uber case is illustrative here. During Travis Kalanick's tenure as CEO, Uber had established a board of directors with up to eleven seats, only seven of which were filled at the time. It's not unusual, by the way, to have some unfilled board seats in anticipation of filling the slots as the business needs develop. Travis effectively controlled three of the seven seats, because they were filled by him, his cofounder, and a third early employee of the company likely sympathetic to Travis. He also had the right to fill the remaining four unfilled board seats at his discretion.

So had the board tried to force a vote to remove Travis from his CEO role, he could have quickly filled the four open seats and thus would have been able to win such a vote. Ultimately, the board applied enough pressure, including a lawsuit filed by one of their major VCs, to convince Travis to resign. This avoided the need for a formal vote by the board.

The other thing to think about is what happens to the board configuration as XYZ Company goes through subsequent rounds of financing. Our perfectly balanced board is likely to be upset. If a new VC leads the next round of financing, they may be likely to ask for a board seat, in which case now the VCs will have two board seats to the one common and one independent.

There are no magic solutions to this problem, but sometimes the founder CEO will ask to add a second independent to provide more balance to the VCs' two seats. Other times, the founder CEO will ask for a second board seat for common, in other words, to match the additional VC board seat with an offsetting common seat. Any configuration is permissible; where we end up is simply a function of the negotiating positions of each of the parties.

Protective Provisions

Recall that the voting rights section didn't really tell us too much about who needs to vote on what things, other than to let us know that each share of stock (both common and preferred) has one vote. But what we really care about is who needs to vote, and in what proportions, to pass various corporate actions.

Delaware law governs the default voting for corporate actions (most startups are incorporated in Delaware because it has the most well-developed set of laws and legal opinions on corporate governance and shareholder rights). It specifies the baseline of whether the common and preferred vote together or separately for various corporate items.

But the protective provisions are really an overlay on top of Delaware law. As long as they don't lessen the foundations of Delaware law, the protective provisions give the parties to a transaction the ability to create some stricter rules of the road. In this term sheet—and in most other venture financings—the protective provisions grant the preferred shareholders (generally the VCs) additional say in various corporate matters.

Just as we saw in the auto-conversion section above, the protective provisions in our term sheet designated the capital "P" Preferred as the class of shareholders entitled to vote on the defined corporate actions. Recall that we talked about the wisdom of this in anticipation of later-stage financing rounds. In general, you want to avoid smaller minority investors in later rounds having greater governance control than they have economic interests. The way to do this is to lump all the independent series of preferred stock together into a single voting class versus allowing each series of preferred to have their own votes. Doing the latter means that each series of preferred can block the other—as we said, that's not a good place to be.

Now, in fairness, there are times later in a company's financing life where a new investor may insist on having at least some of the corporate actions carved out of the capital "P" Preferred voting and decided by a separate series vote. And sometimes this may be appropriate to consider, but best not to set that precedent early in the life of the company.

Where might this come up? When a later-stage investor decides to invest in a startup, she may be investing a significant amount of money, but still end up holding a relatively small ownership position in the company. This is because naturally the valuation for the company should have increased over its various rounds of funding, meaning that a dollar invested at today's valuation buys an investor much less than did a dollar invested many years ago at the Series A round.

As a result, our new investor will have a lot of money at stake in the investment, but likely will be a significant minority from a governance perspective relative to the other VCs who have been investors for a longer period of time and thus at much lower entry valuations. If all the protective provisions, therefore, rely on a majority vote of all the preferred voting together as a single class, the new investor may always find herself powerless to affect the vote; the earlier investors probably control more than 50 percent of the preferred and thus can carry a majority vote on their own.

And their economic incentives could be very different than those of the new investor, given that the amount of capital they have invested is very different and their economic ownership could be very different. For example, there might be acquisition scenarios that produce a great return to our early VCs, but that only provide a return of invested capital to our new investor. It's these types of situations that the new investor will seek to avoid.

One way of doing that is to ask for a separate class vote for the new investor. That is, the new investor's approval is separately required to approve any corporate actions. Obviously, this can be problematic for exactly the scenario I outlined above—the new investor's economic interests may diverge from others, and you are giving her disproportionate voting control relative to her economic interests. An intermediate way of addressing this concern is to not provide a separate series vote for *all* corporate actions, but rather to enumerate a specific list of things that the new investor is most concerned about for which she can have a separate class vote.

Another way to deal with this is to increase the voting threshold for required corporate actions to something greater than a simple majority. What the actual number should be will depend on the specifics of the situation, but the new investor might ask for some number that requires a greater diversity of existing investors to approve the transaction, with the hope that this lessens the likelihood of her always being outvoted by the very early VCs who might control a majority of the preferred shares.

Now that we know who votes, the next question is, what do they get to vote on? You'll see in the term sheet (page 281) that there is a long list of things that the protective provisions give the Preferred shareholder a right to vote on.

We won't cover all the items, but let's talk about a few:

- **(iii)** *Authorization of new classes of stock*—This one is pretty important because it is the mechanism that ensures that the Preferred get a chance to vote on future financings for the company. After all, to sell more stock as part of a new financing round, the company will likely need to issue a new class of stock to the new investor. Sometimes this section just gives a blanket vote to the Preferred to approve (or not) the creation of a new class of stock. In our term sheet, VCF1 and XYZ Company have agreed on a middle ground; the Preferred only get to vote on a new class issuance if it has rights equal to or greater than the rights that the current classes of Preferred have. For example, if XYZ Company wanted to issue a new class of preferred stock that had a liquidation preference that was junior to the preference of the VCF1 stock, arguably they could do that without consent of the Preferred.

- **(v)** *Corporate actions*—This one is also pretty important. It permits the Preferred to vote on an acquisition of the company and a sale of its intellectual property. This makes sense in that VCF1 likely invested in the company in part based on its intellectual property and thus would want to have a say in a sale of that and a sale of the company itself (which would likely include the intellectual property).

- **(vii)** *Liquidation or recapitalization*—If XYZ Company is going to get shut down (liquidated) or recapitalized (meaning that the current capitalization structure is going to get turned on its head), the Preferred will also get to have a say in these matters. We'll talk more about a recapitalization later in the book, but briefly it is a transaction by which the ownership structure of the company is largely reset. For example, preferred shareholders might get forced to convert into common shareholders (to eliminate liquidation preference), or the ownership of existing shareholders might get reduced by what's called a "reverse split." This means that the number of shares that a stockholder has is reduced by some multiple. The purpose of this is to reduce the percentage ownership of these particular shareholders to enable the company to sell stock to new shareholders, such that the new shareholders can own a meaningful percentage of the company.

- **(xi) Increases in the option plan**—Recall that startups generally use stock options to incent employees. As the company grows, it may run out of options in the plan and thus need to increase the option pool in order to grant more equity to its employees. But doing so dilutes the existing shareholders. Hopefully that's intuitive, but any time you have to add more shares to the company, the denominator of total shares outstanding increases, so if VCF1 owns 20 percent of the company before adding the new shares, it will own less than that amount after the addition of the new shares to the option pool. Understandably, then, the Preferred would like to be able to weigh in on the decision to increase the option pool.

When you take a step back from these protective provisions, you'll see that they really are designed to protect the economic interests of the Preferred shareholders. All the enumerated things we talked about above are essentially things that affect the economics of the investment—raising more money (by issuing new shares), selling the company or its intellectual property, liquidating or selling the company, and increasing the option pool. Thus, the protective provisions are really just as they sound—protection against an erosion of the economic value that VCF1 thought it was getting when it invested its $10 million.

Registration Rights

Our term sheet takes a bit of a shortcut by saying that VCF1 gets "customary registration rights." Luckily for practitioners in the field, they understand what that means. This section is not worth spending much time on, not because it's not important, but because it tends to be pretty noncontroversial when the lawyers are advising their clients on key elements of the term sheet. It's also not heavily negotiated because it really doesn't matter until the company is ready to go public and, at that time, the investment bankers will basically tell both the company and the investors what they think the appropriate market terms are for these provisions.

At a high level, this section deals with what happens typically when a company goes public and VCF1 wants to sell its shares in the public market. In general, under US securities laws, shares need to be registered with the SEC in order to be fully liquid. Unregistered shares can be sold only if they comply with various exemptions from registration that the SEC has outlined, but in most cases the volume of shares and the timeline over which those shares can be sold will be restricted. The registration rights section defines under what circumstances VCF1 can either require XYZ Company to register its shares or "piggyback" on a registration of other classes of shares. Piggyback means exactly what it sounds like: if the company is otherwise registering some of its shares of stock, VCF1 gets the ability to piggyback on that registration and have its shares registered as well in the same process.

Pro Rata Investments

We talked earlier about how VCs often reserve dollars for follow-on investments in a company after their initial investment round. The reason for this is that if VCF1 owns 20 percent of XYZ Company today and the company continues to do well, VCF1 might want to invest additional dollars in subsequent financings rounds to maintain its ownership. Otherwise, because a new round of financing entails the issuance of new shares of stock, VCF1 will be diluted by the financing round.

This section gives VCF1 the right, but not the obligation, to purchase its pro rata amount of future rounds of financing to avoid dilution. You'll also note that the right applies only to "major investors," which was defined in the information rights section to be anyone who invests at least $2 million in the company.

This is really just a matter of convenience. If you have a lot of small investors, sometimes it is just a pain to track them down and then wait for them to tell you whether they are going to invest their pro rata amount in the new round of financing. So the major investor definition reserves this right for those who are putting some material amount of money into the company. Of course, the threshold could be set at any level the company and investors agree to.

Pro rata rights seem like a fair thing for existing investors to have, but oftentimes it creates challenges in a financing round. Specifically, when a company is doing really well and the financing round is oversubscribed, meaning there are more investors who want to put money in than the company cares to accommodate, pro rata rights can become an issue.

Why is that? Because the new investor often wants to achieve some target percentage ownership. The reason for this is as follows: the critical scaling limiter for VC funds is the number of board seats that any particular GP can handle. While there are no rules here, it's generally the case that GPs tap out around ten to twelve board seats. So every time a GP takes on a new board seat, that investment decision has an opportunity cost in that it consumes one of a limited number of investments she can make.

Thus, in order to make more investments and scale the firm, VCs need to carefully watch the number of board seats they take and, when they make a decision to take on a board obligation, VCs want to own as much of any company as possible. A cardinal sin of venture investing is picking the right company in which to invest but failing to own enough of the company, such that the returns from that investment don't meaningfully move the needle on the fund's overall returns. Nobody wants to make that mistake, thus the desire to maximize ownership on each investment.

Naturally, the other tension comes from the company itself. There is a finite amount of money the company likely wants to raise at a particular financing round and, correspondingly, a maximum amount of ownership dilution it is willing to accept. So if the company wants to raise a total of only $15 million and sell 10 percent of the company for that amount, the new investor may desire to take the full $15 million. But if the existing investors all have pro rata rights, they are entitled to their portion of the $15 million as well. At some point, either the company has to agree to raise more money (and thus potentially suffer greater dilution) or the new and existing investors have to come to some agreement between themselves.

Stock Restriction

This section packs a lot of punch, so we'll need to break it down into its various sections. Notice that it applies to significant shareholders only; in this case, anyone who owns at least 2 percent of the company's stock.

Let's start with the right of first refusal (ROFR)—this means that if I want to sell some of my stock, I can go to an outside party and get them to give me a price. But before I am allowed to sell my shares to that third party, I need to give the company first (and then the investors) the right to purchase the stock at the same price.

You can think of this provision in two ways.

In the most restrictive version, it really is intended to put a chilling effect on anyone's ability to sell shares. After all, if I am a third-party potential buyer and I know that I have to set a bid price and then give the company and investors the right to match that and thus take the deal away from me, I am not likely to bid in the first place.

The more innocuous interpretation of a ROFR is that it allows the company and its investors to control in whose hands the stock ends up. This is important for many startup companies because they generally don't want potentially unknown investors holding significant shares of the company and thus being able to influence corporate decisions through the stock voting rights. The ROFR gives the company an opportunity to determine if they are comfortable with the third party before they approve the transaction, in which case they will waive the ROFR. If they are not comfortable selling to that third party, the company can pony up the money and effect the purchase itself.

The co-sale agreement is kind of the inverse of a ROFR. A co-sale says that if I offer to sell my shares to a third party (or anyone else), all the other investors get a right to also sell their pro rata portion of shares to that buyer at the same price. In other words, I do all the work to generate a deal for my shares and then risk being cut back because other shareholders can pile onto my deal. For example, if I want to sell 10 percent of my shares, I need to identify a buyer who is willing to make that purchase. If the buyer agrees, then every other shareholder of the company who has the co-sale right gets to sell a corresponding portion of their shares in the transaction. Since the buyer likely doesn't have endless amounts of money, nor an endless appetite to purchase shares, the number of shares that I am ultimately able to sell will get reduced by the number of shares that the other shareholders choose to sell.

You might wonder why either of these provisions exists in the first place. Well, in general they are intended to make it harder (in this case) for common shareholders, in particular the founders, to sell their shares. And why would the VCs want this? Because the VCs are investing in the founders (who are usually the major holders of common stock) and they want to maintain maximum alignment with them to grow the equity value of the company.

So, by restricting their ability to sell the shares, we are all in this together—we all either succeed or fail together, but nobody jumps ship too early.

Now if you look to the last paragraph of this section, you'll see that this alignment seems to be shattering. That section says that everyone (except for the Preferred stock) will have a blanket transfer restriction on stock, other than with approval from the disinterested board members. Cutting through the legal language, the provision says that the common shareholders can't sell at all unless the noncommon board members say it's okay. But the Preferred are exempted from this restriction, freeing them to sell without that approval. That seems a bit one-sided, and it is. Often you will see the more complete version of alignment where everyone is bound by the same stock transfer restrictions—we all hold hands and jump off the bridge together at the same time, or none of us does!

Drag Along

The drag-along provision is intended to prevent minority investors from holding out on a deal to try to get a better deal for themselves. So what it says is that if each member of the board of directors, the majority of common stock, and the majority of Preferred stock all vote in favor of an acquisition, then any of the other 2 percent shareholders (recall this was our major investor definition) gets dragged along in favor of the deal. The presumption here is that if all these other folks have decided that the acquisition is a good thing for the company, there is no reason that a small shareholder should be able to prevent the transaction from happening; tyranny of the minority is outlawed through the drag along.

To provide some protection to these 2 percent holders, note that there are three separate votes required: (1) the board needs to approve; (2) the common voting as a separate class need to approve; and (3) the capital "P" Preferred voting as a separate class need to approve. Thus, there are some protections built in to make sure that the deal hopefully is in fact a good one for the company to pursue.

One other thing to note here: the drag along doesn't apply to the shareholders with less than 2 percent. Why is that? Well, first as a practical matter, acquirers will sometimes close an acquisition with fewer than 100 percent of the shareholders agreeing, as long they get probably more than 90 percent, and all the big players, to agree. Second, you worry less about tyranny of the minority with very small (and often disparate) shareholders—that is, the likelihood of their being able to scuttle the deal or hold out for something better is just much less. So, in a way, we tolerate democracy as long as a democratic process can't in fact affect the outcome!

D&O Insurance

This is a minor (and hopefully) noncontroversial section of the term sheet, but worth a quick mention as we will spend more time on liability later in the book. Recall that when we talked about the GP equity partners agreement, we mentioned indemnification— the idea that the fund can protect individual GPs from having to pay out of pocket for potential lawsuits that arise from their role. That is all true—and VC firms purchase their own D&O (directors and officers) insurance to help cover these potential expenses.

But there's never any harm in being extra careful—wearing both a belt and suspenders is a good way to make sure your pants stay up—so the portfolio company itself also purchases its own D&O insurance to protect its board members and officers against legal liability.

The VCF1 GP who sits on the board of XYZ Company thus has several lines of defense: XYZ's D&O policy first and then VCF1's policy as a backup. And just as the venture firm indemnifies its GPs, XYZ Company will also indemnify its board members and officers. This enables them to be the beneficiaries of the D&O insurance policies.

Vesting

The term sheet sets the rules for the vesting of both employee and founder shares. The employee vesting section—25 percent of an employee's stock vests on the one-year anniversary of their hire (often called a "one-year cliff vest"), and the remaining 75 percent vests in equal monthly increments over the next three years—is pretty standard. It's a total four-year vest, but with the provision that you have to make it through your first full year to vest the first 25 percent.

You'll also notice that the employee section says that the options will have a post-termination exercise period of ninety days. What does this mean? If an employee leaves the company (whether voluntarily or not), she needs to exercise her shares within three months or she will forfeit the options.

While this is the standard provision in most option agreements, companies increasingly are reconsidering this provision as they stay private a lot longer, well past the time period for which the four-year option vesting program was invented. As we noted earlier, it's an anachronism from the days in which companies actually went public around four years from founding, but that's simply not the case anymore: the median time to IPO for venture-backed companies is now in excess of ten years.

So what's the big deal? Well, if an employee leaves the company after four years (or at any time, for that matter), she has only ninety days in which to exercise or forfeit the options. And exercising requires cash, which the employee might not have. Most startup employees accept lower cash salaries in exchange for the upside that equity options might yield, thus cash is often at a premium. If the company were public at the time the employee had to exercise her shares, this problem would be mitigated because the employee could sell some of the shares in the market and use those proceeds to pay for the remaining exercise costs. In addition, many companies offer what is called a "cashless exercise option," which means that the employee can surrender some of her shares to the company in lieu of paying out of pocket for the exercise price.

But not only do you have to come up with cash to pay for the exercise price for each share, but, depending on the type of option you own, the IRS then taxes you on the difference between the then-existing fair market value of the stock and the exercise price. There is unfortunately no cashless option for your tax payments; the IRS accepts only US dollars as payment.

For companies whose stock prices have appreciated significantly, the out-of-pocket amounts can be huge and thus prohibitively expensive for many employees. In some ways, it's a success disaster—that is, employees are penalized for actually succeeding in building a business that is now worth so much (thus they can't afford to exercise their options). This undermines the cash-equity trade-off that many startup employees make—a willingness to accept lower cash compensation in exchange for the potential to earn income from the appreciation of stock options.

As a result, some startups are giving employees more time than ninety days—in some cases up to ten years—to decide whether to exercise the options. This is perfectly legal, but it does have one tax implication for employees.

Remember we talked earlier about incentive stock options (ISOs) and non-qualified stock options (NQOs). Among other things, a difference between the two is that taxes on the spread between the exercise price and fair market value of the stock are owed on NQOs at the time of exercise, whereas they can be deferred to the time of ultimate sale of the stock for ISOs. A critical element of ISOs, however, is that they must be exercised within ninety days of an employee's termination from the company. So while the company's decision to extend the option exercise period for employees has value to the employee by deferring the exercise costs of the option, it converts ISOs into NQOs and thus triggers the tax obligations.

On a positive note, as part of the 2017 tax reform legislation passed by Congress, the tax treatment of stock options has now become more favorable. There are still many details to be worked out, but the new law allows employees to defer taxes for up to five years from when the stock is fully vested. It's possible of course that this may not solve the problem for everyone given the length of time it is taking companies to go public, but this will certainly help a lot of folks.

Let's move on to the founder stock vesting section. Our term sheet says that the founder stock vests ratably over four years, starting from the date on which the founders began providing services to the company.

Surprisingly (or not), this term can often be a source of contention in the negotiation between VCs and founders. From the founder's perspective, she may have been working on this company (or at least this idea) for a while before she engaged with a lawyer to incorporate the company and ultimately raise VC money. Thus, she wants full vesting credit for that time—which makes sense. The VC, on the other hand, is investing largely on the strength of the founder and wants her to be financially incented (in the form of continued vesting of her shares) for as long as possible (as a disincentive for her to leave the company). There is no magic answer to this debate, but often the VC gets comfortable as long as there is some meaningful amount of vesting still to come.

The other provision in this section deals with what happens to the founder stock on an acquisition. The founder would like her stock to become fully vested on an acquisition (this is called "acceleration") because she has done her job, which was to build a company of value. The VC is concerned that if all her shares automatically vest upon the acquisition, then the acquirer will have less reason to do the deal—in many cases, acquirers are buying the talent as much as they may be buying the going concern of the company—because the founder is free to take her money and leave as of the acquisition.

What's contemplated in our term sheet is what's called a "double-trigger acceleration," which is the more common version of acceleration. It means what it says—there are two triggers to the founder getting her acceleration. The first trigger is the acquisition itself, and the second trigger is the founder getting terminated by the acquirer other than for cause or good reason (these are defined terms that require pretty serious bad behavior, often conviction of a crime, on behalf of the founder). This way if the acquirer wants to retain the founder, it has that option without having to worry about her options automatically vesting. And, if the acquirer doesn't want her, then since their termination of her employment prohibits her from fully vesting the shares on the normal schedule, it seems fair that she should be accelerated.

Employee and Consultant Agreements

Recall that when we talked about company formation, we mentioned that, since most of the initial value in a company is a function of any proprietary technology that the company is proposing to commercialize, the VCs want to make sure that the company in fact owns the technology free and clear and can protect it. This section in the term sheet operationalizes that. It says that the company agrees to have all of its employees (and consultants) sign nondisclosure agreements and to assign to the company all the technology that they create while working for the company. This is generally pretty simple and noncontroversial stuff, but, as the Waymo case illustrates, can become more much complicated to the extent that founders or employees are developing technology in the startup that they may have been working on previously at a prior employer.

No-Shop

So we've now successfully negotiated all these terms and are coming to the end of the deal. But there is a difference between signing the term sheet and closing the actual investment. Closing can happen as fast as you can get the lawyers to document everything and complete their due diligence, but as a practical matter, it often takes from two weeks to as much as a month to get from term sheet to closing, which occurs once the parties sign all the agreements and the VC wires its money to the company.

You'll notice that the term sheet itself is nonbinding—that is, either party can decide ultimately that they don't want to proceed with the deal, in which case we are back to square one.

So to provide some hooks into the deal, VCF1 asks for a thirty-day period (it could be shorter or longer, but thirty is pretty standard) in which they tie up XYZ Company. The tie-up is in the form of preventing XYZ from being able to disclose the term sheet to other parties or pursue a deal with somebody else. After all, the last thing VCF1 wants is to have XYZ Company shop this term sheet to other VC firms to see if someone else wants to provide a better deal. The theory is that the parties should hopefully be more committed to one another at this point, so the shopping should have been done before entering into the term sheet stage.

Takeaway: Be Forward Thinking

Okay! We made it through the tour de force of the term sheet or, at least, the more important provisions.

One high-level takeaway from negotiating term sheets is to always be forward thinking about what you agree to in the current term sheet, being mindful that it can have implications for subsequent financings.

In general, simplicity is better. Even if you, the founder, have the negotiating leverage to get some highly favorable term as part of an early-stage financing, it may not always be in your best interest to exercise that leverage, as it may ultimately cost you down the line. Importantly, the same exact sentence is true for VCs.

CHAPTER 11

The Deal Dilemma: Which Deal Is Better?

Now that we have a basic understanding of the major terms of a VC financing, let's put it to use in a hypothetical fund-raising. Let's evaluate a trade-off between two different financing options for our make-believe startup, HappyPets (yes, this is an homage to the famous bubble-era company Pets.com).

In this scenario, we have set out to raise VC money and have had very successful meetings. We are lucky enough to get two term sheets. One term sheet is from Haiku Capital and the other is from Indigo Capital (all names have been changed). As we talked about in chapters 9 and 10, let's evaluate both the economic and the governance terms, starting with the economic terms.

Economic Terms	Haiku Capital	Indigo Capital
$ Invested	$2 million	$4 million
Pre-money Valuation	$8 million	$8 million
Post-money Valuation	$10 million	$12 million
Option Pool %	20% post-money	15% post-money

(continued on next page)

(continued from previous page)

Economic Terms	Haiku Capital	Indigo Capital
Liquidation Preference	1x, participating	1x, nonparticipating
Antidilution Protection	Broad-based weighted average	Full ratchet

How would we evaluate which of these deals is better for us?

Building a Cap Table

Let's start by creating a capitalization table (commonly called the cap table) to help us understand who owns what at the end of the financing. The cap table is a handy way of organizing a company's percentages of ownership over time—for the founders, investors, employees, and any other owners.

Here's what our capitalization table looks like if we were to take the Haiku Capital deal:

Shareholder	# of Shares	% Ownership
Founders	4,000,000	60.0%
Haiku Capital	1,333,333	20.0%
Option Pool	1,333,333	20.0%
Total	6,666,666	100.0%

And this is what it looks like under the Indigo Capital deal:

Shareholder	# of Shares	% Ownership
Founders	4,000,000	51.7%
Indigo Capital	2,580,645	33.3%
Option Pool	1,161,290	15.0%
Total	7,741,935	100.0%

So which do you think you'd prefer, between these two potential deals?

When we look at the ownership of the founders, there is about an eight-percentage-point delta between them. The Indigo deal is more dilutive (meaning the founders own less than in the Haiku deal). Some of this is driven by the difference in the amount of capital being invested by the two firms. The higher Indigo investment of $4 million is good, but that will give the Indigo firm an extra thirteen percentage points of ownership relative to the $2 million from Haiku.

Another difference is coming from the size of the option pool—that 5 percent higher pool in the Haiku deal is coming right out of the founders' pockets. So without that, the Haiku deal would look even more economically attractive to the founders.

What should you do? You should probably first think about whether you can productively put the $4 million Indigo is offering to work versus the $2 million from Haiku. How much do you need the extra $2 million?

As we've discussed before, we at a16z often advise companies that the right amount of money to raise in the current round is what you think you need to hit the required milestones for the next round, generally twelve to twenty-four months later. In other words, you optimize for success in the next round by giving yourselves the right amount of execution runway in the current round. Obviously, more money now generally means more dilution, so this is always a balancing act.

If you had the extra $2 million, would that reduce the risks of your being able to achieve the operating milestones for this financing round? Maybe you could hire additional engineers to help ensure that your development plans stay on schedule. Maybe you could hire a sales team earlier than otherwise, which would help increase your confidence level in the sales targets.

The other way to think about the extra funding is not whether it de-risks your ability to achieve the objectives, but whether it would enable you to achieve even more than you were originally anticipating in this financing round. In other words, if you could get the business to an even better set of milestones, presumably the next round investor would give you even more credit in terms of the valuation she would be willing to pay for the next financing round.

Ultimately this is a trade-off between a known level of dilution now and your best forecast as to what dilution might incur in the next round based on various levels of business achievement. Recall from our discussion in chapter 7 that momentum—and the perception of momentum—does really matter in the competitive world of startups, so you want to think about the funding amount that gives you the highest degree of confidence in being able to maintain momentum from one funding round to another.

So let me ask again: What should you do? Well, actually, that's a trick question! You don't know yet! We haven't looked at the rest of the economic terms, nor the governance terms, to see if they are materially different between the two firms.

Take liquidation preference, for example. Haiku has a 1x, participating liquidation preference, whereas Indigo's is nonparticipating. Recall what that means: Haiku gets to double dip and not only take its $2 million investment off the table first but also then participate in any additional proceeds as if it were a common shareholder.

One way to evaluate these is to look at the payout matrices for the two offers. The payout matrix shows you at different potential exit price points how the proceeds of that exit are divided between the common and the preferred shareholders.

Haiku not only gets its $2 million investment back at any exit valuation above $2 million but also takes 20 percent of the remaining proceeds. In contrast, above an exit price of $12 million, Indigo will choose to convert its preferred shares to common shares and take only its 33.3 percent of the proceeds that equals its level of economic ownership. Depending on how you think about the likely exit options for your company, you might decide that the greater dilution in the Indigo deal is worth it to avoid having the Haiku team participate beyond its liquidation preference at higher sales prices.

Below is the Haiku payoff matrix:

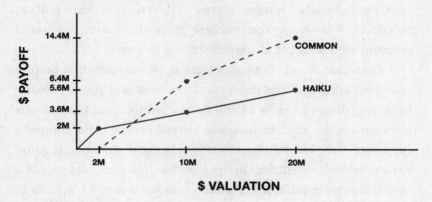

And here is the Indigo payoff matrix:

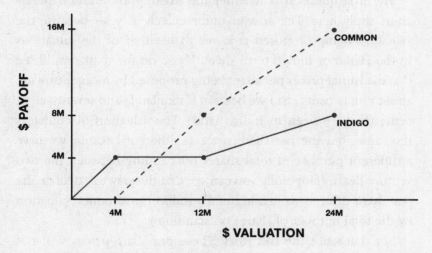

The final economic piece to consider here is the antidilution protection provision. Recall that this comes into play if, in a subsequent financing round, the price of the round is less than the current round price. In that case, the VCs are entitled to some price adjustment on their original shares—the exact amount depending on whether there is broad-based weighted average protection or a full ratchet. The Haiku term sheet has the former; the Indigo term sheet has the latter. Recall that the weighted average formula is friendlier to the common shareholders in that it dampens the effect of a lower-priced round by weighting the price adjustment based upon the relative size of the new financing round. In contrast, the full ratchet is most dilutive to the common shareholders by effectively resetting the purchase price of the previous round investors to that of the current financing proposal.

To illustrate the effect of antidilution, let's assume that despite your best efforts, things don't work out well and you are sitting here in eighteen months having consumed the cash but without having made the requisite progress. You still believe in the company (as do your original venture investors), but your valuation is going to be reflected nonetheless in the less-than-planned progress. As a result, Momentum Capital is willing to invest a new $2 million in the company, but only at a $6 million pre-money valuation.

The first question is whether the existing antidilution provisions apply here. The answer unfortunately is yes—because the valuation being proposed is lower than either of the valuations in the Haiku or Indigo term sheet. If you do the math, you'll see that the initial prices per share being proposed by Momentum are about ninety cents (had we been in Haiku land) and seventy-eight cents (had we been in Indigo land). The valuation of course is the same, but the per-share price is different because we have a different number of total shares outstanding between the two venture deals. (Hopefully you can see that the way to calculate the per-share price is to divide the $6 million pre-money valuation by the total number of shares outstanding.)

But that's not the full story. These per-share prices will not be the prices per share that Momentum ultimately invests in the company. Why is that? Because Momentum wants to invest $2 million and own 25 percent of the company ($2 million divided by the $8 million post-money valuation). However, when we factor in the antidilution protection that Haiku and Indigo each receive as part of the deal, the company needs to issue more shares to them, which in turn dilutes the ownership of Momentum. Thus, we find ourselves in a circular model—the additional shares issued to Haiku/Indigo reduce Momentum's ownership, requiring that we therefore lower the actual price per share to Momentum and thus issue them additional shares, which lower effective per-share price then requires that we recalculate the antidilution protection, and so on.

Eventually we will get our Excel model to iterate enough times to converge on the right answer, but that's no easy task. And now for the painful part: How much are the different antidilution provisions going to cost in terms of additional shares awarded to each of Haiku and Indigo? Let's take a look at the capitalization table for each Momentum transaction.

Here's the capitalization table had we taken the Haiku term sheet and then done the Momentum deal:

Shareholder	# of Shares	# of Shares Issued in New Deal	# of Shares Post-Deal	% Ownership
Founders	4,000,000	—	4,000,000	44.0%
Haiku Capital	1,333,333	156,863	1,490,196	16.4%
Option Pool	1,333,333	—	1,333,333	14.6%
Momentum Capital	—	2,274,510	2,274,510	25.00%
Total	6,666,666	2,431,373	9,098,039	100.0%

And here's the capitalization table had we taken the Indigo term sheet and then done the Momentum deal:

Shareholder	# of Shares	# of Shares Issued in New Deal	# of Shares Post-Deal	% Ownership
Founders	4,000,000	—	4,000,000	19.4%
Indigo Capital	2,580,645	7,741,935	10,322,581	50.0%
Option Pool	1,161,290	—	1,161,290	5.6%
Momentum Capital	—	5,160,290	5,161,290	25.0%
Total	7,741,935	12,902,225	20,645,161	100.0%

That's a pretty big difference—the founders' ownership differs by more than two times between the two options. Often what might happen in practice is that Momentum would make its deal contingent upon Haiku/Indigo (particularly Indigo) waiving its antidilution protection, or at least modifying it to a broad-based weighted average. In addition, Momentum might insist that, in order to lessen the dilutive impact of the round on the founders and employees, the existing investors increase the size of the option pool (and suffer the attendant dilution from that as well) so as to be able to provide additional option grants to the remaining team members. After all, Momentum is unlikely to want to fund the business if it believes that the remaining team is not adequately incented to stay with the business and help return it to growth mode.

Regardless, you want to avoid putting yourself in that pickle if at all possible. Antidilution provisions are very common in venture deals, so it's unlikely that you'll be able to raise venture money without such a provision at all. However, as you've seen, the difference between weighted average dilution versus a full ratchet is very meaningful. So no matter your level of confidence in your entrepreneurship skills, you'd be well-advised to pay careful attention to the full set of economic terms in a term sheet.

Evaluating the Governance Terms

Now that we have a good sense of the different economic terms, let's take a look at the key governance terms in the two original term sheets on the next page.

When we look at the broad difference between the two term sheets, we notice that the Haiku term sheet has used our capital "P" Preferred in its voting thresholds, whereas Indigo has used Series A preferred only. While it's impossible to fully know the implications of this downstream, in general it's simpler to have a capital "P" Preferred vote as the baseline precedent at an early

Governance Terms	Haiku Capital	Indigo Capital
Auto-convert	$50 million IPO or majority of Preferred vote	$100 million IPO or majority of Series A
Protective Provisions	Majority of Preferred vote	Majority of Series A
Drag-Along	Triggered by majority vote of Board + common + Preferred	Triggered by majority vote of Board + common + Series A
Board Composition	2 common + 1 Preferred	1 common + 2 Preferred

stage versus setting up a series-specific vote this early in the company's life cycle. This wouldn't of course have mattered in the Momentum Capital financing round since it came early on (Haiku and Indigo on their own could each control their respective votes), but the governance setup might have influenced the terms that Momentum demanded. For example, if Momentum were following the Indigo term sheet, it might have also demanded a separate set of auto-convert and protective provisions to be voted on only by itself (the Series B).

To be clear, there is no rule that says that all subsequent investors get the benefit of the same terms as did earlier investors, but in my experience this is often the starting point of the discussion: if it was good enough for those investors, why isn't it good enough for me as the new investor? No doubt the best retort to this argument is: "This time things are different."

For example, maybe the company was in a distressed situation in a previous round of financing and thus had to offer slightly more onerous terms to entice an investor. And now the company is firing on all cylinders and can therefore command more company-favorable financing terms. All of these are fair arguments to make—and you should make them if you ever find yourself in this situation—but don't underestimate the value of precedent. It establishes the starting point from which you need to negotiate; whether or not you think that's fair, it's often the way these negotiations go. A little planning when you are doing the current transaction for the eventuality of future transactions can go a long way.

Equally important is the board composition proposed by the two venture firms. Haiku is proposing a common-controlled board—that is, the majority of the board seats are controlled by common. The biggest implication of this is that Haiku on its own would not be able to hire or fire the CEO or control any corporate actions that require board approval. Indigo is less founder friendly in this regard, proposing that it get two boards seats to only one for common. This means that Indigo controls the board and thus has material influence on all major corporate actions.

So with the benefit of the full set of terms—economic and governance—how do you now think about which term sheet is better?

Sorry. It was a trick question again. The whole exercise exists to point out that there are pros and cons to every deal, and there usually is no definitive right answer. Some of the decision depends on how confident you are in the company's future (and yourself as CEO), how much money you really need now to accomplish your goals, and how much you are willing to gamble on the downside in order to give yourself more upside.

A lot of these depend on contingencies that are hard to predict at such an early stage, so in many cases keeping things simple is probably the better course. But, hey, you're an entrepreneur, so maybe taking a gamble is the best way to go!

Importantly, though, as we've tried to point out in this discussion, you need to think beyond valuation alone and consider the combined implications of the full set of economic and governance terms.

CHAPTER 12

Board Members and the Good Housekeeping Seal of Approval

Now that we've raised money and are off to the races, we should turn our attention to the ongoing affairs of the business. The CEO, of course, is responsible for the day-to-day operations of the business (as well as the long-term vision), and I have boundless respect for CEOs and their startup teams. While they are the ones who eat, sleep, and breathe their startups, they are not alone in their care and shepherding of the company. It's critical to understand that a company's board of directors has a role to play in a startup.

Thus, this chapter talks about the role of the board of directors and how the board influences the path of the startup and potentially the ability of the founder to keep steering the ship. Boards, including the founder, also have to operate under various well-defined legal constraints that can materially impact the degrees of freedom of a company. Understanding what those are and how best to accomplish the goals of the startup without going to jail or bankrupting yourself personally is probably worth the effort!

Private versus Public Boards

There are a few important distinctions between boards of private startups versus those of public companies that are worth noting, as they can affect the overall direction and decisions of the startup.

First, for *public companies*, board members are typically elected by the common shareholders. Recall that, in most cases, public companies do not have common and preferred shares outstanding (though it is the case that some public companies—e.g., Facebook and Google—have dual classes of common stock that may have different voting provisions). As a result, other than the potential voting differentials, there is a single class of shareholders who at least in theory have one goal in mind: to maximize the value of the company for the benefit of the common shareholders.

As we've discussed, *private startups* typically diverge from this model. The board composition is generally dictated by the terms negotiated in the course of a financing round. And as a result we tend to have not only multiple types of shareholders—common plus different series of preferred stock—but also often specific enumerated parties that control access to board seats. In our VCF1 term sheet, for example, the board was designated to have a representative from common, one from VCF1, and a third to be elected by the common and preferred together.

Second, the impact of board decisions can also vary between public and private companies because of the presence of the protective provisions that often accompany the VCs' preferred shares. Public companies are much simpler in that respect. If, for example, the board of a public company decides to vote in favor of an acquisition, the acquisition is likely to happen. Of course there is a need for a shareholder vote, but recall that that vote is likely just going to have one class of stock voting, and we certainly don't have different contractual says in the matter (other than the dual-class voting rights) depending on what type of stock a shareholder has.

Again, contrast that with the private startup situation. In the acquisition example, not only does the board need to vote in favor of the deal but also we might have multiple series of preferred stock whose vote is required based upon the protective provisions. If our startup has gone through multiple rounds of financing and we weren't able to stick with the capital "P" Preferred voting threshold in the protective provisions, we could have a preferred series of investor who has a small economic stake in the company but a disproportionate say in the acquisition outcome by virtue of having a series-specific protective provision vote.

Finally, the presence of other terms (in particular antidilution and liquidation preferences) can also affect decision-making in a private startup. In public companies, because we don't have multiple classes of stock with these varying terms, the calculus is pretty simple: grow the value of the equity for the benefit of the common shareholders.

As we'll see in the next few chapters, preferred investors and common investors are not always aligned. Particularly in the case of an acquisition where liquidation preferences may come into play, the interests of the two parties can diverge significantly. So, while the board has certain fiduciary duties to keep in mind—which we'll cover shortly in chapter 13—there are still ways in which the board dynamics and the presence of common and preferred shares can create interesting challenges when trying to make decisions on big corporate actions, such as fund-raising and acquisitions.

Dual Fiduciaries

Here's the fundamental issue to keep in mind when dealing with private startup boards and corporate decision-making in general: the VCs are dual fiduciaries. What does that mean?

Well, as a board member, a VC (just as is the case for public company board members) has a fiduciary duty to the common shareholders of the company. More to come on this in chapter 13, but suffice it to say that this means that the board member needs to always keep in mind how her vote helps maximize the long-term value of the stock held by the common shareholders.

But as a GP in a venture capital firm, she is also a fiduciary to her LPs, who have given her money in order to maximize the value of the investment dollars they have committed to the venture firm. And as we briefly noted above, there are times where the GP's economic interest—as a holder of preferred shares with different rights and privileges—may diverge from those of the common shareholders. Therein lies the rub.

The Role of the Board

Let's come back to the role of the board more specifically. We've hinted at a number of the board's responsibilities, but it would be good to dive into a bit more detail.

Good boards do most of the following things.

1. Hire/Fire the CEO

A foundational role of the board is to put in place the person who has day-to-day responsibility for the operation of the company. The CEO has all her executives in the company reporting to her (and thus she has the ability to hire or fire any of them), and the CEO herself ultimately reports to the board. Well-functioning boards recognize and respect this distinction by giving the CEO the freedom to run the company as she sees fit, subject to the constraint that she is ultimately accountable to the board for the results of the company. Though it can be tempting, particularly in smaller startups, for the VC board member to engage more closely with the CEO's executives, this can inadvertently undermine the CEO's authority and create management challenges for the startup.

And as anyone who has been in a startup before knows, there is a huge knowledge gap between board members and the CEO and other members of the executive team, stemming from the fact that the board members simply aren't in the company's office every day. Without the specific understanding of which employees are capable of doing what, and which product features are most important to the customers—among other things—board members simply aren't immersed enough in the company to meaningfully drive priorities for the business.

All of that being said, this may not stop VCs from overstepping their bounds. After all, many VCs were once CEOs themselves, thus the temptation to get more involved in the company's affairs. And the VCs are generally well-meaning when doing this. Their goal is to help the company become successful, even though the impact of their actions could well be the opposite. When VCs find themselves getting too entangled with the day-to-day operations of the business, you as the CEO should engage with your VC board member to understand why. It's possible that your VC may simply not be aware she is doing this, or there may be a deeper concern she has with your abilities as a CEO that is causing her to increase her level of engagement. Uncovering if either or both of these are present is a good thing for you to do as CEO.

As we talked about in chapter 10, this board responsibility is why board composition is often a hotly contested issue in term sheet negotiations. If the common shareholders control the board by having more board seats, that effectively neuters the VCs' ability to remove the founder CEO from her role. And the opposite of course is true: if the VCs control the board, the founder CEO might have concerns about whether the VCs will be trigger-happy and remove her from the business prematurely.

2. Guidance on Long-Term Strategic Direction for the Business

Consistent with the commentary above about the need to allow the CEO the appropriate level of freedom (and accountability) to drive the company's strategy, the board does have a role in at least providing guidance and review of that strategy.

For example, to execute the CEO's strategy might require a certain budget (or the need to raise additional capital): these are areas where the board's input is both expected and desirable. After all, we know that, particularly in the case of additional financing, the board will need to vote to approve an action at some point, and the protective provisions will likely grant the VCs a separate voting approval as well. So, if for no other reason than beginning to build consensus around these activities, good CEOs bring these discussions to their board for input well before they are asking for a formal vote.

Aside from items that might ultimately require formal board votes, startup boards are also good places for seeking input on strategic areas of focus, given that experienced VCs tend to have a wider aperture through which to provide guidance. In many cases, a startup CEO might be in that role for the first time, whereas a tenured VC might have sat on tens (or more) of boards over the course of her career, and thus simply have seen more game film that could help inform discussions. Again, that doesn't mean that the VCs should dictate the strategy to the CEO, but they often can provide lessons learned from prior experiences that can be helpful to a CEO who is doing some of these things for the first time.

3. Approving Various Corporate Actions

Startup boards also play an important part in approving corporate actions. We mentioned approving financings above, and of course major acquisitions or divestitures of assets need to be approved by the board.

Specific to compensation, the board also approves a number of important things.

First, in order to issue stock options to an employee, the board must first determine the appropriate fair market value of the stock. Under US tax laws, if companies issue stock options to an employee where the exercise price of the option is below the then-existing fair market value of the stock, the employee is liable to pay taxes at the time of the grant on the difference between the strike price and the fair market value. Nobody wants that, and boards don't want to have created tax problems for employees in retrospect by having the IRS challenge fair market value at a later date.

To prevent this, companies will often hire an outside firm to render what's called a 409A opinion. This is a financial analysis the firm conducts that arrives at a fair market value for the common stock and on which the board can rely to approve this value as the exercise price for options. A 409A opinion is generally good for up to twelve months, as long as there has not been a material change in the company in that time period—e.g., a new financing round or major changes in the financial performance of the business. Thus, as a matter of course, boards will update the 409A coincident with a new financing, or at least every twelve months. For those of you who have joined startups, this is why your offer letter may tell you how many options you are receiving but not tell you the exercise price; it's only once the board has approved the fair market value and taken the corporate action to authorize the granting of options that you will know precisely your exercise price.

Another compensation-related function of the board is to adjust the size of the option pool as needed to enable the company to make new-hire grants or provide additional options to existing employees. Recall from chapter 9 that our goal is to set the size of the option pool at the time of a financing to be sufficient to handle the company's forecast hiring needs until the time of a subsequent financing. Best laid plans don't always work, though, and the board is often called upon to increase the size of the option pool prior to a next financing. Hopefully in most cases this is because the company is doing so well that it has accelerated its hiring and thus needs more options to accommodate. Oftentimes, though, it's because the initial forecasting was a bit imprecise.

Good boards should also review CEO and broader executive compensation every one or two years. When we discussed stock vesting, we noted that VCs are always keeping an eye on the amount of vested versus unvested stock for founders (as well as other key members of the team). This is because the VCs want to ensure that the people most critical to the company's success have sufficient economic incentive to remain important contributors over the long term. Unvested stock options provide this incentive by tying economic rewards to continued tenure with the company.

As a result, good boards should both evaluate the performance of the CEO on a regular basis and, where appropriate, ensure that key contributors have sufficient unvested equity to incent the desired behavior. As we've noted before, doling out stock options is not costless, as the option pool may need to be expanded to accommodate this, and the pool's expansion dilutes the VCs' ownership in the company. So VCs will want to ensure that any such expansion is really likely to increase the value of the company as a way to offset the percentage ownership dilution they will feel in the short term.

4. Maintaining Compliance and Good Corporate Governance

We are going to explore the various legal duties of board members in chapter 13, but recall that we talked earlier about how the directors and officers generally want to protect themselves from taking on personal liability for any legal mishaps of the company. That's a good goal, but it requires that the board operate consistent with its legal duties and maintain good corporate governance. So an important role of the board is to simply meet on a regular and consistent basis to keep members informed of the business, enabling them to act in a manner that is consistent with their fundamental role of increasing long-term shareholder value for the common stock and, particularly in the case where the value doesn't materialize, protect themselves against personal liability.

You'll hear lawyers talk about this as protecting against a piercing of the corporate veil. That's a fancy way of saying that boards want to make sure that they get the benefit of the limited liability that a corporate structure is intended to provide. The way to do this of course is to satisfy the various legal duties that boards owe the company and its shareholders—e.g., holding regular board meetings that reflect the board's deliberations about the state of the business and ensuring that board members don't get too entangled in the day-to-day of the business.

5. VC-Specific Roles

There are also nonlegal/nongovernance roles that VC board members often play with the goal of helping to improve the prospects for the business. Many times a VC board member is an informal coach to the CEO. Again, because a VC generally has had the benefit of simply having seen more startups in action or been a founder herself, she is often in a good position to be a helpful mentor and coach. Admittedly, this can be a little weird in that the CEO of course ultimately reports to the board and can be removed by the board, so she might be a little reserved in her willingness to open up to the VC board member. Nonetheless, this is an area where VCs can be helpful.

Another informal role of the VC board member is to open her network to the benefit of the CEO. Sometimes this may be to introduce potential executive candidates or external advisors for the company. Other times it may be to introduce potential corporate customers or partners. And some VCs have institutionalized this beyond the board member herself to include teams of others at the venture firm to help with this activity.

6. The Board's Non-Roles

We've hinted at this earlier, but the board's non-roles are as important as its roles. Most starkly, the role of the board is not to run the company or dictate the strategy, in particular the product strategy; that is the job of the CEO. There is no way that the board members—independent of how much they engage with you as the CEO—understand the detailed capabilities of the company in a way that they can meaningfully influence product strategy. Only you know what each organization is capable of delivering and how the orchestration of those deliverables can ultimately be accomplished. Good boards recognize this distinction; bad boards overreach.

As painfully obvious as that sounds, some boards do in fact cross this line sometimes. The board's mechanism to "run" the company is to evaluate the CEO and coach, or ultimately fire, her if they don't like the way the company is being run; it is not to interfere with the CEO's ability to manage her team directly nor to dictate a particular product strategy.

If you see this kind of overreach from the board, you should address it directly with your respective board members. The innocuous explanation may be that you have inexperienced board members who simply need to be reminded of the best ways in which they can be helpful. The more serious explanation may be that the board is losing confidence in your ability to continue running the company—and this is simply their way of demonstrating that. Either way, as CEO, you want to know!

More generally, a big part of your job as CEO is to manage the board. That might sound odd in that managing typically applies to your direct reports—whom you have the ability to hire or fire—whereas you serve at the pleasure of the board. That notwithstanding, there are several things you can do with your board to help manage them indirectly.

First, set the right expectations up front about what you want from your board members. Many CEOs like to do regular one-on-one meetings with board members to ensure that they have time outside of the board meeting to share information and receive feedback. In addition, do you expect them to help you identify future members of the executive team, interview candidates for executive roles, open their Rolodexes to identify sales prospects, etc.? This goes without saying, but you should also set expectations about how you intend to run the board meetings—e.g., do you expect people to have read the deck beforehand and plan to use the meeting largely as a discussion of open questions?

Second, get agreement among your board members as to how they will provide you feedback. Some boards ask a single member to consolidate feedback from all the others and deliver it one-on-one to the CEO. Others may have an executive session with just the board and the CEO at the end of each meeting to provide group feedback. There is no required mode of operation, but you should both make clear your interest in hearing the feedback and agree on the best avenue.

Third, make sure that you and your board agree on engagement outside of a board meeting with members of your executive team. Good board members will make sure that you know if a member of the exec team has reached out to them to meet, and provide appropriate feedback to you as the CEO if critical questions are being raised. Bad board members will interfere with your relationships with your direct reports and likely raise concerns among your team about your viability as the CEO.

Finally, you need to orchestrate the board meeting itself and the agenda. This doesn't mean not sharing bad news or being selective in your disclosure of important information to the board, but it does mean figuring out what topics are worthy of board discussion and not spending time on topics that are appropriately delegated to you as the day-to-day manager of the organization. Sitting down with your board members at the outset to solicit their feedback on what they would like to see as part of the board agenda is a great way to avoid missing the mark during the board meeting.

CHAPTER 13

In Trados We Trust

As we've mentioned, in performing their jobs as board members, directors are generally entitled to protection from liability. But doing so requires that they fulfill their core legal duties to the common shareholders of the company. Let's take a look at what those duties are and how directors can ensure that they get the benefit of them.

A word first on this chapter. I am sure that some of you might be tempted to skip it because we are going to be talking about legal things, and we've already fairly exhaustively talked about board members. I get it. You may have other more exciting things to do right now (like, maybe, work on your startup?) but allow me to at least put in a plug for this material.

It's one thing to start a company and have it fail. That sucks, no doubt, but at least you gave it your best and didn't lose all your money in the process (at least I hope that's the case). But it doubly sucks if you fail and then you end up in a legal battle for years beyond that trying to defend yourself from any number of decisions you made (or didn't make) that are now being second-guessed by some of your shareholders.

If you didn't bankrupt yourself from the company's failing, the chances are pretty high that you will do so on the legal bills alone that accompany a lawsuit. Nor is it great to have your company succeed, make a bunch of money, and then find that some of your earlier shareholders feel as though they were screwed eight years prior and lost a lot of money as a result. Coming out on the losing end of that suit may mean that some of the gains you thought you had earned will disappear in the form of legal fees or a monetary damages award.

You don't want to be in either of those situations—whether as a founder CEO or as a VC board member. And you don't have to, because if you take the time to read this section, you'll see that there are some common-sense ways to help prevent you from getting into trouble.

Of course, all the usual caveats apply here—I am not your lawyer and am not providing you formal legal advice here (in fact, I'm not really a lawyer at all since the state of California says I am now an inactive member of the bar and thus not properly licensed to practice law). So when you start your company, and if you ever find yourself in a legal quagmire, hire a real lawyer to help you navigate your way through. The path is pretty well-worn.

Let's start by reviewing the duties of a board member.

Duty of Care

The duty of care is a foundational responsibility of a board member. At its most basic level, the duty of care says that you need to be informed about what's going on in the company to perform your basic role of maximizing value for the common shareholders. Specifically, you need to keep informed consistent with what a reasonable person would want to know in order to be able to evaluate the company's prospects.

You're not required to be prescient and see around corners to predict how some incredibly smart computer science student from

Stanford is going to eat your company's lunch. All you have to do is be informed—read the board materials, show up at the meetings, don't sit on your iPhone the whole time texting your bookie about the spread on the upcoming WWE match, and ask relevant questions. The joke is that you can probably satisfy your duty of care by not being asleep at the board meeting. I'm not sure that anyone has actually ever tested this, but that ought to give you a sense of the relatively low bar you have to clear.

Duty of Loyalty

The duty of loyalty requires that a director not self-deal or enrich herself. Rather, she should be motivated solely by what is in the best interests of the company and its common shareholders.

As we'll see shortly, while this sounds pretty straightforward, in the particular case of venture-funded startups, navigating the duty of loyalty can prove challenging. That's because of the dual fiduciary problem we talked about. How does a VC board member balance her duties to the company and her duties to her LPs if in fact those are in conflict? Where there have been legal cases brought against venture capital firms (and there are not very many in total), they almost always focus on this basic question.

Duty of Confidentiality

This is just as it sounds. If you are on the board of a company, you need to keep confidential any information that you learn in the course of your tenure.

We talked earlier about the opportunity costs of a VC making an investment. Among the reasons for this are that a VC can only sit on so many boards, so every time she fills up a slot on her dance card, she necessarily reduces her availability to invest in other companies. Another form of opportunity cost comes from conflicts: as a VC you can't really invest in Facebook and Friendster or Lyft and Uber. Rather, the decision to invest in a company likely means that you are conflicted out of other companies that are directly competitive. To be clear, there is no prohibition against this, but the convention of the business makes this hard to do—as a VC you are lending your name and your firm's brand to your investments, so it's hard to invest in direct competitors without creating challenges for both companies in the marketplace.

Where this gets difficult—and the reason I am raising this in the context of the duty of confidentiality—is when companies pivot. It's pretty easy at the time of an investment to know if the company you are proposing to invest in is competing directly with some other company; thus, navigating the potential conflict at time of investment is manageable. But we know that startups pivot all the time. Some pivots are small tweaks, but others could result in the company entering into entirely new businesses, the result of which may bring them into conflict with another investment that is already in a VC's portfolio.

We at Andreessen Horowitz dealt with this early in our firm's history. We initially invested in the seed round of Mixed Media Labs in 2010. Founded by Dalton Caldwell, Mixed Media was building a mobile phone photo-sharing application. As I mentioned earlier in the book, we also invested in the seed round of Burbn, which at the time was building a mobile location-sharing application (similar to Foursquare). Thus, at the time of our initial investments, there was no conflict. Burbn later pivoted into the photo-sharing space, ultimately becoming the very successful Instagram that was acquired by Facebook for $1 billion in 2012.

When Burbn and Mixed Media Labs both later decided to raise A rounds, this conflict was apparent. We were not on the board of either company, so this did not create any fiduciary questions regarding the duty of loyalty, but it did raise the broader conflict question we've been talking about. We ultimately invested in Mixed Media as part of its A round (and another VC went on to lead the Burbn A round), deciding that the best way to honor the

conflict was to give the tie to the company that had started originally in the photo-sharing space versus the one that had pivoted
into the space. This was not an easy decision given our respect for
both companies—and, to be clear, we had no formal investment
restrictions to constrain our behavior—but this is how we ultimately resolved the conflict.

Where these situations get more difficult, however, is when VC
firms have existing investments *and board seats* in companies that
ultimately pivot into another existing investment. Then the duty
of confidentiality does come into play, requiring that the firm take
various steps to ensure that the board members can satisfy their
legal obligations.

The most common way to handle this situation is to create
what's known as a Chinese wall between the GPs who sit on these
competing boards (let's take the case for now where there are
different GPs involved). A Chinese wall is basically a formalistic
way to restrict information flow between parties. In this situation,
any material information that one GP learns in the context of her
board service will not get shared with the other GP. By cordoning
off the flow of information, the individual GPs can generally satisfy their duties of confidentiality.

In the case where a single GP holds both board seats, there
are a few options. If the GP wishes to retain both seats (and the
companies are both in agreement), then disclosure of the conflict
and recusal are the primary mechanisms to manage this situation.
Thus, in a board meeting where material areas of conflict arise,
the GP would make sure the other board members know of the
potential conflict, and she would often recuse herself from that
portion of the meeting.

The more directly competitive the companies are, the harder
this becomes, as more and more aspects of the board meeting
may give rise to potential conflicts. Thus, in such a situation, it may
ultimately require that the GP reassign the board seat to another

partner in the firm, enabling them to utilize the Chinese wall process to ensure protection of confidential information.

Duty of Candor

The duty of candor requires that board members disclose to shareholders all the requisite information they need to be informed on important corporate actions. For example, if the company is undertaking an acquisition, the duty of candor would require providing the shareholders all the relevant information on the deal: how it came to pass, why the board thinks it's in the best interest of the shareholders, what the economic terms look like, etc.

What you'll find as you sit on boards is that the duties of care and loyalty are really the heart of the fiduciary duties that tend to come into play. It's not that the other two are not important, but just that if startup company boards get themselves into trouble—or at least need to think about their fiduciary duties in greater detail—it will in most cases implicate the duties of care and loyalty.

Common versus Preferred Stock

If you were paying careful attention, you might have noticed that when talking about duties of the board, we've been referencing common stock only. That is, we've said that the primary fiduciary duty of a board member is to optimize for what is in the best long-term interests of the common shareholders. But what about all the preferred stock shareholders that exist in our typical venture-backed startup?

Well, it turns out that board members do not owe fiduciary duties to the preferred stock. Instead, the courts have long said that preferred rights are purely contractual in nature; that is, they are negotiated by the parties to the financing agreement at the time of the funding. And—probably most important—they are negotiated by sophisticated parties who can take care of themselves. After all, nobody should have to worry about protecting the big bad VCs.

So a preferred shareholder could in fact sue if she felt as though the contractual rights that she had negotiated for were being violated—i.e., she had a protective provision vote that the company ignored in undertaking a corporate action. But she could not sue (or, more correctly, she could sue but would lose) alleging that the directors violated their fiduciary duties to her, because in fact none are owed.

And that really is the fundamental issue behind the difference between how boards need to treat common and preferred shareholders. The basic assumption is that the preferred can look out for themselves, but that there really is no way for the common to do so. Thus, we need to impose fiduciary duties on the board members to protect the little people—those are the common shareholders. As a result, if you find yourself in a sticky situation and are trying to figure out how to weigh things in the balance, you'll want to honor the contractual rights that the preferred has, but you need to make sure that you are keeping the best interests of the common paramount. Sometimes easier said than done.

The Business Judgment Rule (BJR)

Now that we're familiar with the duties board members owe, the question is, how do we know if we are in fact satisfying them and thus keeping ourselves out of trouble? Enter the business judgment rule, or BJR.

As a general policy matter, we want people to sit on boards. We've decided as a society that people being willing to spend some of their time as board members helps improve the prospects of maximizing the long-term value of the common shareholders. And if every time somebody on a board made a decision they feared that they might be held personally liable for, it's likely that people would no longer want to sit on boards. We've also decided that it's really hard for courts to second-guess decisions that a board makes after the fact, since they might not have a full appreciation of all the considerations that were factored into the board's decision-making process.

As a result, directors are generally entitled to a pretty lax standard of review known as the business judgment rule. In simple terms, the BJR says that the courts are loath to second-guess a board decision as long as, at the time the decision was made, the board acted on an informed basis, in good faith, and with the honest belief that the action taken was in the best interest of the corporation and its common shareholders.

Importantly, the decision need not have ultimately been right. Rather, the courts will look to evaluate the *process* of the decision-making to ensure that it complies with the duty of care: Did the directors inform themselves of the facts, did they read the board materials, did they take the time at a board meeting to discuss the issue? Essentially, was there a clear record of an informed, deliberative process? That's it; if you did that, then you can get the outcome wrong and still be protected from legal liability.

In fact, it's even a bit more favorable than that to the board members. In legal terms, the board members are presumed to have done these things. This means that it is up to the plaintiff (the person who is challenging the board's decision) to prove otherwise; she has the burden of proof to convince the court that the process was bad and thus led to a bad decision. This is a pretty high hurdle to jump and the reason why boards really want to stay within the protections of the BJR; it's a good comfort blanket in which to wrap yourself.

How do you do this?

Well, of course, the first thing to do is to in fact follow a good process. But the other critical item is to make sure that you keep good minutes of the meetings to reflect the frequency and level of deliberations. That doesn't mean you have to capture every word that is said in the meeting—and good lawyers know how to do this well—but it does mean that you want enough in the record so that if you ever have to defend yourself against a fiduciary duty claim, the record will support your good process.

This is why you always start the next board meeting by approving the minutes from the prior board meeting. That is your chance to make sure the record is accurate and to be able to show a court later on that you followed a good process in discussing the issues, recording them, and ultimately approving that the minutes accurately reflect what transpired.

Entire Fairness

Given how pro–board member the BJR is, do we even need to worry about all this fiduciary duty stuff? After all, it doesn't sound as though there really is much room for board members to be held personally liable as long as they don't sleepwalk through board meetings.

This is where the duty of loyalty comes into play. It turns out that there is a way to get outside of the BJR cocoon: show (or at least allege at the outset) that the board of directors violated its duty of loyalty, putting its own interests ahead of the common shareholders.

How do you do that?

There are a number of ways, of course, the most obvious being to show that there was in fact fraud or some egregious self-dealing. But, while that can certainly exist, it's pretty rare and also often pretty tough to prove.

The easier way to do this is to show that a majority of the board members were conflicted in some manner (e.g., dual fiduciaries), and that conflict led them to enjoy a financial benefit from the transaction (e.g., an acquisition or a financing) that was not equally shared by the common shareholders.

We're going to go through a live example of this shortly to understand the nuances in more detail, but essentially what this does is change the burden of proof in the case and give the court more latitude to look into the details of the business transaction. If you read the legal cases in this area, you'll see that the courts are basically willing to substitute their own judgment for that of the board if they conclude that there really were not disinterested, qualified decision-makers on the board faithfully representing the common shareholders.

In doing so, the courts abandon the BJR and move to a new rule called "entire fairness." There are a couple of important facets of the entire fairness standard.

First, as mentioned above, the burden of proof changes. That means that, unlike in BJR, where the board members were presumed to be acting with good process and the plaintiff bore the burden to overcome that presumption, in entire fairness the board members don't get any such presumption. In fact, the directors bear the burden to prove that they were acting in the company's best interest. I realize for some of you that might not seem like a big deal, but when it comes to defending yourself in court, having the burden to prove your case is much more difficult than coming in with a presumption of fair dealing.

Second, the courts will now dive much deeper into the decision-making process and analyze two specific aspects of the deal.

They will first test the fairness of the process itself, asking all the same questions about the board's deliberations that they would ask in the business judgment rule context, but again this time with the board members themselves having to provide affirmative proof to the court that their process was good. The courts will next test the fairness of the price achieved by the board (in the venture case, that is often the price of the acquisition or of a financing round).

So entire fairness means that the board members need to prove two things: (1) the process was fair and (2) the price was fair (which really means what the common shareholder got from the deal).

Finally, I mentioned this before, but this would be a good time to repeat it. A huge difference between violations of the duty of care versus violations of the duty of loyalty is that directors can't indemnify themselves against breaches of duty of loyalty. So if you lose a duty of care case, that's certainly no fun, but at least you won't have personal liability for the ultimate damages. Not so with violations of duties of loyalty; losing may mean digging into your own pocket for real dollars and cents.

In Re *Trados*

To see how this plays out in practice, let's turn to the seminal Delaware case that covers the fiduciary duty topics in the context of an acquisition. Recall that I mentioned there aren't many VC cases out there, so this one is pretty important.

Trados, like most VC tales, starts off with a promising startup. Trados successfully raises multiple rounds of venture financing from very well-respected firms. In fact, Trados raised a total of $57.9 million over its lifetime and, for a while, seemed to be making good progress. Unfortunately, things start to go sideways about five years into its life cycle, and the board decides to sell the company. The board ultimately accepts a $60 million acquisition offer.

In connection with the venture money Trados raised over the years, it accumulated liquidation preference equal to the $57.9 million in capital it had raised. The liquidation preference was 1x, nonparticipating—recall that means that the investors have a choice to take their liquidation preference off the top, or convert into common shares and take the amount reflecting their ownership, but not both. In the case of the $60 million acquisition offer, all the venture investors were better off taking their 1x liquidation preference, and that is what they elected to do.

Now, had things stopped right there, it's possible that this case never would have been brought, and we would be deprived of the ability to read about it. The VCs could have taken their $57.9 million in liquidation preference, and the remaining $2.1 million would have gone to the common shareholders. That's definitely not a great outcome for common, but maybe the common shareholders would have decided not to fight about this. In fact, they'd probably have had a hard time finding a lawyer who would be willing to take on their case, as the likelihood of winning was pretty remote.

Whither the MIP?

However, there's another important fact to add to the story.

Once the board decided to pursue a sale of the company, they instituted a management incentive plan, or MIP. Think of a MIP as essentially a carve out from the acquisition proceeds designed to incent the management team to work diligently toward an acquisition. In this case—and in most cases where you put a MIP in place—the board probably had a pretty good idea that the acquisition offers would not be sufficiently attractive to pay back the liquidation preference and leave much left over for the common shareholders (and, importantly, the employees of the company whom the board wanted to incent to try to sell the company).

So the board put in place the MIP—the precise amount was based on some percentage of the deal and varied by size of the acquisition. At the $60 million acquisition offer, the MIP paid out $7.8 million to identified employees of the company, heavily weighted toward a few senior executives.

In essence, the VCs agreed to carve out that money in part from their liquidation preference. As a result, the $60 million in acquisition proceeds were ultimately distributed as follows: $52.2 million to the VCs (less than the $57.9 million that they were entitled to under their liquidation preference), $7.8 million to the MIP participants, and zero to the rest of common.

A 5 percent owner of common stock, who was dismayed to learn that his ownership stake was now worthless, sued the company and the board, claiming that the deal was not fair. The board, after all, owes fiduciary duties to the common shareholders and, in this case, the plaintiff alleged that the fact that common received nothing from the deal while the investors and participants in the MIP got the benefit of the $60 million proved that something was fishy.

Conflicted Board?

The initial question that the court had to resolve in Trados is which standard of review—the business judgment rule or the entire fairness standard—applied. Recall that we talked about the importance of this because it determines which party carries the burden of proof: if the business judgment rule applies, the plaintiff has to prove the unfairness of the process, but if entire fairness applies, the defendants (in this case the VCs and the company's officers) have the burden of proof.

To determine if the board faced actual conflicts that caused it not to be disinterested and independent, the court does an exercise of counting the heads on the board. In essence, the court goes through the individual board members to determine whether or not each is independent. If a majority of the board is not disinterested, then the board itself is conflicted and entire fairness applies. In the Trados case, the board has seven directors, so if at least four are not independent, the problem is solved. Let's look closely at this, since it is really the key takeaway for anyone sitting on a venture-financed company board.

First, the VCs: it turns out that three of the directors represent VC firms that are part of the $57.9 million in liquidation preference. This is not surprising at all, as the company had gone through several rounds of financing, so it wouldn't have been unusual for the lead investor in each round to ask for a board seat. But the court comes down pretty hard on the VCs.

The court says that they are conflicted for two reasons.

Because they have a liquidation preference, the VCs' cash flow rights cause them to diverge from the common shareholders. You know this by now, having read this book (and thought about the payoff matrices), but the court says it explicitly: the VCs gain less from increases in the value of the company than they suffer from decreases in the value of the company as a result of the liquidation preference.

Does that make sense? It means that if the acquirer paid $45 million (instead of $60 million), the preferred would lose a dollar of proceeds for every dollar decrease in the purchase price; the VCs would feel that in their pocketbooks. But, if the acquirer paid $75 million for the company, because the VCs were still well underwater relative to the valuations at which they originally invested, they wouldn't have converted to common and thus still would have received their liquidation preference only. Thus, they were not very incented to argue with the acquirer for a marginally higher price because it provided no economic benefit to them.

However, that was not the case for the common shareholders. For every incremental dollar of acquisition price, the common shareholder would have received a corresponding dollar increase in their payback. This is because once the VCs elect to receive their liquidation preference as nonparticipating preferred shareholders, they do not participate in any additional upside. Rather, all those proceeds flow to the common shareholders.

The court also finds the VCs conflicted because of what the court calls the VC opportunity cost model. That is, the court says VCs don't like to spend time on losing companies (because of the economic trade-offs noted earlier in this book), preferring to spend it on companies that could have real potential economic upside to their funds (and thus improve their at-bats-per-home-run average). As a result, they are motivated in cases like Trados to get as much of their liquidation preference back as quickly as possible, but then not to spend more time pushing up the price. Doing so doesn't benefit them much, and spending the time has a high opportunity cost of time not spent on winning companies.

Unfortunately for the VCs in this case, there are some not-so-choice quotes in the record from one of the VCs that made it much easier for the court to find them conflicted. One particular VC stopped trying to spend any time with the company other than to show up for the acquisition-related board calls, told the CEO to get the M&A deal done quickly, and explicitly said that he'd rather be spending time on other potential upside companies. None of that is probably surprising, but note to self: you probably don't want that kind of stuff in the legal record when trying to defend yourself in court.

Let's pause for a second to digest this.

A ton of lawyers and legal practitioners have tried to ascertain what all this means, but I think the conservative reading of the case says that, if you are a VC board member who has liquidation preference (i.e., basically every VC) and you are selling the company for a price that is way out of the money (i.e., you are not going to convert into common, but instead take your liquidation preference), you should probably assume that you are conflicted. You may be able to make a bunch of arguments to show otherwise, but you don't want to be doing that in a courtroom after the deal has been closed. Rather, you'll want to make sure that you do all the right things while you are a sitting board member to increase the likelihood of keeping yourself clean.

Okay, we're not off to a very good start here, as we are three for three board members conflicted right out of the gate.

Let's look at the two people representing the common shareholders—the CEO and the president. The CEO received $2.3 million from the MIP, and the president received $1 million. So, at first blush, the court says they are potentially conflicted in that they received something from the acquisition that was not available to the other common shareholders. But, the court says, the real question is whether those benefits were material; getting them by itself doesn't automatically conflict them.

And how do we figure out materiality?

The court does a simple economic analysis. For the CEO, it turns out that the MIP payment represented about 20–50 percent of his net worth and was ten times the compensation he had been receiving in his CEO role. Those were sufficient to deem them material. For the president, the MIP payment represented about the same percentage of his net worth as was the case with the CEO, plus he was getting a job at the acquiring company that was very material to him. So the court said it was reasonable to think that his support of the deal could have been influenced by these material benefits.

Now we are five for five. The court could have stopped here (since we only needed to find four to get to a majority), but why stop when you are having fun? So we now look to the two independent directors.

What could possibly not be independent about the independent directors? Well, it turns out that one of the independents had a longtime relationship with one of the VCs who was on the board, having been an investor in the VC's fund (including the one that had Trados in its portfolio) as well as a CEO of two of the firm's portfolio companies. This independent director had also received shares in Trados through an acquisition of another company in which he was an investor, as was one of the conflicted VCs. The court looked at all this and concluded that all the relationships created a sense of owingness to this VC that could have compromised the independent director's independence. By the way, the plaintiff didn't bother challenging the independence of the second independent, so we did in fact have one out of seven that was truly independent.

We've talked about the takeaways here with respect to the VC directors, but we now have some more guidelines to follow stemming from this case.

First, if you have executives who are representing the common shareholders on the board and they get benefits from the deal that are material to them (e.g., as a percentage of their net worth) and not otherwise shared with the rest of the common, there is a pretty good presumption that they are conflicted.

Second, calling someone an independent doesn't make them so. Putting a buddy on the board who owes his career and well-being to you as an investor, portfolio company CEO, or serial board member can create conflicts. Of course, all these things are very fact specific, but you're now on notice that you need to do this factual analysis at the time you are thinking about a transaction to make sure you don't have a conflicted board.

Applying Entire Fairness

With the court having concluded that the board was indeed conflicted, the deference normally afforded the board under the business judgment rule no longer applied. So the court used the entire fairness standard to review the case. Recall that there are two elements to entire fairness: (1) fair process and (2) fair price.

On fair process, the court basically throws the book at the board. There are too many things to go through them all, but here are a few that the court noted.

First, the VCs were too interested in getting their money out versus trying to balance this with the interests of common. Examples of this that the court cited included that (1) the VCs were very involved in hiring and managing the bankers on the deal; (2) they kept the president on a short leash with respect to operational decisions in the company to maximize the M&A prospects; and (3) they rejected the CEO's financing proposals and purportedly brought him in just to sell the company.

Second, the court also objected to the handling of the MIP. Among other things, the court said that boards need to be very careful when the presence of the MIP itself takes away money from the common. Recall in this case that, without the MIP, common would have received $2.1 million—not much, but better than the zero they received. But, because the MIP essentially took common from something to nothing, the court got excited. In fact, the court noted that common contributed 100 percent of its proceeds ($2.1 million) to fund the MIP, whereas the preferred contributed only 10 percent of its proceeds (reducing its take from $57.9 million to

$52.5 million). The court didn't give us a bright-line rule here, but it did say that the board should have considered whether there was a more equitable way to fund the MIP.

And, finally, there were lots of other elements of the process that the court said evidenced a lack of fair dealing. For example, there was testimony from the board members themselves that they never really considered the interests of the common share-holders, and there was nothing in the official minutes of the board meetings to counter that assertion. The court also objected to elements of the voting process. In particular, the court noted that the president's participation in the MIP was increased (from 12 to 14 percent of the proceeds) during the course of the deal negotiations, and it appeared that this increase influenced his willingness to vote in favor of the deal. Maybe it wasn't a pure quid pro quo, but it looked and smelled a bit like it.

So we're down to the last piece—the only way to save the defendants is if the court determines that the price common received was fair. In other words, was the common in fact worth more than zero?

At the risk of spoiling the punch line, this is the part of the case that takes many people by surprise. If you actually read the full opinion and have gotten up to the point of the court's beginning to review the fairness of the price, you would have given 100 to 1 odds that the defendants are going to get crushed. Everything in this case up until this point feels as though the VCs in particular are going to have to come out of pocket and pay some of their winnings back to the common.

And then the clouds part and the sun starts shining again—for the VCs, that is.

We won't go through the full analysis, but the court reviews a bunch of expert testimony (each side of course has their own expert to testify about the value of the company) and ultimately concludes that the common got exactly what they deserved. That is, the company was pretty much worth zero before the acquisition, so the common got exactly what it was owed.

Here's the reasoning: Trados could not secure any additional funding (and the court reiterates the general proposition that the VCs have no obligation to put good money in after bad if they don't feel like doing so), thus it had no chance to be able to execute on its business plan. In the absence of being able to execute on the plan, Trados "did not have a realistic chance of generating a sufficient return to escape the gravitational pull of the large liquidation preference . . .".

Saved by the bell! After taking a pretty good tongue-lashing for the first three-quarters of the court's opinion, the defendants emerge victorious.

Now, before you start celebrating (depending on where your sympathies lie), everybody spent a ton of time and money on legal fees on this case, so there were real costs, notwithstanding the somewhat Pyrrhic victory for the defendants. And you as an entrepreneur or a VC don't want to hang your hat on the fair price part of this analysis; if you get to that point, the chances are pretty good that any given court on any given day could come to a different conclusion.

Trados Takeaways for the Rest of Us

So, what should you take away from *Trados* to help you best navigate the boardroom dynamics, particularly in a ho-hum acquisition scenario?

- It's probably a good starting assumption that most VC-backed startups do not have independent boards. The VCs (preferred) are likely conflicted by virtue of their liquidation preference and, if the common board members have material participation in a MIP, they, too, may be conflicted. And even independents may not in fact be independent.
- If you find yourself in that situation, you're probably best to assume therefore that the entire fairness test is going to be

applied to your situation. If so, you need to really pay careful attention to demonstrating a fair process and/or a fair price. As we'll mention in a minute, it's probably easier to get to a fair process than to rely on getting to a fair price.

- Given that, how do you ensure a good process? Here's a laundry list of things to consider—not all might be relevant for your situation, but the more you can incorporate, the better:

Hire bankers. Often, hiring a banker is a good way to run a comprehensive process of soliciting bids from multiple parties, understanding of course that sometimes it's not economically efficient to do so. If you can't do so, at least make sure that the company directly reaches out to a number of parties as part of the acquisition process. The other role of a banker (which really goes more to the fair price prong of the test) is to have a banker issue a fairness opinion. This is a financial analysis the banker presents to the board at the time of the deal opining that the financial terms of the transaction are within a band of reasonable prices. Utilizing a third party to do this (versus the board itself) is an important protectant for the board.

MIPs are often good tools to incent management, so we shouldn't conclude from *Trados* that you should avoid them. But if you do implement a MIP, be careful about making changes to it too close in time to the decision to vote on a pending deal. In the *Trados* case, the fact that the president might have received an increase in his MIP participation in order to vote for the deal raised a lot of concerns on the part of the court. The other thing to think about is the relative contribution to the MIP of common versus preferred. Again, recall in *Trados* that the court didn't like the fact that the common funded 100 percent of its proceeds into the MIP, whereas the VCs funded only 10 percent. There is no magic number here, but a better allocation (and in particular a discussion of this in the minutes) would have gone a long way toward helping make the process look better. If the VCs had carved out an additional $2 million from their proceeds (the amount that common would have received but for the MIP) to give to common, I suspect the case may have been much easier to decide in their favor.

Sometimes boards try to set up special committees to wall off conflicted board members and to give special consideration to the interests of common shareholders. As a practical matter, this is tough in many venture-backed company boards just given the likely conflicted nature of a number of the board directors. But where you have the ability to do this, special committees can provide great insulation from charges of self-dealing.

Another procedural mechanism to protect the board is to implement a separate vote of the disinterested common shareholders. Recall that in most cases, a majority vote of the common and a separate vote of the preferred are often sufficient to approve a deal. But voluntarily adding a separate vote of the most disenfranchised set of shareholders—the disinterested common—is a good way to ensure that they are comfortable with the transaction. Again, this can sometimes be hard to implement in practice, but worth considering nonetheless.

Although this may sound counterintuitive, often you want to be careful not to have the board members too overreaching in their engagement with the company around the acquisition. If you recall in *Trados*, one of the VCs selected the banker and was reportedly keeping the president on a short leash to make sure he was unilaterally pursuing the acquisition alternative. While this may have been helpful in getting to the outcome, too much entanglement can be viewed by the court as the board member's failing to consider the full range of potential options available to the company.

Most importantly—and really most simply—you need to demonstrate that the board understands the potential for conflicts, is taking the time to talk about them and their implications for common shareholders, and is looking for ways to mitigate the conflicts. The easiest way to start this is to have the company's lawyers come to a board meeting and basically walk the board through its fiduciary duties (or you could just assign all your board members to read this book). Once you do so, document it in the minutes so it's in the permanent record as having occurred. When you have board meetings, make sure you also talk about the common shareholders and what, if anything, you are doing to help them. At a minimum you need to show that you are not ignorant of the potential conflicts, even if you can't find ways to resolve them to your complete satisfaction.

CHAPTER 14

Difficult Financings:
When Bad Things Happen
to Good People

We spent a bunch of time in chapter 13 talking about the role of the board and its fiduciary duties surrounding an acquisition that reflected a very mediocre outcome for the company. While we of course hope that all startups can continue to raise capital at prices higher than they raised previously, sadly that is not always the case. Sorry to continue the buzzkill theme for a little while longer.

In this chapter, we are going to spend some time reviewing how to navigate difficult financings. As it turns out, the same fiduciary duty principles that we talked about in the acquisition context apply to the famously dreaded down-round financings.

As noted previously, a down round is what happens when a company raises funds at a lower valuation than the previous round. By the way, there are lots of flavors of down rounds. Sometimes we have a new investor who comes in to lead a round that is normal in most respects other than that the valuation is lower than the previous round. Other times we have a down round that is led by the existing investors in the company—and, as we'll talk about, this raises a lot of the core fiduciary duty questions from before.

Other times, we have what is called a recapitalization of the company (led by either a new investor or existing investors). A recapitalization not only often includes a much lower valuation than the company has previously raised at but also can include reductions in the liquidation preference and even reverse splits of the stock to reduce the equity ownership of existing investors.

We Are Where We Are, and Something Needs to Change

These difficult situations can, unfortunately, often be a part of the entrepreneurial process. Understandably so, founders oftentimes try to maintain a smiling face and look for other ways to finance the business. We've seen this many times at a16z. When the going gets tough, nobody starts the conversation with a recapitalization proposal; rather, the entrepreneur or the board often thinks first about providing what's called a bridge financing. Generally that means a cash infusion from the existing investors in the form of a convertible note or as an extension to the last round of financing (basically, just reopening the last round and having existing investors invest on those terms).

While each of these can seem like the easier path, they are often the wrong way to proceed because they don't really solve the underlying problem: for a variety of reasons, the business just did not develop the way in which the board and the founder had originally planned.

Perhaps the market developed more slowly than anticipated, the initial product missed the mark, thus causing the company to be in market with the correct product later than anticipated, the sales engine didn't materialize as expected, or the management team took too long to hire and get functional. Whatever the cause, it's smart to take a hard look at reality and say, "We are where we are, and something needs to change."

In nearly all these cases, the company has probably grown expenses beyond the level that it can rationally support at this stage. That's understandable in that the hiring plan anticipated a set of milestones that now appear further out than originally contemplated. As a result, kicking the can down the road by not taking the hard actions required to get the company back on a solid footing—including addressing the current cost structure alongside addressing the right capitalization structure—generally does not work.

What a down round or recapitalization does, when properly executed, is to reset the company and allow it to restart the journey toward success. It's painful, no doubt, for both the company and the existing investors, but if everyone still believes in the mission, this is the most likely path to success.

In the absence of doing so, the company may continue to move forward but is likely to face another challenge when seeking to raise its next round of financing. For when the time comes to raise additional capital, the new downstream investor is likely to feel that both the company valuation and the amount of liquidation preference are beyond the actual state of the business. And nothing can be more damaging to a business than having to reset once again after it is just starting to regain some of its momentum.

It is entirely possible to emerge successfully from a down round, but it is also entirely possible that, despite everyone's best efforts, the CEO and the board don't believe there is a viable path forward for the business and there are no acquisition alternatives. Sometimes the only remaining path is to wind down the company.

But let's not go there quite yet. Let's look first at other options. Remember, "Live to fight another day" is sometimes the right answer.

Reducing Liquidation Preferences

Let's talk first about the reduction or elimination of liquidation preferences.

We talked earlier about the auto-convert in a term sheet. This is the provision that governs the circumstances under which the preferred stock can be converted into common stock—either voluntarily or automatically. In the voluntary category, we noted that often the term sheet defines some level of voting threshold from either the capital "P" Preferred or the different series of preferred stock that are required to convert preferred shares into common. Among other things, the main reason to do this is to eliminate the liquidation preferences that the existing preferred has accumulated.

It may seem odd that VCs would ever voluntarily do this, but in the case where they believe in the prospects for the business but realize that the overhang of the current liquidation preferences may disincent the current employee team or make it unpalatable for a new investor to put money into the company, the potential for upside from their equity holdings may entice them to forgo their current preference.

In some cases, VCs will create an incentive for other existing investors to participate in the recapitalization by offering a mechanism called a "pull-up." There are lots of flavors of pull-ups, but the basic idea is to give a participating VC credit for the new dollars she is putting into the company by allowing her to pull up some of her old liquidation preference into the go-forward capitalization. In other words, instead of wiping out 100 percent of her liquidation preference, she can carry forward some portion of it as an inducement to invest in the new financing round.

In really difficult situations, the VCs may also agree to a reverse split of their existing stock holdings. That is, they convert their existing preferred into common, and then their ownership in the company is reduced by reverse splitting (maybe by as much as 10 to 1) their existing stock into an ownership percentage that is a fraction of what they own. Why would they do that? Well, similar to the liquidation preference situation, the VCs may want to give the company (and its employees) a fresh start by reducing the dilution they face in the wake of a new influx of capital at a low valuation and to attract outside capital into the company. This of course is a pretty extreme measure to undertake, so it does not happen very often.

As you might imagine, in situations like the ones we are discussing, it is often difficult to bring new, outside money into the company. As a result, down-round financings or recapitalizations, if they happen, are more often led by the existing VCs in the company.

This raises lots of the same fiduciary duty questions that we saw in the troubled M&A situation. The scenario tends to unfold as follows: the company is in trouble; there are no outside investors who want to inject capital into the business; the existing VCs decide that they want to give the company another shot but want to invest at a low valuation that reflects the true state of the company; and five years later the company turns out to be a smashing success and then the VCs (and the rest of the board) find themselves at the wrong end of a lawsuit from a disenfranchised, heavily diluted common shareholder who wants to challenge the validity of the original recapitalization. No good deed goes unpunished.

Learning from the *Bloodhound* Case

To prove to you that I don't just make this stuff up, let's look at one case in particular that highlights these issues. I decided on this one because it has such a great name—*Carsanaro v. Bloodhound Technologies* (let's call it *Bloodhound* for short).

Here are the facts.

The plaintiffs in this case are founders and early employees of a health-care company that goes through various rounds of financing, some of them led by existing VC investors. As is often the case, the company has a bit of a troubled history, but the existing investors keep funding the company, and somehow the company pulls through and ultimately gets sold for $82.5 million.

At first blush, that sounds like a decent outcome, but when you look beyond the surface, you see that our plaintiffs get only $36,000 from this acquisition (the common shareholders as a group got less than $100,000). The rest of the money went mostly to the preferred to satisfy their liquidation preference and to a $15 million MIP. Not surprisingly, the plaintiffs sue the company and the board, alleging that the various dilutive financings that happened along the way violated the board's fiduciary duties to the common shareholders.

As did the court in Trados, the Bloodhound court analyzed the various board members to determine whether the majority of the board was conflicted or disinterested. As we saw before, the VC directors who also participated in many of the inside financings were deemed to be conflicted. And in two of the inside financings, the then-sitting CEO was awarded a significant option grant contemporaneous with the financings.

On the one hand, this doesn't seem too crazy; the CEO is going to be heavily diluted by the down-round financing, so it's not unusual for the VCs to want to reincent the CEO by giving him more options. On the other hand, the proximity of the option grant to the approval of the financing round raises questions about the independence of the CEO board member. And that's what the court was bothered by: there was at least an appearance that the board member's vote was essentially bought in exchange for the option grant. Those optics aren't good.

Having concluded that a majority of the board was conflicted, the Bloodhound court then proceeded to evaluate the transaction under the two-pronged entire fairness standard—fair process and fair price.

The court was not happy with the process. Among the things the court cited were that

- the board failed to do a market check—meaning that they agreed on the terms for the insider-led financings without having really canvassed outside investors to see if they were interested in bidding for the deal;

- the board needed the consent of a majority of the common stock to approve the financings, yet engaged in some shenanigans to fudge this. In one case, the board didn't provide full information on the transaction to a key common shareholder and, more generally, the board didn't provide full disclosure of certain elements of the transaction to other common shareholders;
- the board failed to update the terms of the financing transactions in light of improved company financial performance; and
- the terms were not approved by a majority of the disinterested board members.

So what should we take away from *Bloodhound* as it relates to the proper process a board could go through in a down round or recapitalization situation? Below are a few things to keep in mind:

- It's really important to do a market check and run a full process with outside investors. You may think that no one else will ever touch the financing given the company's performance to date, but best practices suggest that you need to canvass your options. It's a good thing to get noes from a lot of potential investors before you proceed with an inside-led round. This shows that you were not trying to hoard the opportunity for yourself but rather reacting to a true lack of market interest. If you can hire a banker to run this process, even better.
- Be careful not to entangle new option grants to employees too closely with the inside financing. It's customary to want to re-incent the team, but doing so after the financing closes (versus before) and employing a compensation consultant to gauge the size of an appropriate grant would help eliminate any suspicion that an executive board member's vote was contingent upon her receiving a new option grant.
- Give other investors (and particularly major common shareholders) the opportunity to participate in the deal. We call this a rights offering, and the basic idea is to give everyone on the capitalization table the right to participate pro rata in the deal

on the same terms. You'll find in practice that most people will turn down this offer, but the fact of offering it to them is a very good prophylactic against future litigation.

- Implement a go-shop provision in the insider financing round. Recall that we talked about no-shops in chapter 10. A no-shop prohibits the company from taking your term sheet and showing it to others to induce them to potentially bid with better terms. A go-shop is exactly the opposite. It specifically allows the company to shop your term sheet to other potential investors and is often used in insider-led rounds. This is the proactive version of a market check. Give the company the proposed terms and let them see if any outsider is willing to match or beat those terms.

- As was the case in the acquisition context, to the extent you can get approval of the deal from a majority of the disinterested directors, or you can get approval from the disenfranchised common shareholders, these will be very helpful. Understandably, sometimes the board composition or shareholder dynamics make this impractical.

Finally, make sure the minutes of the board meetings reflect the board's understanding of the potential conflict of an insider round and demonstrate an attempt to take into account the interest of the common shareholders. Get the company's lawyers to reeducate board members on fiduciary duties and reflect the deliberations in the official minutes of the board meetings.

Success after a Down Round

While a down round is no doubt challenging, it's not the end of the world! There are ways to set the company up for success, assuming you do in fact raise new capital. After all, if you are going to go through all the pain of the down round or recapitalization process, it would be a real shame to come out the other end without a clear plan for achieving success.

Naturally, one very important point of consideration should be how you and your team will be properly incented to continue maximizing the value of the business after the financing round. There are a few ways to achieve this.

First, as noted above, hopefully the existing VCs have considered some form of reduction in the total liquidation preferences. It may not be realistic for them to give up all their preferences, but many forward-looking VCs will recognize that some reduction is required to align incentives properly for the management team and employee base. There is no magic number to solve for here, but you should have a discussion with your existing VCs about the range of reasonable near-term exit valuations that the company might achieve and size the remaining liquidation preferences appropriately to give the common shareholders at least a shot at earning some return on their equity.

Second, because the issuance of new shares at a lower price will dilute the existing management and employee holdings, you may want to consider increasing the option pool and providing for new grants to the remaining employees. Oftentimes, in connection with a recapitalization, the company has to reduce its employee base (because the company may need to be rightsized for the state of the business and to achieve a lower cash consumption target). As a result, you may have some employees exiting the business with stock options that are well out of the money, meaning that the exercise price of those options substantially exceeds the current value of the shares. Most departing employees will not, therefore, choose to exercise those options, at least not at that time. If your options permit them to be exercised for years to come post-termination of an employee, they may very well remain outstanding for that amount of time. If, however, those departing employees choose not to exercise their options, they will come back into the pool and be available for the company to regrant to those employees who are part of the go-forward business. I realize of course that it's no fun to be having these discussions about options essentially being forfeited by employees who are no longer part of the company, but this does in fact often happen in these situations.

In addition, though, it is often reasonable for the board to also increase the size of the option pool on its own to create a greater ability on the part of the company to reincent its remaining employees with new options. Recall that, as we discussed earlier, increasing the option pool is not free; it means that everyone of course has her ownership diluted in proportion to the size of the increase. But by allocating new options to the remaining employees, the company can more than offset this dilution in the form of the additional stock grant. The investors, therefore, will bear the brunt of the dilution, but again if they believe in the go-forward plan for the business, they will often agree to this as a means of properly aligning economic incentives.

A final mechanism to consider in this circumstance is the implementation of a management incentive plan (MIP). We first talked about this with Trados, and, as that case showed, there are certain legal considerations to be mindful of when considering a MIP. Nonetheless, a MIP is often implemented in recapitalization or down-round scenarios in which a near-term sale of the business is being contemplated.

There are many ways to structure a MIP, but essentially think of the MIP as a mechanism by which the investors with liquidation preference agree to make some amount of the acquisition proceeds available first to defined employees in the company, before they take their liquidation preference. In general, the amount of a MIP ranges from 8 to 12 percent of the purchase price of the acquisition, and the beneficiaries of the MIP are agreed upon by the board. These beneficiaries are typically those employees who are most critical to getting the acquisition completed.

The other element you commonly see in a MIP is a prohibition against double-dipping. This means that, if it turns out that the acquisition price is higher than anticipated and thus the common shareholders do in fact get to participate in the acquisition proceeds, the MIP proceeds will be reduced dollar for dollar. The rationale for this is that the purpose in implementing the MIP was to incent employees who otherwise wouldn't receive any acquisition proceeds because of the presence of the liquidation preference, so if that turns out not to be the case, we no longer need the MIP.

Operationally, the payout for a MIP follows the same payout of the acquisition proceeds. So, for example, if all the acquisition proceeds are paid out to investors immediately on closing of the transaction, the MIP proceeds will also be paid out then. If, however, some of the proceeds are withheld until a future date—we'll talk later about this concept when we cover escrows in the mergers and acquisition section—then the MIP payout will follow accordingly. The form of payout will also be the same as that paid to other shareholders—cash, stock, or a mixture of the two.

If, however, the board views the recapitalization as a fresh start for the business to try to execute on a stand-alone path, a MIP can actually create the wrong incentives. In such a case, the MIP could provide the management team (or whoever are the beneficiaries of the MIP) a short-term incentive to sell the company versus playing for the longer term. For example, if you as CEO could receive a $2 million payment through the MIP by selling the company in the short term, you might orient your time toward that path, even though you might stand to earn a lot more money if the company remains stand-alone and ultimately goes public five years hence. Perhaps you think the risk of that latter path is too great, such that less money now with certainty seems more attractive. Thus, you and the board should carefully consider what behavior you are trying to incent.

The bottom line in these situations is to ensure that the company is set up for whatever appropriate path the board and the employee base are heading down. If we all agree to play for a home run, then maximizing the long-term equity incentives of everyone involved is the right play. If we are just viewing this new financing as a short-term bridge to an acquisition, the MIP may make more sense.

Winding Down

Sometimes, despite everyone's best efforts, the CEO and the board just don't see a viable path forward for the business, and there are no acquisition options. At this point, the only remaining path is to wind down the company.

If you find yourself in this situation, there are a few important things to consider as an executive or director.

First, depending on the number of employees that you have, you may need to consider something called the WARN Act. There are both state and federal WARN statutes: the federal law applies to companies with more than one hundred employees, whereas some states (including California) apply the rule to companies with only fifty employees. While WARN was originally intended to deal with mass layoffs, particularly in manufacturing companies, WARN is applicable to any company at those employee levels that is planning to shut down and therefore lay off all its employees. In these circumstances, WARN requires that you provide these employees sixty days' notice of such a shutdown, and, in the event you fail to do so, a company can have liability for up to sixty days' worth of wages for those employees. While the law is not completely settled here, it is unlikely that individual board members and executives would have personal liability (beyond the liability for the corporation) for WARN violations.

There is an exception to WARN liability under what is called the "faltering company exception." This gives a company more latitude around the sixty-day WARN notice requirement if the company is actively pursuing financing for the business and believes that providing notice would significantly jeopardize the likelihood of being able to obtain that financing. For example, if you were worried that providing the notice would cause all your engineers to leave the company, and this exodus of employees would dissuade a potential investor from injecting capital into the business, you may be able to utilize the faltering company exception. Doing so of course requires a legitimate capital-raising process that the company reasonably believes could result in an investment. So startups that find themselves in this situation will want to keep an active log reflecting all the financing outreach they are undergoing, and the board minutes should reflect all these activities appropriately.

Another thing to consider in this situation is potential liability for employee wages and accrued vacation. The general rule here is that you cannot keep employees working beyond the point at which you can pay payroll—seems pretty straightforward. For example, if you have $100,000 in the company bank account and your daily payroll exceeds this amount, you cannot keep employees on the books, even if you still have two weeks before the next official payroll cycle and think you might be able to raise new capital before then. If you do so and fail to raise the money, officers and directors could have *personal* liability to pay these expenses. Note, this is different from potential WARN liability, which likely attaches to the corporation only; in direct employee wages, compensation may have to come directly out of the officers' and directors' own pockets.

A second area of potential personal liability is accrued vacation. Let's say your company has a two-week annual paid vacation policy. Employees accrue (or earn) this vacation as they work during the year—for example, if we are now halfway through the year, employees will have accrued one week's worth of that vacation. That accrual has an economic cost to the company equal to the employees' wages that they would otherwise get paid for that one week. Once this vacation is earned, it belongs to the employee and is now a liability of the company. This is why, for example, if you quit your job, in addition to your final paycheck, your employer will typically pay you an additional amount of money equal to your accrued vacation.

In the shutdown context, accrued vacation therefore is another expense for which officers and directors can have personal liability. And this number can get pretty big if you are not keeping an eye on it. Some companies, for example, allow employees to carry over from one year to the next accrued vacation time that they may not have used in any given year. So an employee with long tenure who hasn't been using all her vacation each year can have a sizable accrued vacation expense on the company's books. To avoid this, many companies have a use-it-or-lose-it vacation policy, which wipes the vacation liability off the books at the end of each year, so that in any given year, no more than two weeks' worth of vacation liability will be present.

As a result of these potential liabilities, startups that find themselves in a potential wind-down situation will want to review these topics with the board regularly and ensure that they don't accidentally find themselves on the losing end of both the company's dissolving and former employees' seeking personal liability for employment-related expenses. As we noted earlier in the book, this is another place where being diligent about documenting board meeting notes to reflect the board's diligence can pay huge dividends.

What happens to other expenses that the company may have taken on for which it doesn't have the money to pay? For example, what about expenses owed to manufacturers who may be developing the product or to other outside contractors who are performing some work for the company? The good news—at least for the officers and directors—is that these entities are generally treated as unsecured trade creditors in a wind-down situation. This is a fancy way of saying that they are largely screwed. They need to line up along with anyone else who is owed money by the now-defunct company and see if there are any remaining scraps from which they can be paid.

The one significant exception to this is when the company acts in bad faith with respect to these creditors. For example, if you know that a wind down is inevitable, but you still choose to enter into a new contract with a vendor knowing that there is no way to ever pay them, the vendor might have a claim that you acted in bad faith and therefore sue you for liability. These claims are pretty hard for them to ultimately win, but, as we talked about earlier in the *Trados* discussion, you don't want to tempt fate here, nor do you want to spend a bunch of time and money fighting legal claims post–wind down.

In addition to raising equity, many startups these days also raise some form of debt. We are not talking here about convertible debt that is most commonly used during seed financing rounds, but rather debt that comes from a commercial bank or a specialized debt provider. Most debt is cheaper than equity, mainly because it doesn't involve issuing more shares (which we all hope in the startup case are ultimately worth a lot of money). As a result, many startups choose to supplement their equity raises with some amount of bank debt.

Thus, in the wind-down context, we also need to think about debtors, different from how we think about the equity holders. That is because the equity holders know that they are the lowest on the repayment totem pole in the event of a wind down; they will generally get nothing and understand that as part of the original bargain they made when they purchased the equity. Debt holders, however, are higher on the totem pole and thus are generally first in line to collect any remaining money a company may have. They are not only ahead of equity holders, but also ahead of the unsecured trade creditors we talked about before (who are themselves ahead of the equity holders).

Importantly, though, the board does not owe fiduciary duties to the debt holders. Thus, even when the company is facing the situation where they might need to wind down, the board's fiduciary duties still run only to the equity holders. In practice, though, boards will take extra care in these situations to maintain constant communication with the debt holders and try to make every effort to pay back at least part of the debt in connection with a wind down.

CHAPTER 15

Exit Stage Left
(The Good Kind)

If you just read chapter 14, you're probably in need of a big breath of fresh air and positivity. Here it is on a silver platter, and it comes in the form of a successful realization of the entrepreneurial life cycle.

Let's fast-forward your startup to success and imagine that you are starting to think about exiting. This time, we are talking about good exits, as opposed to the not-so-exciting last-ditch acquisition alternatives we reviewed in the previous chapters.

Venture-backed companies often exit either through an acquisition by another company or via an IPO. We are using the term "exit" somewhat euphemistically here in that, in the case of an IPO, the company itself is not exiting anything (in fact it's entering a new chapter of its life as a public company), but oftentimes the VCs are exiting their ownership positions in the company. They have achieved what they set out to do: invest in the early stage of a company and grow the equity value of their investment to the point where they can return capital to their LPs. This is a VC exit.

We'll go through the IPO exit more in this chapter, but we will also address another and more common type of exit: the acquisition, where another company purchases yours.

Getting to Know You

Before we jump in to some high-level discussion of acquisition terms and considerations, let's walk it back a bit first. One important consideration for all startups—whether you intend to remain stand-alone or may one day seek to be acquired—is to spend time understanding who your likely eventual acquirers might be and finding ways to engage with them. This notion often sounds counterintuitive to many strong entrepreneurs. They wonder, Why would I want to tip a potential competitor or acquirer off to what I am doing by proactively reaching out to them?

Well, it goes without saying that you don't need to expose any of these players to your core intellectual property, trade secrets, or detailed road maps. But that being said, building relationships is important nonetheless—and you can choose to disclose whatever level of information with which you are comfortable. Even if you are not interested in an acquisition, these companies may often be good business development partners as they likely have existing sales channels into some of the markets you are planning to enter. Some of the best acquisitions often stem from relationships that begin as business development partnerships.

Most importantly, companies get bought, not sold. That is, it's very difficult to wake up one day and decide you want to sell your company and assume that you can just call up a bunch of potential suitors and have them champing at the bit to acquire you. Sometimes that indeed happens, but the far better strategy is to have potential acquirers solicit your interest in being acquired. When any of your potential acquirers decides it's time for them to think about making an acquisition in your space, you want to be on the list of potential candidates. It's a bit like the high school dance—you want to be invited to the dance (hopefully by more than one suitor), even if you ultimately decide not to go. But not receiving the invite can be painful.

Acquisitions and Key Terms

We're discussing acquisitions first, because that is the predominant form of exit in the VC world. There was a time—most of the first twenty to thirty years of the history of venture capital—where exits were fairly evenly distributed between acquisitions and IPOs. But as we discussed earlier in the book, starting in the late 1990s (excepting, of course, the dot-com bubble of 1999 and 2000), the number of IPOs started to decline fairly precipitously. As a result, if you look at VC exits today, more than 80 percent come via acquisition, a far cry from the fifty-fifty split between acquisitions and IPOs that dominated most of VC history.

Let's cover some of the important terms that boards often consider when evaluating an acquisition offer.

Not surprisingly, price often tops the list. But price alone is not the only thing to think about. Often the form of consideration can influence the board's view of the price. For example, if the acquirer is proposing to exchange its shares for the shares of the acquired company, then the board will want to undertake a valuation analysis of the buyer's shares—are they overpriced, underpriced, or fairly valued?

To deal with the fact that it often takes time between the announcement of a transaction and the final closing, boards may ask for some price protection in the event that the acquirer's stock price moves meaningfully in that interim period. There are various ways to do this, but a common one is to create a "collar"—essentially, you create a reasonable upper and lower bound of stock price movement and, as long as the stock stays in those bounds, the price doesn't change, but any movements beyond that are accounted for. This is the pricing equivalent of an insurance policy; you look to cover extreme moves in either direction.

Another aspect to consider in terms of a stock acquisition is whether the stock the acquired company receives is freely tradable. Assuming that the acquirer is a public company, one would hope that if she received stock in that company, she could sell it immediately to lock in her proceeds. Sometimes, however, if the amount of stock is material, the acquirer may not register the acquisition stock immediately, thus requiring that the recipients of its stock sit on it for some period of time. Obviously, this introduces market risk to the acquired company's shareholders.

Importantly to employees of the acquired company, how are employee options affected in the case of an acquisition? In particular, what if you are only two years into the vesting of your options and the company decides to sell itself? There are a number of possibilities that should be outlined in your stock option plan, so let's go through each of them:

Scenario 1. Your unvested options get assumed by the acquirer. This means that, if you are given the opportunity to stay with the acquirer and choose to do so, your options continue to vest on the same schedule (albeit as part of the equity of the acquirer). Seems reasonable, unless you decide this wasn't what you signed up for, don't want to work for the new employer, and quit. In that case, you would forfeit the opportunity to vest the remaining two years of your option grant.

Scenario 2. Your unvested options get canceled by the acquirer and you get a new set of options with new terms (assuming of course you decide to stay with the acquirer). The theory behind this is that the acquirer wants to reincent the potential new employees or bring new employees in line with its overall compensation philosophy. Again, seems reasonable, though of course it's a different plan than the one you originally agreed to.

Scenario 3. Your unvested options get accelerated, meaning that they automatically become vested as if you already satisfied your remaining two years of service. We talked about this earlier in the vesting section of the term sheet and noted that there are often single- or double-trigger acceleration provisions in options granted to executives. Not surprisingly, acquirers don't like single triggers, because they at least want the option to retain good talent without having to give them wholly new option grants. Double triggers help address the concern about single triggers (which are rare) by giving the acquirer a chance to hold on to strong talent. Still, it is very unusual for most employees to have either of the above forms of acceleration. Those are typically reserved for senior executives where it's highly likely in an acquisition scenario that they won't or can't be offered jobs at the acquirer—for example, you can't have two CFOs for a single company—and thus won't even have a chance to vest out their remaining shares.

The broader employee issue consideration is which employees of the acquired company are considered critical to the go-forward business. Often you will have an acquirer put together a list of key employees that it wants to retain (and often as part of this there may be some material amount of financial incentive in the form of equity grants to those individuals from the acquirer) and what percentage of those employees are required to in fact come over to the acquirer as part of the deal.

You can imagine that this sometimes creates potential holdout issues—i.e., if I know I am on that list, do I ask for some additional consideration in exchange for agreeing to join the acquirer? As such, the selling company wants to keep the required acceptance rate as low as possible, whereas the acquirer wants to get as many as possible of those whom it considers to be the key employees to come over.

To get to the desired outcome, the acquirer will create a closing condition (meaning that it doesn't have an obligation to close the acquisition until the condition is met) that requires some agreed-upon percentage of the key employees to have accepted their offers of employment to work at the acquirer. There is no magic number here, as it depends greatly on whether the main reason for the acquisition is to get access to the talent, or if there is a more general ongoing business that the acquirer is trying to get hold of.

Speaking of closing conditions, another important one in most deals is the set of voting approvals the seller is required to get. We've talked before about protective provisions and which votes are in fact required for a deal. Although most companies will require only a majority of common and preferred (voting as separate classes, meaning that a majority of each group needs to approve the transaction) to vote in favor of a deal, acquirers will often demand a higher threshold. By the way, this is also where drag-along provisions come into play; they are a handy mechanism to force at least a subset of often larger investors to vote in favor of a deal even if they are not thrilled about it. Acquirers will often want to see at least 90 percent of the shareholders vote in favor of a deal; the main purpose here is to reduce the surface area of potential shareholders who may ultimately object to the deal and potentially seek legal redress.

In most acquisition scenarios, the buyer doesn't pay the full purchase price up front. Rather, it puts some percentage of the purchase price into an escrow account (this just means an account that is managed by a third party) to cover potential surprises it may discover after the deal closes. Escrow sizes vary but are often between 10 and 15 percent of the purchase price. The term of the escrow account also varies, but is often between twelve and eighteen months post-closing. The types of contingencies that the escrow is intended to cover often include, among others: (1) basic representations from the company (e.g., its share count is accurate); (2) any litigation that might arise after closing relating to something the company did before closing; and (3) ownership and any potential claims against intellectual property.

There are x-number of bells and whistles that can apply to the escrow. Sometimes, for example, the acquiring company agrees to a minimum dollar threshold below which it will eat the costs and not access the escrow. Other times, if the dollar threshold is exceeded, the acquirer will hold back the full amount of the claim, or it may only hold back the amount in excess of the threshold. Sometimes, the escrow amount is the only remedy that an acquirer has for breaches of the agreement; other times the acquirer can sue the company to recover amounts in excess of the escrow. And, finally, the time frames may vary by type of claim. Some claims, for example, that arise after the twelve-to-eighteen-month escrow period are simply irrelevant, whereas others (sometimes intellectual property claims) may survive beyond the escrow period.

Another big-picture economic item—and, trust me, we have glossed over a lot of issues that practitioners in the field spend a lot of time on—deals with our favorite topic: indemnification. In general, the buyer wants the selling company to indemnify it from any number of claims that may arise post-closing. The escrow is of course intended to be the first line of defense for such claims, but buyers often look for more protection.

The big negotiations in this area tend to center on a few areas.

First, which claims can be covered beyond the escrow account? That is, if a third party brings a big intellectual property claim and it has a damage amount greater than the escrow, can the acquirer get that excess money back from the sellers? If there is a limit on the recovery, is it capped by the purchase price of the acquisition, or can sellers be on the hook for even greater amounts? And, finally, can individual members of the selling group potentially be on the hook for liabilities that other members of the selling group either don't have the money to pay or otherwise refuse to pay? In other words, can one seller be forced to pay more than her pro rata share of the damages, or is she responsible only up to her pro rata amount?

Finally, let's mention exclusivity periods. Recall that we talked about no-shops in chapter 10, which essentially prevent a startup from shopping a term sheet with other potential investors for some reasonable period of time (often fifteen to thirty days) for the purpose of allowing the investor who has proposed the deal time to finish due diligence and complete legal docs.

The same concept exists in acquisition, and goes by the term "exclusivity period." This is the time between signing of the term sheet and (hopefully) closing of the transaction during which the seller is engaged to the buyer. The form of that engagement generally means that they can't shop the term sheet to other buyers, nor can they solicit interest from other potential buyers. Not surprisingly, buyers want this period to last as long as possible, but for many startup deals, the time frame should really be gauged by the amount of remaining due diligence and legal documentation time required. Thus, thirty to sixty days tends to be the reasonable range of exclusivity period for such acquisitions.

Acquisitions: Board Responsibilities

What does a board have to do when considering an acquisition offer?

Recall that we talked about the business judgment rule as the default form of review of corporate actions, and entire fairness in the case where you have a conflicted board. There is an intermediate legal standard in the case of normal acquisition transactions. For the sake of clarity, note that we are talking here about situations where you don't have a conflicted board and are considering what we like to think about as a good acquisition transaction.

The responsibilities of the board in this circumstance are generally referred to as "Revlon duties," named after the Revlon legal case that codified the standard of review for acquisition-related activities. (There was a case subsequent to Revlon called Paramount that further clarified the board's duties; nonetheless, most people still refer to Revlon as the moniker for board acquisition duties.)

In short, Revlon says that, while the board has no obligation to sell the company, if the board decides to proceed down that path, it must seek to maximize the value of the common stock. This means that the board must act in good faith to get the best price reasonably available (and explore all reasonable options to get the best price). And the courts are permitted to retrospectively review both the board process and the reasonableness of the price in determining whether the board satisfied its Revlon duties.

These duties apply in most acquisition scenarios where, as the courts have said, there is no tomorrow for the common shareholders. That is, this is the last chance for the common to enjoy the economic value of its holdings, so the board should do what they can to get the best price reasonably available. Thus, the time-based focus of the board shifts from maximizing the long-term value of the common shareholders to focusing on maximizing the short-term value via the transaction. This is often thought of as an intermediate level of review between the business judgment rule and the entire fairness standard that we reviewed previously.

As we covered in the previous sections, the process matters here.

To satisfy *Revlon* duties, boards should: (1) run a broad outreach to multiple potential acquirers, with the help of bankers where possible; (2) consider other possible paths forward (e.g., is there a financing alternative whereby the company remains a stand-alone entity to maximizes shareholder value?); (3) consider incorporating a go-shop provision into an offer they receive from an acquirer to permit other competing bids to surface; and (4) document a well-vetted process that shows the board considered all available possibilities to maximize shareholder value.

The board is not obligated in all cases to take the highest price; it just has to reasonably maximize shareholder value. So, for example, the board can take a slightly lower offer if it feels that the offer is more likely to close or the form of consideration (stock versus cash) is more favorable. Ultimately, the processes of negotiating with the buyer and evaluating the various alternatives are likely to be sufficient as long as the price is within a range of reasonable prices.

There is much more to cover here in the acquisition context—and this is the reason why M&A agreements often run into the hundreds of pages—but we've covered some of the high-level considerations.

Obviously, an acquisition can be a great validation of what you—as an entrepreneur—have tirelessly built over the years.

Sometimes, it's an opportunity to keep building and realizing your product vision, albeit with a new set of owners and colleagues. Other times, it may be the end of a chapter and the opportunity to either take a break or begin anew the startup process.

Amid all the excitement of the deal, what should you as CEO be thinking about in the M&A context?

First, your employees. As noted above, you'll be asked to help the acquirer figure out which employees are going to be part of the go-forward team and which, unfortunately, may need to look for new opportunities. For those who are staying, part of your job will be to make sure they are properly incented financially and organizationally to help deliver whatever the acquirer is seeking to achieve from the deal. Key to this will be understanding—and potentially influencing—the organizational structure that the acquirer is contemplating post-acquisition: Will your team get folded intact into an existing organization, will the team get distributed across various functional organizations in the company, or will the business be run as a separate entity (with or without you as the leader)? Depending on the answers to these questions, the acquirer will be looking to you not only to help place employees in the best spot but also to help make sure that the employees are excited and well prepared to execute on the business plan.

For those employees who may not have an opportunity to come along as part of the acquisition, you of course want to make sure they exit the business with the same level of respect and appreciation for their accomplishments as when you first welcomed them onto the team. As noted above, hopefully these employees are able to at least enjoy the financial benefits of the acquisition while they go on to new adventures. Regardless, the startup community is a small one, and many people are repeat players in the ecosystem, so your reputation will be earned—and remembered—based upon how you treat departing employees.

Once all those issues are sorted, then it's time for you to finally think about yourself. If you are a critical part of the post-acquisition organization, you should expect to spend a lot of time with the acquirer, planning for what things will look like post-acquisition. You will of course have had a number of conversations with the acquirer during the pre-deal phase, but the hard work of integration remains.

Overview of the IPO

Let's move on to the IPO, the other major form of exit for a venture-backed company.

Although you wouldn't know it from the current trends, the IPO was once the most sought-after prize for venture-backed startups. From 1980 to 2015, the median time to IPO for a venture-backed company was about seven years; since 2010, though, that has increased to more than ten years. There are lots of reasons for this— we mentioned a few earlier in the book.

Putting aside the reasons why more companies are choosing not to go public, let's focus for a second on why companies do in fact go public.

- **Raising capital**—This is an obvious one, but interestingly has declined in importance over the years as a major driver for companies to go public. It used to be that companies needed to go public because the private market tapped out pretty quickly when you started to contemplate raising $100 million-plus financing rounds. Now those are a dime a dozen, and we see some companies raising billions of dollars in the private marketplace—e.g., Uber, Lyft, Airbnb, and Pinterest, among others. There's an ongoing chicken-and-egg debate about what created this—did the big financial players start investing in the private markets because startups were delaying going public, or did startups start delaying going public because they could raise huge sums of money in the private markets? It's not worth debating here, other than to note that the attraction of the public markets as an important source of large capital raises is clearly diminished.

- **Branding**—There also once was a time when startups were not on the front page of every news source and not followed by popular, dedicated technology reporters. As a result, for many companies, an IPO was an important public branding event— an opportunity for them to tell their story directly to their customers and to the broader financial community, helping drive new business along the way. Today, who hasn't stayed in an Airbnb, taken a ride with Lyft, or pinned on Pinterest? And if you haven't personally done these things, you have certainly read about them in the popular press, even if you live outside of Silicon Valley. So, strike number two against going public is there; the branding value of the coming-out event just simply isn't as needed as it once was.

- **Liquidity**—Finally, a partial check in favor of this one. Even employees who have stock options (and, of course, investors) and love their company will ultimately want some ability to convert their appreciated investments into cash. As we mentioned before, to sell your stock, it either has to be registered (for which the IPO process is an important first step) or you have to have some other exemption from registration. Thus, selling your stock in the private markets is far more challenging than just hitting the SELL button from your Schwab account once the company has gone public. In most cases, if you want to sell your private stock, you need to find a third-party buyer (who is sophisticated enough to legally purchase your shares) and, at a minimum, get the participation of the company whose shares you are trying to sell to effect the transaction. As we noted earlier, sometimes as an employee you may not even have the right to sell the stock—for example, if you have a blanket transfer restriction on your shares. And, in cases where that doesn't exist, you might be bound by a right of first refusal, which you'll recall might prevent buyers from engaging, since they know that the company could ultimately usurp them by buying the shares itself. In some startups today, the companies are offering partial liquidity to employees through the form of tender offers. This is a structured sale often organized by the company in which the employee is allowed to sell some portion of her shares to an approved set of buyers at periodic intervals, maybe once per year. It helps release the pressure valve a bit for employees, but doesn't go all the way toward providing a liquid market for broader stock sales. Thus, an IPO still has real value in achieving the liquidity goal.

- **Customer credibility**—This one is particularly relevant for companies that sell critical technologies to other companies (i.e., B2B). In some cases, the potential customer who may be contemplating a purchase of a network security device wants to know that the startup is going to be around for a while and not go bankrupt tomorrow and leave the customer high and dry. Thus, being a public company and having transparent financials for your customers to review can sometimes remove an impediment to the sales process. Of course, private companies can also share their financials with potential customers (and being a public company in and of itself doesn't mean that you can't go bankrupt), but the financial discipline and visibility associated with being a public company can often be helpful in B2B selling.

- **M&A currency**—Technology companies build products. Those products have product cycles that hopefully go up and to the right for a long time. However, as with all things, what goes up often comes down, and a product's growth when it gets to the end of a product cycle is no different. Thus, to maintain growth, technology companies need to either build or acquire new products to ride the wave of another product cycle. Acquisitions do tend to be an important part of that strategy for technology companies and, while companies can of course make acquisitions while they are still private, it's easier to do so when you have a public currency. Why? Because the stock market gives you a daily report card in the form of your stock price to tell the seller exactly what your stock is worth if the acquirer is proposing to use it as currency for an acquisition. In the private world, because of the discontinuous nature of private financings, there's always a healthy debate about how to value the stock on any given day.

The IPO Process

Assuming a startup does in fact decide to go public, the process is a well-worn and highly orchestrated one.

It starts with picking the investment banks, otherwise known as the underwriters. This process is often euphemistically called the "beauty contest" or "bake-off," as it involves various banks pitching their wares to the startup.

There are several important factors that a startup might consider in picking a bank. First, their domain expertise in the industry, including who the research analyst is who is likely to publish research on the company post-IPO. (Research analysts generally work for investment banks and interact frequently with institutional investors who may be buying or selling a public stock. Some of that interaction comes in the form of published research reports that lay out their thesis on the stock, including its potential for generating financial returns to shareholders. For a newly public company, research analysts are even more important, as they help educate the institutional investors, particularly in the early days post-IPO where the company is not yet well known.) Second, their relationships with institutional investors who could be buyers of the IPO (and, in some cases, relationships with retail investors). Third, the strength of the banks' sales and trading desks to not only place the stock at the IPO with institutional investors but also help create an orderly trading environment, particularly in the first few weeks following the IPO. And, finally, their capabilities post-IPO to be able to help with M&A advice, follow-on financings, debt issuances, and other capital markets issues. And, of course, relationships factor in a lot; many bankers are picked on the basis of having cultivated the board and CEO relationships for a long time prior to the bake-off.

Once the banks are picked (and, by the way, there tends to be a lead underwriter and several co-underwriters on the overall team), the company will often host a kickoff meeting with the banks. The meeting's purpose is exactly as the name suggests— to kick off the process by presenting the company's products, strategy, go-to-market, and financial information. The idea is to help educate the bankers on the nuances of the business so they can both advise the company and begin to think about how they will market the company during the IPO.

The biggest labor component of an IPO tends to be the process of drafting the prospectus. This is a highly formalistic legal document that is mostly intended to provide all the relevant disclosures required by prospective investors. It provides some narrative about the company, but most of the pages are filled with detailed financial disclosures and a litany of all the risks that investors are taking on should they elect to buy the stock. It's not intended to be a marketing document but is really designed to disclose information and risks and, ultimately, to provide legal protection for the company and its board should something go awry once the company is public. In that case, you hope that the prospectus highlighted the risk that ultimately befalls the company! If not, expect to be on the receiving end of a class action lawsuit from those investors who purchased the stock in reliance on the prospectus.

Congress passed the JOBS Act in 2012 to try to streamline both the information requirements of the prospectus and other components of the process of going public. To qualify for filing an IPO under the JOBS Act, a company needs to be an "emerging growth company, or EGC." An EGC is a company that has less than $1 billion in revenue in its most recent fiscal year. As a result, most venture-backed startups qualify as EGCs.

The benefits of being an EGC are numerous.

- **Testing the waters**—An EGC is allowed to meet with potential investors (as long as the investors meet certain asset size requirements) as a mechanism to get feedback and to build the relationship ahead of the IPO. This is really valuable since, in the absence of doing this, companies get to spend typically one hour only with an institutional investor during the course of the sales meetings surrounding the IPO itself. The full set of IPO-related sales meetings is called the road show, as it is usually entails a seven-to-ten-day set of meetings with investors in various locations across the US and sometimes Europe. Testing the waters helps both parties have more time to evaluate the opportunity and takes some of the pressure off of the more constrained road-show meetings.

- **Confidential filings**—An EGC is allowed to file its initial prospectus with the SEC confidentially, versus the past practice of having the filings be public. The reason this matters is that it takes time once a company files its prospectus for the SEC to review it and provide comments and, in this interim period, the company is restricted in some of its external communications. Violations of these restrictions—called "gun jumping"—can cause the SEC to delay the company's IPO until the market has cooled off from the communications. Ultimately, the SEC is worried about companies trying to hype their stock before the offering and thus potentially causing investors to make investment decisions without fully considering all the risks. In the absence of a confidential filing, the communications restriction means that all the company's financial information is sitting in the public domain for competitors and reporters to take apart, yet without the company's ability to meaningfully respond. Thus the confidential filing ensures that the company is not a sitting duck in the period during which the SEC is completing its review. By the way, confidential filings started with EGCs, but as of the end of 2017, the SEC changed its own filing rules to extend confidential filing privileges to all IPOs, even if the company is not an EGC.

- **Financial and regulatory disclosures**—EGCs enjoy lighter regulatory and disclosure requirements both in the prospectus and post-IPO. For example, an EGC is required to provide only two years of historical financials in its prospectus and is not subject to a requirement that its auditors opine on the company's internal controls. Essentially, the JOBS Act scaled down the regulatory costs of becoming a public company.

Once an EGC has mostly completed its back-and-forth with the SEC on its prospectus, it will make the prospectus publicly available (i.e., take the covers off of the confidential filing) and begin the formal marketing phase of the deal. It is also at this time that the underwriters will provide an initial filing price range and offering size for the transaction, with the understanding that these numbers may move up or down during the course of marketing based upon investor feedback. As noted above, the marketing process is called a road show, and entails exactly that: traveling around the country (and sometimes Europe) to do a seemingly endless number of one-hour pitch meetings to institutional investors.

During the road show, the underwriters are doing what's called "building the book." That is, they are talking with the various institutional investors and trying to get a sense of how much demand there is for the offering at different prices (in relation to the initial filing price range the underwriters had set). Once the marketing period has finished, the underwriters and the company will assess the strength of the book and make a decision on how many shares to ultimately sell and at what price. At this point, the SEC needs to weigh in one final time to declare the prospectus effective, permitting the underwriters to distribute the shares to investors and start the public trading of the stock.

Pricing an IPO is one of the more challenging aspects of the process, and undoubtedly leaves at least one of the parties unhappy. Here's the challenge: the underwriters are repeat players in the IPO process (as are the institutional investors who purchase IPO shares), whereas the company by definition likely only ever goes public once. Thus, the incentives for the underwriters are to price the IPO appropriately so that it trades well in the aftermarket; as I've said many times in this book already, the world is a much happier place when things go steadily up and to the right, and stock prices are no exception. The incentive for the company going public is of course to achieve a good long-term stock trajectory but also to raise as much money as possible with the least amount of dilution possible. After all, the company gets the proceeds from selling the IPO shares, but it does not benefit directly in the form of cash on its balance sheet with the subsequent appreciation of the stock price.

Estimating the right selling price for the stock, however, is more art than science. If the underwriters price it too high, then the stock is at risk of trading below this price on the first day of trading. This is called "breaking issue price" and can be a very bad place for a company to be, in part because so much of how a stock trades is based on sentiment, and negative sentiment can become a self-fulfilling prophecy.

Recall what happened to Facebook on its first few days as a public company. Granted, we won't ever be able to disentangle the effects of the trading glitch in the Nasdaq market that day from the underwriters' decision to set the initial price at $38 per share, but both may have contributed to the sell-off in the stock. Facebook stock fell all the way to $14 per share before eventually recovering and is now trading at nearly four times its IPO price.

On the flip side, if the underwriters set the initial price too low and the stock trades way up in the aftermarket, the institutional investors may be happy because of the appreciation, but the company will feel as though it left a lot of money on the table or unnecessarily suffered dilution. Interestingly, when I was a banker at Credit Suisse First Boston in the dot-com bubble, we held the record for the largest one-day IPO increase in a stock price. The company was VA Linux, and the stock, which was priced at $30 per share in the IPO, traded immediately (on the opening trade) to $300 per share and then closed on the first day of trading at

$242.38, an 8x increase in one day. Funny enough, at that time, we actually celebrated and marketed this as our brilliance in leading the IPO; in retrospect, that was a pretty sure sign that we completely misjudged the real market price for the stock!

After this initial pricing dance, in the first thirty days post-IPO, the underwriters are allowed to stabilize the trading price of the stock. The primary mechanism by which they do this is through what's called the "green shoe" (named after the first company, Green Shoe Manufacturing Company, for which this technique was deployed).

The green shoe allows the underwriters to sell to the market up to an additional 15 percent of stock at the time of the IPO; essentially it oversells the IPO but retains the right to purchase those shares back within thirty days from the company at the IPO price. So if the stock price goes up, then the underwriter exercises the green shoe by buying the shares back and distributing them to the institutional investors to whom the overallotted shares were sold. If the stock price goes down below the original sale price, the underwriters can just go in the market and buy shares back at the lower market price and thus they do not end up exercising the green shoe.

We started this section by talking about liquidity being one of the reasons to go public, but so far we've said nothing about liquidity. For investors, liquidity is still a ways off, since they are generally required to execute a lockup agreement that restricts their ability to sell stock for the first six months post-IPO. The reason for this is price stabilization as well; we worry that if the VCs (or founders and executives who own a lot of stock) dump all their stock immediately, it could have a big impact on the trading price. Even once the lockup expires, VCs may still be restricted depending on whether they remain on the board of directors (and might be subject to the company's trading policy, which restricts the time intervals during which officers and directors can trade) or on how much stock they own (there are sometimes volume limitations associated with large holders).

Employees and executives, too, are usually subject to the lockup agreement. After that, other than for executives, who may have restrictions based on the company's trading policy, employees are generally free to trade their shares.

Finally, that long journey from startup to liquidity is in sight. But how do venture capital firms ultimately achieve liquidity for their LPs, and when do they decide to seek liquidity? The decision to seek liquidity varies among firms, so it is important for you as an entrepreneur to have this discussion with your particular firms, assuming you are lucky enough to get to an IPO.

Recall that when we talked about LPs and the Yale endowment we mentioned that VC is but one asset class to which most institutional investors allocate capital—public equities, real estate, debt, etc., being among the other classes. As a result, most venture LPs take the view that, once a portfolio company goes public, the default should be that the VC exits its position in the stock by returning cash or stock back to its LPs. The reasoning behind this is that LPs pay VCs to invest in and manage private company exposure, but generally have separate fund managers on whom they rely for managing public stocks. If an LP wants to own Facebook shares, she has a public manager who is skilled in that area; she doesn't need her VC to do that for her.

That doesn't mean that VCs are required to exit public shares immediately. Remember that a function of being a limited partner is that you are in fact at the mercy of the GP's decision to exit or not. But in practice, many VCs will take the position that they will seek to exit public shares in some reasonable proximity to an IPO, unless they still have a thesis such that there is material upside still available in the stock. The definition of "material" varies by VC, but most would probably agree that if the stock is likely to go up at the same general rate as the overall market, that doesn't qualify. So the bar to continue holding for a longer period of time usually requires a stronger conviction in the remaining upside in the stock.

The decision to exit can also be affected by whether the VC is remaining on the board of directors of the company post-IPO or by whether they remain a significant shareholder (typically meaning that they hold a position in excess of 10 percent of the stock). Either of these conditions can impose restrictions on the VC's ability to exit the stock, by limiting either the windows in which they can exit (e.g., a board member will often be prohibited by the company's insider trading policy from exiting in a closed window, which typically occurs within certain times of an earnings release) or the volume of shares they may sell at any given time.

Once a VC makes the decision to exit its position in whole or in part, the VC can do so either by selling the shares in the open market and returning the cash proceeds to its LPs or by distributing the shares themselves directly to the LPs. As with other aspects of the GP-LP relationship, this is a GP-only decision. There are a number of considerations in this decision, including the overall trading liquidity of the stock, and the VC's opinion as to whether doing a mass sale or distribution could materially weaken the stock price, as well as the desire (or not) to trigger taxes to the LPs and the GP (a sale of stock for cash is a taxable event, whereas the distribution of shares defers taxes until the recipient herself decides to sell the shares).

As an entrepreneur, you will want to be mindful of the VC's deliberations around sales or distributions, as they may have an impact on the stock. In particular, if a stock is thinly traded (meaning there is not a lot of regular trading volume in the stock), a meaningful sale or distribution could cause a material decline in the stock price. Similarly, the signaling of a large VC exiting the stock alone might have an impact on the trading sentiment of the stock.

As a result, sometimes the company's board will seek to mitigate the potential deleterious effects of VC exits by organizing what's called a secondary offering of shares. Just as in an IPO, this is an offering coordinated by the company and its underwriters in which the company seeks to orchestrate a sale of shares to oftentimes existing institutional investors who want to add to their holdings in the stock. As distinct from an IPO, however, the shares being sold are secondary, meaning they are owned by someone else, rather than being newly issued by the company. These shares are often those owned by executives or VCs who may have not already exited their holdings. Thus, the proceeds of such a stock sale do not go to the company but rather to the holders of the shares who are selling into the market. The main benefit of this process in lieu of having VCs simply distribute shares independently to their LPs or sell on their own is to give the company an opportunity to place the shares in friendly institutional hands and thus minimize the negative price pressure on the stock.

However accomplished, the sale or distribution of shares by a VC completes the often ten-or-more-year cycle of having invested in a startup and seeing it through to a successful exit. And the circle of life for the participating VC begins anew: looking for the next potential IPO candidate.

While an IPO may ultimately be an exit for the VCs—and provide broader liquidity for you and your employees—it also reflects a new chapter for you as CEO. You've now got a new set of co-owners in the company—namely, public institutions that will be able to grade your performance daily in the form of the stock price. And of course a new set of governance rules by which to live.

Most importantly, however, you also need to think about how you keep your key employees focused on delivering on all the promises that you outlined to your investors during the course of the road show. This can be a real challenge, particularly given that the liquidity that many early employees will have achieved via the IPO may change their go-forward financial incentives. In addition, the daily reminder of apparent success (or failure) that the stock price represents can become a distraction from keeping people's eyes focused on the long-term prize of executing your product plan.

These are of course first-class problems to have, given that you have achieved what a very small minority of venture-backed entrepreneurs ever do: getting your company from founding to a successful IPO. And thus a new day begins.

CONCLUSION

The World Is Flat

If you made it this far, congratulations to you, and might I suggest that you find some hobbies?

Seriously, though, I hope I have been able to give you a better perspective on how the venture industry works and how startup companies can best navigate their way through their interactions with venture capital firms.

As I mentioned at the outset, this book isn't intended to be the VC bible. But I do hope this book is like your own Alohomora incantation from Harry Potter—the spell you need to unlock some fairly heavy, opaque doors, behind which are the inner workings, incentives, and decision-making processes of VCs. In short, I want to shine a light on what makes VCs tick, what the VC life cycle is, and why all this matters to you as a startup founder, employee, or partner.

The decision to raise capital from a venture firm is a huge one, and my personal motto about most things is *Better to be informed*.

The Evolution of VC

When Marc Andreessen and Ben Horowitz started Andreessen Horowitz, they were contemplating building a different type of venture firm from those already in the market. In particular, we decided to hire a lot of noninvestment, nonfinancial personnel to work closely with our startups to help them achieve their goals of building large, self-sustaining companies. Today, in fact, a16z employs about 150 people, and two-thirds of the employees are focused on post-investment engagement with our portfolio companies.

We thought at the time, and continue to think today, that this was part of a broader evolution in the VC industry through which money alone would no longer be the primary source of competitive differentiation.

The thesis was that money had been the scarce resource through much of the industry's first thirty to forty years, and, because the VCs controlled access to money, they had the power as a result. Over the more recent ten or so years, money is no longer a scarce commodity—there are plenty of VC firms with lots of capital and many more non-VC firms that provide significant amounts of particularly later-stage capital into the venture ecosystem—and thus something other than money will serve as the source of competitive differentiation in the marketplace. For a16z, investing in a team of post-investment resources is one way in which the firm hopes to compete among a group of other very successful and competitive venture firms. There are of course other ways to achieve that differentiation in the marketplace, and no doubt new models will continue to emerge.

How did we get to this point where capital ceased to be a scarce resource? We talked about this briefly in the introduction to this book, but a few things happened along the way. First, starting in the early 2000s, the costs required to start a new company began to fall precipitously.

As cloud computing began to take off, the unit costs of all these hardware and software products began to fall. A variant of Moore's law was sweeping through every segment of the technology stack. At the same time, software development systems also progressed, and engineering efficiency increased correspondingly. Today, developers can go to Amazon Web Services or competing providers and rent compute utility on demand, providing incremental pricing coupled with dramatically lowered input costs. Thus the costs required to start a company have fallen significantly, and therefore the amount of money that startups need to raise at an early stage has declined accordingly. This is a good thing overall in that it means there is a lot of new company experimentation that can be had with only small amounts of actual capital put at risk. This is why you have seen such an increase in the number of early-stage companies being funded.

Commensurate with this decline in costs, a new form of early-stage financing developed. In the old days (roughly pre-2005), angel investors were individuals who invested small amounts of money in startups out of their own checkbooks. However, as the costs of starting a company fell, the institutional seed market began to develop. Over the past ten years, likely more than five hundred new seed firms have been formed, most of which have fund sizes less than $100 million, and many with fund sizes below $50 million. But unlike the angel investors of old who invested their own money, most of these firms are funded by the same types of institutional LPs who fund larger VC firms. The proliferation of these firms has also contributed to the increase in the number of seed-funded startup companies.

Ironically (or maybe not), at the same time that it has become cheaper to start a company, it has become more expensive for companies to win. That's because the world is flatter than ever before. Whereas the US once dominated the venture scene, funding as much as 90 percent of global venture capital investments just about twenty years ago, today the rest of the world is roughly on par with the US in terms of share of the venture capital funding pie. As a result, startups face competition in virtually every global market in which they seek to compete. The good news is that the end markets for successful companies are bigger than ever (we've never before seen a company achieve what Facebook has done—grow from zero to a $400-plus billion market cap company in fourteen years); the bad news is that winning those markets requires a lot of capital to simultaneously capture each one.

And with this change has come two important financing trends.

First, many of the traditional venture capital firms have increased their fund sizes to be able not only to fund startups in the very early stages, but also to be a source of growth capital throughout their life cycles. Second, as companies have elected to stay private longer, more nontraditional sources of growth capital have entered the financing market. Whereas public mutual funds, hedge funds, sovereign wealth funds, family offices, and other strategic sources of capital had traditionally waited for startups to go public before they would invest growth capital, nearly all these players have now made the decision to invest directly in later-stage startups while they remain in the private markets. This is the most viable way for such institutional investors to capture the appreciation attendant to startups; that appreciation has essentially shifted from post-IPO to largely pre-IPO.

Consider the following example. Microsoft went public in 1986 at a $350 million market capitalization. Today, Microsoft has a market cap of approximately $800 billion. That's more than a 2,200x increase in market cap *as a public company*. No doubt the venture investors in Microsoft did fine themselves in terms of return on their investment, but if a public market investor held Microsoft since its IPO, she would have made more than Accel made on its pre-IPO Facebook investment—talk about public venture returns!

In contrast, Facebook went public at a $100 billion market cap and now trades around $400 billion. Absolutely nothing to sneeze at, particularly given that the company's value has increased four times in about six years. Just to have some fun, though, for the public market investors to eventually earn the same multiple on their Facebook holdings as has been the case for their Microsoft holdings, Facebook would have to reach a market of more than $220 trillion. To put this into context, global domestic production—the sum of the entire economic value in the world—is about $80 trillion.

Now, I realize these numbers are crazy and this comparison may not be apples-to-apples, but it illustrates a very important point in the overall capital markets. Companies are definitely staying private longer, resulting in more of the appreciation of startups going to those investors in the private markets, at the expense of those in the public markets. This means that normal retail investors, who rely on public stock price appreciation to fund their retirement accounts, may be losing out on a real portion of economic growth.

Regardless of your policy views, private capital is becoming a commodity, and this is why access to capital alone no longer provides significant differentiation for most venture capital firms. And yet, despite our having tried something new to differentiate our service offering at a16z, my partner Marc likes to keep us ahead of the curve by often asking whether we are in fact simply the most advanced dinosaurs—the implication being that we may think we look differentiated relative to others, but we are always at risk of being the last generation in the evolutionary chain of traditional venture firms.

What Might Be the End of Venture Capital as We Know It?

- Crowdfunding is one alternative—in 2017, roughly $1 billion was raised through crowdfunding efforts in the US, an increase of about 25 percent from the previous year. Obviously, this is much smaller than the more than $80 billion of venture capital financing that year, but nothing to dismiss.

- Initial coin offerings (or ICOs) for digital tokens is another potential candidate to replace venture capital. In 2017, roughly $4 billion was raised via ICOs, about 5 percent of the total US venture capital investments. Some have argued that ICOs are a mechanism for founders to raise both institutional capital and retail capital without having to rely on VCs to finance their growth.

These funding sources ultimately represent two sides of the same coin—each is a way to democratize access to capital beyond the more centralized venture ecosystem that exists today. In that respect, they are part of the very same trend on which Andreessen Horowitz founded its business—capital is no longer a scarce resource, and thus returns will not accrue to those individuals or firms that provide access to capital only.

This is, I think, the fundamental answer to whether crowdfunding, ICOs, or some other new financing mechanism that we can only dream of today will supplant venture capital. If money remains abundant, and value creation in startups (or digital coins) remains a function of being able to build large, self-sustaining businesses, then the firms that provide meaningful value to entrepreneurs beyond just being a source of capital likely have an ongoing role to play. It's certainly possible that those firms may not be the traditional venture model that we see today, but could also include a whole new variety of organizations that combine capital availability with value-add aimed at helping entrepreneurs achieve their business goals.

And this takes us right back to where we started this book. VCs and entrepreneurs working together to achieve wonderful things.

Here's What I Believe about Good VCs

Good VCs help entrepreneurs achieve their business goals by providing guidance, support, a network of relationships, and coaching.

Good VCs recognize the limitations of what they can do as board members and outside advisors as a result of the informational asymmetry they have with respect to founders and other executives who live and breathe the company every day.

Good VCs give advice in areas in which they have demonstrated expertise, and have the wisdom to avoid opining on topics for which they are not the appropriate experts.

Good VCs appropriately balance their duties to the common shareholders with those they owe to their limited partners.

Good VCs recognize that, ultimately, it is the entrepreneurs and the employees who build iconic companies, with hopefully a little bit of good advice and prodding sprinkled in along the way by their VC partners.

If VCs remain good, they won't become dinosaurs.

The World Is Flat

I am very privileged to be part of an incredibly dynamic industry that, while small in terms of relative capital, contributes an enormous amount to the technological development and the economic growth of the global economy. For many years, as noted earlier, the US has occupied a special place in venture capital. As a country, the US has benefited tremendously from the startup and VC communities, and we need to continue to encourage more people in the US and across the world to pursue careers in these industries. Eliminating the information asymmetry barriers between entrepreneurs and VCs is one step in helping to achieve this goal.

The world is undeniably flat—and the global playing field has never been more open to startup opportunities. I hope at some small level that this book helps inspire more people to think about the role they can play in this increasingly important ecosystem to improve the growth prospects and financial well-being of people all across the globe.

APPENDIX

SAMPLE TERM SHEET
[COMPANY XYZ, INC.]

TERM SHEET FOR
SERIES A PREFERRED STOCK FINANCING

This term sheet dated as of January 17, 2018, summarizes the principal terms of the proposed Series A Preferred Stock financing of Company XYZ, Inc., a Delaware corporation (the "**Company**"), by Venture Capital Fund I ("**VCF1**"). This term sheet is for discussion purposes only, and except as expressly set forth below, there is no obligation on the part of any negotiating party until a definitive stock purchase agreement is signed by all parties and other conditions set forth herein are met. The transactions contemplated by this term sheet are subject to, among other things, the satisfactory completion of due diligence. This term sheet does not constitute either an offer to sell or an offer to purchase securities.

OFFERING TERMS	
Security:	Shares of Series A Preferred Stock of the Company (**"Series A Preferred Stock"**).
Aggregate Proceeds:	$10 million in new capital, all of which shall be from VCF1 (for at least 20% of the post-closing fully diluted capitalization of the Company) (the **"Investor"**).
	In addition to the new capital described above, to the extent the Company has any outstanding convertible notes and/or SAFE securities, such instruments shall convert into shares of capital stock (the **"Note Conversion Shares"**) pursuant to their terms.
Price per Share:	The per-share purchase price of the Series A Preferred Stock (the **"Original Purchase Price"**) shall be based upon a $50 million **post-money** fully diluted valuation (which includes all new capital described above, the Note Conversion Shares, the unallocated pool described below, and all other rights to acquire shares of the Company's capital stock).
Capitalization:	The pre-money capitalization shall include an ungranted and unallocated employee option pool representing at least 15.0% of the fully diluted post-closing capitalization (after giving effect to the issuance of the Series A Preferred Stock, any Note Conversion Shares, and any other rights to acquire shares of the Company's capital stock), exclusive of any shares of Common Stock or options to acquire shares of Common Stock that have been previously issued, granted, promised, or otherwise committed by the Company (verbally or in writing) prior to the closing of the Series A Preferred Stock financing (the **"Closing"**).
Use of Proceeds:	The proceeds shall be used for working capital and general corporate purposes.

TERMS OF PREFERRED STOCK

OFFERING TERMS	
Dividends:	The holders of any prior series of preferred stock, Series A Preferred Stock, and all future series of preferred stock (together, the **"Preferred Stock"**) shall receive an annual 6% per-share dividend on a pari passu basis, payable when and if declared by the Board of Directors (the **"Board"**), prior and in preference to any declaration or payment of dividends on the shares of the Company's Common Stock (the **"Common Stock"**); dividends are not cumulative. For any other dividends or distributions, the Preferred Stock participates with Common Stock on an as-converted basis.
Liquidation Preference:	In the event of any liquidation or winding up of the Company, the holders of Preferred Stock shall be entitled to receive prior and in preference to the holders of Common Stock an amount equal to the applicable Original Purchase Price per share for such series of Preferred Stock (as adjusted for stock splits, stock dividends, recapitalizations, etc.), plus any declared but unpaid dividends on such shares (the **"Liquidation Preference"**). After the payment of the Liquidation Preference to the holders of Preferred Stock, the remaining assets shall be distributed ratably to the holders of the Common Stock.
	A merger, acquisition, sale of voting control, sale of substantially all of the assets of the Company, or any other transaction or series of transactions in which the stockholders of the Company do not own a majority of the outstanding shares of the surviving corporation (but excluding the issuance of stock pursuant to customary venture capital financings by the Company) shall be deemed to be a liquidation or winding up (a **"Liquidation Event"**) and shall entitle the holders of Preferred Stock to receive at the closing (and at each date after the closing on which additional amounts [such as earn-out payments, escrow amounts, and other contingent payments] are paid to stockholders of the Company) the greater of (1) the amount they are entitled to receive as holders of Preferred Stock above or (2) the amount they would be entitled to receive had such holder of Preferred Stock converted such shares into Common Stock prior to the closing. Subject to the Protective Provisions herein, treatment of any such transaction as a Liquidation Event may be waived only with the consent of the holders of a majority of the Preferred Stock, voting as a single-class on an as-converted basis.

TERMS OF PREFERRED STOCK *(cont.)*

OFFERING TERMS	
Redemption:	No redemption.
Conversion:	The holders of Preferred Stock shall have the right to convert the Preferred Stock, at any time, into shares of Common Stock at an initial conversion price of 1:1, subject to adjustment as provided below.
Automatic Conversion:	The Preferred Stock shall be automatically converted into Common Stock, at the then-applicable conversion price (i) in the event that the holders of a majority of the outstanding Preferred Stock consent to such conversion or (ii) upon the closing of a firmly underwritten public offering of shares of Common Stock of the Company pursuant to a registration statement under the Securities Act of 1933 for a total offering of not less than $50 million (before deduction of underwriters' commissions and expenses) (a **"Qualified IPO"**).
Antidilution Provisions:	Proportional antidilution protection for stock splits, stock dividends, recapitalizations, etc. Except as further described below, the conversion price of the Preferred Stock shall be subject to adjustment to prevent dilution on a broad-based weighted average basis in the event that the Company issues additional shares of Common Stock or securities convertible into or exercisable for Common Stock at a purchase price less than the then-effective conversion price; except, however, that without triggering antidilution adjustments, (1) Common Stock and/or options therefor may be sold, issued, granted, or reserved for issuance to employees, officers, or directors of the Company pursuant to stock purchase or stock option plans or agreements or other incentive stock arrangements approved by the Board, (2) shares of Common or Preferred Stock (or options or warrants therefor) may be issued to leasing companies, landlords, company advisors, lenders, and other providers of goods and services to the Company, in each case approved by the Board (including at least one director elected by the Preferred Stock [a **"Preferred Stock Director"**]), (3) shares of Common or Preferred Stock (or options or warrants therefor) may be issued to entities in connection with joint ventures, acquisitions, or other strategic transactions, in each case approved by the Board (including a Preferred Stock Director), (4) securities may be issued pursuant to stock splits, stock dividends, or similar transactions, (5) Common Stock may be issued in a Qualified IPO, (6) securities may be issued pursuant

TERMS OF PREFERRED STOCK *(cont.)*

OFFERING TERMS	
Antidilution Provisions (cont.):	to currently outstanding warrants, notes, or other rights to acquire securities of the Company (the foregoing issuances described in subsections [1] through [6] shall be referred to as the **"Exempted Securities"**), and (7) securities may be issued in any other transaction in which exemption from the antidilution provisions is approved by the affirmative vote of a majority of the then-outstanding Preferred Stock.
Voting Rights:	The Preferred Stock will vote together with Common Stock and not as a separate class except as otherwise provided herein for Preferred Stock or as otherwise required by law. Each share of Preferred Stock shall have a number of votes equal to the number of shares of Common Stock then issuable upon conversion of such share of Preferred Stock. For all votes of the Common Stock, each share shall have one vote.
	Subject to the Protective Provisions below, the Company's Certificate of Incorporation will provide that the number of authorized shares of Common Stock may be increased or decreased with the approval of a majority of the Preferred Stock and Common Stock, voting together as a single class, and without a separate class vote by the Common Stock.
Board of Directors:	The Board shall initially have three directors. The holders of Series A Preferred Stock, voting as a single class, will have the right to elect one member of the Board (who shall be designated by VCF1). The holders of Common Stock, voting as a single class, will have the right to elect one member of the Board, to be the CEO. The remaining member of the Board will be an outside industry expert approved by the other members of the Board. The parties shall enter into a voting agreement with respect to the election of the directors.
Protective Provisions:	For so long as any shares of Preferred Stock remain outstanding, in addition to any other vote or consent required herein or by law, the vote or written consent of the holders of a majority of the outstanding shares of Preferred Stock, voting together as a single class on an as-if converted basis, shall be necessary for effecting or validating the following actions (whether consummated by merger, amendment, recapitalization, consolidation, or otherwise): (i) any amendment, alteration, or repeal of any provision of the Certificate of Incorporation or the bylaws of the Company (the **"Bylaws"**); (ii) any increase in the authorized number of shares of Preferred Stock or Common Stock; (iii) any authorization,

TERMS OF PREFERRED STOCK *(cont.)*

OFFERING TERMS	
Protective Provisions (cont.):	designation, or issuance, whether by reclassification or otherwise, of any new class or series of stock or any other equity or debt securities convertible into equity securities of the Company ranking on a parity with or senior to the existing Preferred Stock in right of redemption, liquidation preference, voting, or dividends or any increase in the authorized or designated number of any such new class or series; (iv) any redemption or repurchase with respect to Common Stock (excluding shares repurchased upon termination of an employee or consultant pursuant to a restricted share purchase agreement); (v) any agreement by the Company or its stockholders regarding an asset transfer, license of intellectual property out of the ordinary course of business, acquisition, or a Liquidation Event; (vi) any action that results in the payment or declaration of a dividend on any shares of Common Stock or Preferred Stock; (vii) any voluntary dissolution or liquidation of the Company or any reclassification or recapitalization of the outstanding capital stock of the Company; (viii) any increase or decrease in the authorized number of members of the Company's Board; (ix) any borrowings, loans, or guarantees in excess of $500,000; (x) any interested party transaction, unless approved by the Board (including a disinterested majority of directors); or (xi) any increase to the Company's stock option plan. There shall be no separate series votes of any series of Preferred Stock.
Information Rights:	The Company shall deliver to a purchaser of $2.0 million or more of the Preferred Stock (a *"Major Investor"*) its audited annual and unaudited quarterly financial statements prepared in accordance with US GAAP, consistently applied. In addition, the Company will furnish Major Investors with monthly financial statements compared against plan and will provide a copy of the Company's annual operating plan prior to the beginning of the fiscal year. Each Major Investor shall also be entitled to standard inspection and visitation rights. These provisions shall terminate upon a Qualified IPO or Liquidation Event.
Registration Rights:	Customary registration rights.

TERMS OF PREFERRED STOCK *(cont.)*

OFFERING TERMS	
Right to Make Pro Rata Investments in Company Offerings:	In the event the Company proposes to offer equity securities to any person (excluding Exempted Securities), Major Investors shall have the right to purchase their pro rata portion of such equity securities. Major Investors shall have twenty (20) calendar days after delivery of a notice from the Company describing such offering to elect to purchase their pro rata portion. Any such equity securities not subscribed for by a Major Investor may be reallocated among the other Major Investors. Such right of first refusal will terminate immediately prior to a Qualified IPO or upon a Liquidation Event.
Stock Restriction:	Each current and future holder of 2% or greater of the Company's Common Stock post-financing will execute a Right of First Refusal and Co-Sale Agreement with the Investor and the Company pursuant to which the Company and then the Investor will have a right of first refusal with respect to any shares proposed to be sold by the holders of Common Stock. Any shares purchased by the Company will be returned to treasury. The Right of First Refusal and Co-Sale Agreement will also contain a right of co-sale providing that before any such holder of Common Stock may sell any of his shares, he will first give the Investor an opportunity to participate in such sale on a basis proportionate to the amount of securities held by the seller and those held by the Investor. Such agreement shall contain exceptions for transfers to affiliates and transfers for estate planning purposes, but shall not include exceptions for any other transfers or pledges of stock. In addition, no stockholder shall be a party to any Stock Sale unless all holders of Preferred Stock are allowed to participate in such Stock Sale and the consideration received pursuant to such Stock Sale is allocated among the parties thereto as if such Stock Sale were a deemed liquidation event. A *"Stock Sale"* means any transaction, series of related transactions, or series of unrelated transactions in which a person or entity, or a group of affiliated (or otherwise related) persons or entities acquires more than fifty percent (50%) of the outstanding voting stock of the Company. The Right of First Refusal and Co-Sale Agreement will terminate upon a Liquidation Event or a Qualified IPO. The Bylaws will contain a blanket restriction on the transfer (including pledges and other hypothecation of shares and proceeds from the future transfer of such shares) of Common Stock and founder stock without disinterested Board approval, but not a corresponding restriction on transfers of Preferred Stock.

TERMS OF PREFERRED STOCK *(cont.)*

OFFERING TERMS	
Drag Along:	Each current and future holder of 2% or more of the capital stock of the Company will be required to enter into an agreement providing that in the event a majority of the Board, holders of a majority of the Common Stock (voting as a separate class), and holders of a majority of the Preferred Stock (voting as a separate class) have approved an acquisition of the Company, whether by merger, sale of assets, sale of stock, or otherwise, such holder will grant any necessary consents or approvals reasonably determined by the Board to be necessary in order to approve or participate in the acquisition of the Company subject to customary limitations.
Purchase Agreement:	The investment shall be made pursuant to a Stock Purchase Agreement by and between the Company and the Investor, which shall contain, among other things, appropriate representations and warranties of the Company, covenants of the Company reflecting the provisions set forth herein, and appropriate conditions of Closing, including an opinion of legal counsel for the Company and the issuance of a management rights letter to the Investor.
D&O Insurance:	The Company shall covenant to maintain directors' and officers' insurance, with a limit of at least $2.0 million and other terms satisfactory to the Board.
EMPLOYEE MATTERS	
Vesting:	Except as otherwise approved by the Board, options issued after the Closing to employees, directors, consultants, and other service providers of the Company will have a post-termination exercise period of no more than ninety (90) days and be subject to vesting as follows: 25% to vest on the first anniversary of (i) the date of commencement of providing services to the Company in the case of new hires or (ii) the date of grant in the case of refresh grants, with the remaining 75% to vest in equal monthly installments over the next thirty-six (36) months thereafter. Shares of capital stock held by the founders will be subject to a forty-eight- (48-) month vesting schedule with the vesting commencement date relating back to such founders' commencement of full-time services to the Company. Such vesting will be subject to, in the event that there has been a Liquidation Event, 100% acceleration in the event of a termination without "cause" or "good reason."

TERMS OF PREFERRED STOCK *(cont.)*

OFFERING TERMS	
Employee and Consultant Agreements:	Each employee and consultant of the Company shall sign (or shall already have signed) a proprietary information agreement providing that (i) he is either an at-will employee or a consultant of the Company, as the case may be, (ii) he will maintain all Company proprietary information in confidence, and (iii) he will assign all inventions created by him as an employee or consultant during his employment or service to the Company.

OTHER MATTERS	
No-Shop:	The Company agrees that, through the earlier of (i) thirty (30) days from the date this Term Sheet is executed by the Company and a VCF1 and (ii) the date on which VCF1 notifies the Company in writing of its intention not to continue to pursue the proposed purchase of Series A Preferred Stock, neither the Company nor any director, officer, employee, or agent of the Company will, directly or indirectly, solicit, initiate, entertain, or encourage any proposals or offers from any third party relating to the sale of the Company's capital stock (other than customary grants of options pursuant to the option plan), any merger or consolidation of the Company, the dissolution of the Company, or the acquisition of a material portion of the Company's assets, or participate in any discussions regarding, or furnish to any person any information with respect to, any such transaction.
Confidentiality:	This Term Sheet and any related correspondences from the Investors are to be held in strict confidence and not disclosed to any party other than the Board, existing investors in the Company, Company employees who reasonably need to know, and their legal counsel without prior approval of such Investors.
Closing:	Except for this provision and the provisions contained herein entitled "No Shop" and "Confidentiality," which are explicitly agreed by the Investor and the Company to be binding upon execution of this Term Sheet, this Term Sheet is not intended as a legally binding commitment by the Investor or the Company, and any obligation on the part of the Investor or the Company is subject to satisfactory completion of legal due diligence by VCF1, satisfactory business and technology due diligence by VCF1, and completion of legal documentation to the satisfaction of VCF1.

TERMS OF PREFERRED STOCK (*cont.*)

OFFERING TERMS	
Legal Counsel and Fees:	Upon the closing of the transaction, the Company shall bear its own legal fees and expenses and shall pay the reasonable fees and expenses of VCF1 not to exceed $35,000.

The foregoing correctly reflects our mutual intentions as a basis for proceeding toward negotiation of definitive agreements.

COMPANY XYZ, INC.	VENTURE CAPITAL FUND I, L.P.
By:	By:
Name:	Name:
Title:	Title:
Date:	Date:

ACKNOWLEDGMENTS

When Marc Andreessen and Ben Horowitz reached out to me in 2008 to ask if I would join them on the a16z journey, I have to admit that I hesitated. I was living in North Carolina at the time, working for Hewlett-Packard, and my family was enjoying the welcome respite from the fast-paced excitement of the Bay Area. And, not to mention, it was the summer of 2008, the beginning of what would become the global financial crisis that would decimate the financial services industry and throw the global economy into a financial tailspin.

I'll never forget being on a call with Ben in September 2008— the precise weekend that Lehman Brothers would go bankrupt— discussing the plans for the a16z business and questioning whether we'd be able to raise a new venture fund. In many ways, it seemed to defy the odds, but then again, I'd seen this story before.

I'd joined LoudCloud at the beginning of 2000 in what turned out to be the height of dot-com euphoria. Less than twelve months later, we had to "adjust" our financial plan to the new realities of the dot-com bust. And, as I discussed in this book, we went public in 2001 in the crosshairs of the technology meltdown, ultimately navigating our way through a massive restructuring and the sale of the LoudCloud business to EDS, followed by the launch of Opsware as a public company with exactly one client (EDS).

But, in ultimately deciding to join Marc and Ben on the a16z journey, I recalled what I had told my wife when I made the original decision to join LoudCloud: "While it's impossible to predict whether we'll ultimately build a successful business, I know that the journey will be an amazing one."

And having the privilege to work with two individuals as successful, ambitious, and intellectual as Marc and Ben has been truly that. I come to work every day knowing that I will be challenged to think differently and to respond to new opportunities, never relying on precedent as the answer for why we do something, but rather being forced to think through everything from first principles.

Thus, in many ways, the decisions to join LoudCloud in 2000 and a16z in 2008 were IQ tests. Lucky for me, I passed the tests.

This book would not have been possible without those decisions, as the opportunities and the platform that those experiences—and Marc and Ben personally—provided me, set the stage for the learning that I hope to have conveyed throughout this book. And for that I am eternally grateful to the two of them.

I also want to thank all my teammates at a16z, who are too numerous to name individually here, and whose contributions to the success of the firm are equally too numerous to call out individually. They are the ones who have made the firm successful and helped build the a16z platform to a point where we have the ability to communicate directly with entrepreneurs in forums such as this book.

Special thanks to a few folks who reviewed early versions of the manuscript and provided helpful feedback: Joe Grundfest, professor at Stanford Law School, who taught me everything I know about securities regulation; Bobby Bartlett and Adam Sterling, professors at UC Berkeley Boalt School of Law, who have been great partners in broadening the knowledge of the VC ecosystem to new investors, particularly those outside Silicon Valley; and Peter Stamos, CEO of Stamos Capital Partners, who always forces me to expand my thinking around financial management.

Of course, any mistakes in this book are mine and mine alone. Hopefully, they are relatively few and far between.

To my parents: Thank you for instilling in me a love of learning and for providing me the strong foundation on which I've relied for so many years.

And, ultimately, to my loving wife, Laura, and my three amazing, crazy fun, and inspirational daughters, Ashlee, Alexa, and Amanda: Without your love and support, I am nothing.

NOTES

3   **42 percent of all US company IPOs:** Will Gornall and Ilya Strebulaev, "The Economic Impact of Venture Capital: Evidence from Public Companies," Stanford Graduate School of Business Research Paper No. 15-55, November 1, 2015; Tim Kane, "The Importance of Startups in Job Creation and Job Destruction," Firm Formation and Economic Growth, Kauffman Foundation Research Series (Ewing Marion Kauffman Foundation, July 2010).

Chapter One: Then and Now

10   **$36 billion went into new startups in 1999:** Thea Singer, "Where the Money Is," *Inc.*, September 1, 2000; *National Venture Capital Association Yearbook 2016* (NVCA and Thomson Reuters, 2016); *National Venture Capital Association 2018 Yearbook* (NVCA and PitchBook, 2018).

10   **On March 10, 2000, the Nasdaq index:** Heather Long, "Tech Stocks Aren't at Bubble Levels," CNN Business, March 10, 2015, https://money.cnn.com/2015/03/10/investing/nasdaq-5000-stocks-market/index.html.

11   **Nasdaq P/E ratio today is under 20:** "Nasdaq PE Ratio 2006–2018," Macrotrends.net, accessed December 18, 2018, https://www.macrotrends.net/stocks/charts/NDAQ/nasdaq/pe-ratio.

11   **Cisco's market cap peaked at about $555 billion:** Paul R. La Monica, "Cisco Is the Market's Comeback Kid," CNN Business, March 15, 2018, https://money.cnn.com/2018/03/15/investing/cisco-comeback-best-dow-stock/index.html.

11   **Nasdaq index began a precipitous decline:** "The Dot-Com Bubble Bursts," Editorial, *New York Times*, December 24, 2000, https://www.nytimes.com/2000/12/24/opinion/the-dot-com-bubble-bursts.html.

Chapter Two: So Really, What Is Venture Capital?

30 **median ten-year returns in VC:** Cambridge Associates, "US Private Equity Was Strong, US Venture Capital More Middling in Second Quarter of 2017," January 8, 2018, https://www.cambridgeassociates. com/press-releases/us-private-equity-was-strong-us-venture-capital-more-middling-in-second-quarter-of-2017.

35 **Accredited investors:** US Securities and Exchange Commission, "Accredited Investors," https://www.sec.gov/fast-answers/answers-accredhtm.html.

39 **Accel Partners:** JP Mangalindan, "Timeline: Where Facebook Got Its Funding," Fortune, January 11, 2011, http://fortune. com/2011/01/11/timeline-where-facebook-got-its-funding.

40 **investments in companies by VC firms topped $84 billion:** National Venture Capital Association 2018 Yearbook (NVCA and PitchBook, 2018).

41 **VC firms raised about $100 billion:** National Venture Capital Association 2018 Yearbook.

41 **global buyout industry raised about $450 billion:** Joshua Franklin, "Global Private Equity Funds Raise Record $453 Billion in 2017: Preqin," Reuters, January 4, 2018, https://www.reuters.com/article/ us-privateequity-fundraising/global-private-equity-funds-raise-record-453-billion-in-2017-preqin-idUSKBN1ET23L; Christine Williamson, "Hedge Fund Assets End 2017 at Record $3.2 Trillion—HFR," Pensions & Investments, January 19, 2018, https://www.pionline.com/article/ 20180119/ONLINE/180119827/hedge-fund-assets-end-2017-at-record-32-trillion-8211-hfr.

41 **concentration of venture-backed companies in the US public markets since 1974:** Gornall and Strebulaev, "The Economic Impact of Venture Capital."

Chapter Three: How Do Early-Stage VCs Decide Where to Invest?

46 **"I knew nothing about airlines":** "Herb Kelleher: Father of Low-Cost Airline Travel Dies at 87," BBC News, January 4, 2019, https://www .bbc.com/news/world-us-canada-46755080.

Chapter Four: What Are LPs and Why Should You Care?

53 **Financing a whaling venture:** Tom Nicholas and Jonas Peter Akins, "Whaling Ventures," Harvard Business School Case Study 9-813086, October 2012 (revised December 9, 2013).

54 **the 1930s passage of the Glass-Steagall Act:** Kurt Jaros, "The Men Who Built America: J. P. Morgan," Values & Capitalism," http://www .valuesandcapitalism.com/the-men-who-built-america-j-p-morgan.

60 **the endowment tops $25 billion:** Josh Lerner, "Yale University Investments Office: February 2015," Harvard Business School Case Study 9-815-124, April 2015; Yale Investments Office, 2016 *Yale Endowment*.

Chapter Six: Forming Your Startup

102 **$245 million in Uber equity paid to Waymo:** Aarian Marshall, "Uber and Waymo Abruptly Settle for $245 Million," *Wired*, February 9, 2018, https://www.wired.com/story/uber-waymo-lawsuit-settlement.

107 **US Congress passed in 2002 the Sarbanes-Oxley Act:** Sarbanes-Oxley Act of 2002, July 30, 2002, https://www.govinfo.gov/content/ pkg/STATUTE-116/pdf/STATUTE-116-Pg745.pdf.

107 **SEC began promulgating various rules:** Nicole Bullock, "SEC Urged to Review Rules for Equity Market Trading," *Financial Times*, March 30, 2017, https://www.ft.com/content/ac12e7b0-14c9-11e7-80f4-13e067d5072c.

Chapter Eight: The Art of the Pitch

130 **for $1 billion:** Megan Garber, "Instagram Was First Called 'Burbn,'" *Atlantic*, July 2, 2014, https://www.theatlantic.com/technology/ archive/2014/07/instagram-used-to-be-called-brbn/373815.

Chapter Thirteen: In Trados We Trust

213 **Burbn later pivoted into the photo-sharing space:** Garber, "Instagram Was First Called 'Burbn.'"

220 **Trados raised a total of $57.9 million:** In re Trados Incorporated Shareholder Litigation, 73 A.3d 17 (Del. Ch. 2013).

228 **"did not have a realistic chance of generating a sufficient return:"** In re Trados Incorporated Shareholder Litigation, p. 111.

Chapter Fourteen: Difficult Financings

243 **WARN Act:** Worker Adjustment and Retraining Notification of 1988, https://www.law.cornell.edu/uscode/text/29/chapter-23.

Chapter Fifteen: Exit Stage Left

261 **filing an IPO under the JOBS Act:** Equity Capital Formation Task Force, *From the On-Ramp to the Freeway: Refueling Job Creation and*

Growth by Reconnecting Investors with Small-Cap Companies (November 11, 2013).

264 trading at nearly four times its IPO price: Shayndi Raice, Ryan Dezember, and Jacob Bunge, "Facebook's IPO Sputters," *Wall Street Journal*, updated May 18, 2012, https://www.wsj.com/articles/SB1000 1424052702303448404577411903118364314.

INDEX

Note: Page numbers in *italics* refer to illustrations.

ABOUT THE AUTHOR

SCOTT KUPOR is managing partner at Andreessen Horowitz. He has overseen the firm's rapid growth to one hundred and fifty employees and more than $7 billion in assets under management. He is also a cofounder and codirector of the Stanford Venture Capital Director's College and teaches venture capital and corporate governance courses at Stanford Law School and the Haas School of Business and Boalt School of Law at UC Berkeley. He is vice-chair of the investment committee for St. Jude Children's Research Hospital and was previously the chairman of the board of the National Venture Capital Association.